Practical SSADM

Version 4+

A Complete Tutorial Guide

Practical SSADM
Version 4+

A Complete Tutorial Guide

Second Edition

Philip L. Weaver, Nick Lambrou and Matthew Walkley

FINANCIAL TIMES
Prentice Hall

An imprint of **Pearson Education**

Harlow, England · London · New York · Reading, Massachusetts · San Francisco · Toronto · Don Mills, Ontario · Sydney
Tokyo · Singapore · Hong Kong · Seoul · Taipei · Cape Town · Madrid · Mexico City · Amsterdam · Munich · Paris · Milan

Pearson Education Limited
Edinburgh Gate
Harlow
Essex CM20 2JE
England

and Associated Companies throughout the world

Visit us on the World Wide Web at:
http://www.pearsoneduc.com

First published in Great Britain in 1993
Second Edition published in 1998

© Financial Times Professional Limited 1998

The rights of Philip L. Weaver, Nick Lambrou and
Matthew Walkley to be identified as Authors
of this work have been asserted by them in accordance
with Copyright, Designs and Patents Act 1988

ISBN 0 273 62675 2

British Library Cataloguing in Publication Data
A CIP catalogue record for this book can be obtained from the British Library

10 9 8 7 6 5 4
05 04 03 02 01

Printed and bound in Great Britain by Redwood Books, Trowbridge Wiltshire

For Sam and Molly

Contents

Preface

Structured Systems Analysis and Design Method (SSADM) is the standard Information System development method for UK government projects, and has become a de facto standard for the UK private sector. It also forms the core of numerous courses at HND, BSc and MSc levels.

SSADM is a well tried and comprehensive method. It takes a top-down approach to system development, in which a high level picture of system requirements is built and then gradually refined into a detailed and rigorous system design. This is achieved through the careful and staged application of a range of standard techniques, several of which are used more than once during the life of an SSADM project to meet different objectives. The whole process is controlled by the structural framework of SSADM.

This book is aimed at anyone wishing to learn *how* to apply SSADM version 4+. It does not aim to justify the use of SSADM or of structured methods in general. It has been written to appeal both to students with no previous knowledge of systems analysis and design, and to practising analysts who want to use SSADM and may be thinking of sitting for the Information Systems Examining Board Certificate in SSADM.

Students frequently complain that SSADM is presented to them in a disjointed manner, one technique at a time. This leaves them with no sense of the purpose, interdependence or context of these techniques, or of how SSADM is used within a real project. The material in this book follows the default structure of the method very closely. It introduces techniques as and when they are needed in a project, and uses a comprehensive case study to illustrate their application. In this way the reader learns about techniques in a natural way, rather than being presented with them in isolation. Learning is reinforced through the extensive use of exercises, with suggested solutions given in Appendix D.

The entire method is covered, beginning with Requirements Analysis and ending with Physical Design, with a final section on Feasibility. No specific technical environment is assumed in the book, as this would have the effect of alienating a large proportion of readers, and in any case would rather go against the philosophy of SSADM.

SSADM is an 'open' method in the sense that anyone is free to use it, without paying any fees or infringing copyright laws. As a result many support agencies have been set up to offer advice on its use. The addresses of some of them are given in Appendix E.

Appendices also include an SSADM glossary of terms, suggested further reading and a comprehensive cross-reference of steps, techniques and products.

Acknowledgements

First and foremost we owe thanks to Anna, Phillip's wife, without whom this book would simply never have been written. Her expertise and efforts on the PC made the whole thing possible, and her constant encouragement when the going got tough were invaluable.

We also owe many thanks to our University colleagues Jackie Croft and Angelos Stefanidis for their thorough technical review of the book and for many discussions on the finer points of SSADM.

There are many other people who have helped in the writing of this book, some unwittingly (such as the students on our courses) and others more overtly, in particular: Andy MacWilliams for his review of the very first draft; John Cushion at Financial Times Management for his advice on editorial matters and general approach of the first edition; Penelope Woolf and Michelle Graham for editing the second edition; and Joseph Howarth for his meticulous proof-reading.

Finally we would like to thank Learmonth and Burchett Management Systems (LBMS) for their permission to use those parts of SSADM notation which are their copyright, notably the Jackson structures.

1 Introduction

The aim of this chapter is to do a little scene setting. The Structured Systems Analysis and Design Method (SSADM) is a highly structured and rigorous method of systems development, and newcomers can all too easily find themselves lost in a mass of detail with no sense of where they are heading. Hopefully by reading this chapter some of these feelings should be avoided. We will begin with a brief look at what structured methods, and SSADM in particular, are all about. We will then discuss some of the major principles and terminology of SSADM, and will finish with a short overview of the SSADM process itself.

1.1 Structured Methods

Most information systems share a common life-cycle. This is not to say that they are all developed and operated in the same way, but that they will all pass through the same basic phases in their lifetime.

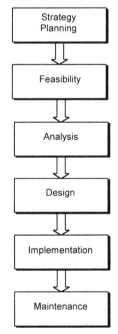

Figure 1.1 - Development Life-Cycle

Figure 1.1 illustrates one version of this life-cycle. There are many variants on this with some people breaking down these phases and others merging them. The important thing is to form an overall picture of how systems are developed and brought into production:

Strategy Planning

In most organisations there will be a formal mechanism for deciding which areas of the business require new or enhanced computer systems. This may be referred to as strategy planning or something similar, but will always involve assessing the relative priorities of different areas, with a view to initiating one or more development projects.

Feasibility Study

Before system development begins in earnest we may need to establish its feasibility, although sometimes there is no choice in the matter; we simply have to provide computer support to remain competitive or to comply with legislation. The ideas that come out of strategy planning are often vague and untried so some assessment of their feasibility will have to be carried out before we spend too much time and effort on projects that cannot be cost justified or that are technically impossible.

Systems Analysis

Once the project is underway our first task is to establish the requirements of users, and hence of the business. At this point we may have some idea of the eventual shape of the system, but the main thing is to concentrate on what it should deliver, rather than how it should deliver it.

System Design

We then translate the user requirements gathered during systems analysis into a computer system design, which details exactly *how* they will be satisfied.

Implementation

The system design provides a blueprint for building, testing and introducing the new system. It is during implementation that programs are finally constructed and hardware is installed. We will also need to provide training for users and assistance in cutting over to the new system.

Maintenance

This is often referred to as the production or operational phase, and covers the period when the system is up and running in support of the business. In the developers' eyes it is definitely the *maintenance* phase, where the system will need to be kept up to date in responding to changing requirements and system errors. In terms of the total development effort required over the life of a system it has been estimated in the past that 70% has been expended in the maintenance phase.

In the early days of systems development (1960s and 1970s) each individual developer or project team would devise their own method of moving through the life-cycle, often influenced by hardware and software considerations, but always driven by personal likes and dislikes. This was all very well for the individual analyst or programmer, but did not always lead to the best system design, or to the easiest of systems to maintain. Most of the problems with systems developed in this way were due to poor communication of ideas, between users and developers, or between a system's designers and its maintainers, and to lack of rigour which led to errors and omissions.

Initial efforts in overcoming these problems were directed at the programming or implementation end of the life-cycle. Conventional programming methods tended to result in code that was as clear as day to the person who wrote it, but was virtually incomprehensible to anyone else (the classic 'spaghetti code'). This meant that it was difficult to maintain or debug. Structured programming methods aimed to overcome this problem by providing a series of steps and diagrammatic program design techniques that ensured that code was well structured and easy to follow, was based on consistent and effective design principles, and was accurately specified. Their structured nature also meant that programming activities could be managed and quality controlled more effectively.

As a result program quality improved greatly, but this still left a much larger problem: there is no point in producing wonderfully coded programs that fail to provide the facilities that users need to support the business. So attention turned to the earlier phases of the life-cycle and in particular systems analysis and design. The result has been a whole range of 'Structured Systems Development Methods', now more commonly known simply as 'structured methods'.

Structured methods consist of two basic elements:

(i) A *default structure* of steps and tasks which the project team should consider following.

(ii) A set of techniques to be applied in each step that provide (largely diagrammatic) *structured* definitions of user requirements and system components.

Many claims have been made about the effectiveness and benefits of structured methods over conventional methods. The main one is that they result in systems that more closely match the needs of users because user requirements have been more fully understood and communicated from the outset. They do this by applying rigorous techniques that force analysts to examine the business problem thoroughly, and by improving communication through the use of structured diagrams that are easily understood and less ambiguous than text. By providing a firm structure of steps and checkpoints throughout the life-cycle, projects can be carefully managed and personnel can be used and targeted effectively.

Structured methods move the project forward through analysis and design, using techniques that gradually transform user requirements into a system specification, and which interrelate and cross-reference with each other as they do so. In this way they ensure that information is not lost, which is a danger with conventional methods that leap suddenly from a set of analysis activities (techniques is probably too generous a term), using a largely textual specification of requirements, to another set of design activities, possibly carried out by an entirely different team.

It is also claimed that structured methods reduce the costs of a system, but it must be stressed that this is over the entire life-cycle and not just the analysis and design phases. It is precisely because more effort is spent during analysis and design that the resulting system should require less maintenance (due to higher quality, greater flexibility and fewer errors). Bearing in mind that maintenance accounts for 70% of the development cost of a system, any savings in this area are likely to outweigh increased costs in other phases.

Finally, by using a consistent set of techniques and steps for the development of all systems within an organisation, personnel from one project should be able to transfer to another with minimal retraining. Most structured methods are self-documenting in the sense that they produce a comprehensive description of the system and how it operates as part of the analysis and design process. This removes the need to set up a separate documentation task once the system is in production (a notoriously onerous task), and again ensures consistency.

1.2 SSADM

SSADM was originally developed by Learmonth and Burchett Management Systems (LBMS) following an investigation by the Central Computing and Telecommunications Agency (CCTA) into adopting a standard Information System (IS) development method for use in UK government projects. It was launched in 1981 and by 1983 had become mandatory for all new government developments. This gave SSADM a large toehold in the structured methods market.

Since 1981 SSADM has been considerably updated, largely in response to practical feedback, leading to the current version (number 4.3) released in 1996. It now occupies a dominant market position and is in many ways the de facto standard for information systems development, both in government and industry. In 1988 the Information Systems Examinations Board (ISEB), a subsidiary of the British Computer Society (BCS), introduced an examinable qualification which has now become a requirement for consultants on government projects. Readers who are interested in obtaining the latest SSADM qualification should approach the ISEB to obtain a list of approved course providers; to maintain standards one has to attend such a course before being allowed to sit the relevant ISEB examinations.

1.3   Life-Cycle Coverage

SSADM covers most of the system life-cycle from feasibility study to system design (see Figure 1.2).

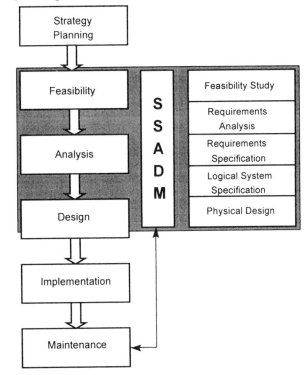

Figure 1.2 - SSADM Life-Cycle

It assumes that strategy planning will be carried out before an SSADM project is undertaken. Core SSADM is not explicitly intended for use in the maintenance phase. However it does make maintenance easier by providing accurate documentation of the system's operations, which can be used as the basis for enhancements designed using SSADM techniques.

1.4   SSADM Concepts

Although detailed descriptions of SSADM concepts will come in later chapters, it is worth looking at some of the major ones now, along with a brief overview of SSADM's underlying philosophy.

User Involvement

On too many occasions in the past users' views and requirements have been totally lost or overridden by analysts and designers who have marched in and taken over a project. It is a prerequisite for SSADM that user commitment and involvement are agreed right from the start. Most of SSADM's techniques can be taught to users without any prior experience of IS development, who can then participate fully in the project.

The Three Views of SSADM

SSADM looks at a system from three different, but highly interdependent perspectives.

The first is that of functionality or processing. This looks at the way in which data is passed around the system and the processes or activities that transform it, i.e. it sets out the functions provided for users by the system.

The second is that of data. An IS exists only to store and act upon an organisation's data. By understanding the true nature and structure of the data we get to the real heart of the system. Data structures are far more constant than processing or functions, which tend to change fairly frequently; so it is the data view that forms the backbone of SSADM. In this sense SSADM belongs to the family of structured methods referred to as 'data driven'.

The final view looks at the effects of time and real world 'events' on the data held within the system. Whereas the function and data views are rather 'snapshot' in nature, the event view is dynamic; it is specifically designed to model system behaviour over time.

Top-Down Approach

In many ways SSADM provides a top-down approach, where a high level picture is drawn up and subsequently refined into ever lower levels of detail. This not only applies to individual techniques, but to the way that one technique takes over from another when the earlier one has fulfilled its high level role.

Separation of Logical and Physical Models

One extremely important concept in SSADM (as in most rigorous methods) is the distinction between logical and physical views of system components.

Physical components are those that actually *physically* exist within the real world (or will exist in the future). They represent things as they are, warts and all, complete with constraints imposed by organisational, political or technical factors. For example in the physical world, there may be two processes associated with producing an invoice; filling in the invoice details and calculating the invoice cost. The reason for the separation of the two tasks may be purely organisational, i.e. the job descriptions or policy in the accounts office dictate that one job holder (e.g. clerk) carries out the description task, and another (e.g. accounts supervisor) carries out the other. The fact is that there are two distinct *physical* processes.

Logical components are those that represent a picture of what underlies the physical components. In a sense they give a picture of what physical components would look like in an ideal world, free from real world constraints. Using the invoice creation example from above, the logical view would be one of a single activity: creating the invoice. The fact that the process is split in reality is irrelevant; we are only carrying out one 'business' process.

Another example of physical and logical views of a system component might be the invoice itself. In physical terms we have a single object: the invoice. In logical terms we have information about several objects: the customer being invoiced; the items detailed in the invoice; the quantities and costs of each invoice line and of the total invoice.

1.5   Overview of SSADM

SSADM consists of three main components:

- The default structure or framework of an SSADM project
- A set of standard analysis and design techniques
- The products of each technique

1.5.1   Structure

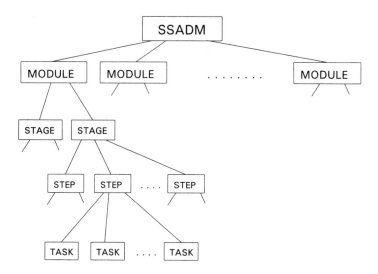

Figure 1.3 - SSADM Structure Breakdown

The structure of SSADM might appear a little complex at first, but will make more sense as we begin to look at the method in more detail. Figure 1.3 illustrates the breakdown of the life-cycle into a hierarchy of modules, stages, steps and tasks.

Each module represents a major SSADM phase, and is made up of one or two stages. Where a module contains two stages, one will be an analysis or design stage, and the other will be a project decision stage.

Each stage is made up of between two and eight steps, which provide the framework for applying and controlling the development techniques. The tasks to be carried out within each step define how the techniques should be used, and specify the required standard of the products output from the step. SSADM can be considered to be a product-driven method in that project management will be largely concerned with monitoring the quality and completeness of products, rather than with monitoring the application of the techniques that create them. The products of a technique can vary according to the step in which it is being used, as we can see from the cross-reference in Appendix F. This book will introduce techniques and products within the context of the steps of SSADM. Individual tasks will only be listed where they serve as a useful way of summarising a step. This is because while tasks are very helpful in breaking down a project into easily manageable pieces of work, they do not provide the most natural way of explaining or introducing the method.

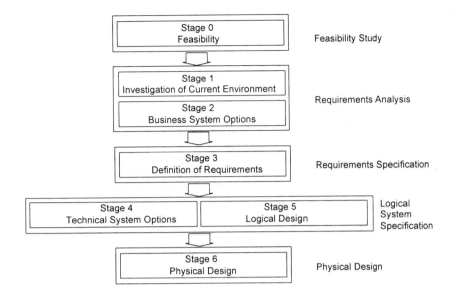

Figure 1.4 - The Stages of SSADM

Figure 1.4 shows the breakdown of SSADM's modules and stages. A brief description of each *stage* is given below:

Stage 0 - Feasibility

The scope of the proposed IS project is defined using some of SSADM's core techniques to produce a high level overview of processing and data. Several options for taking the project forward to a full SSADM study are looked at and a single option is selected on the grounds of benefits versus costs. A decision to abandon the project might be taken if the project is found to be unfeasible.

Stage 1 - Investigation of Current Environment

In many cases the new computerised information system will be intended as a replacement or extension of existing systems (which may be fully computerised, entirely manual, or a combination of the two).

In this situation we will begin the full analysis of requirements by modelling the current system with a view to drawing out existing problems and new requirements. In previous versions SSADM was heavily criticised for concentrating on old systems, rather than looking to new systems. In version 4 the emphasis is very much on the required system, and current systems analysis has a number of points to commend it as a vehicle for uncovering user requirements (if used properly):

- **Retained Functionality**. Although the current system must have limitations (otherwise we would not be thinking of replacing it) it will usually be providing a large degree of support for the business, which will have to carry forward to the new system. If we analyse this support carefully, then we may well understand the core functionality required of the new system.

- **User Confidence**. By demonstrating our ability to understand and model the current system, we will increase the confidence of users in our ability to understand the requirements of the new system. By beginning with a scenario that they already know well, users will be encouraged to take an active role in system modelling.

- **Identification of Requirements**. Many analysts find that the most effective way of uncovering user requirements is by discussing the shortcomings of current systems. By analysing and reviewing current operations closely with users our chances of identifying a complete set of requirements are greatly increased.

- **Familiarisation**. Current systems analysis is an effective way for analysts to become familiar with the business area under investigation. In particular it will be of great help in establishing common terms with users.

- **Project Scoping**. The scope and complexity of the new system can often be deduced quite effectively from those of the current system.

Stage 2 - Business System Options

At the end of Stage 1 we should have a reasonably comprehensive statement of user requirements. We now examine this and put together several options for solving the business problem (or a subsection of the business problem) represented by this statement. Although we will need to take into account some generic physical or technical aspects, our attention will be directed towards defining business (or logical) solutions, and not towards describing any specific technical environment.

A single option will be selected as providing the shape and direction for detailed requirements specification.

Stage 3 - Definition of Requirements

Stage 3 lies at the heart of an SSADM project; it is where user requirements are transformed and refined into detailed and precise specification of *what* the system is required to do. Many of SSADM's most powerful modelling techniques are applied in this stage, and we move firmly from analysis into design.

Stage 4 - Technical System Options

Stage 4 is carried out in parallel with Stage 5 (Logical Design). The specification resulting from Stage 3 should provide us with enough information to propose alternative technical environments to implement our system design on. In many cases we will have no choice of hardware and software, but where we do have some discretion we will draw up several options for hardware, software and development platforms, and help management to select a single option for use in physical design.

Stage 5 - Logical Design

In Stage 5 we will take the system design process as far as is possible without reference to a particular technical environment. The resulting design will be logical in nature and so capable of implementation on a variety of platforms. It will also act as a more or less permanent model of *how* the system satisfies user requirements. The logical nature of the design means that it should reflect underlying business rules and activities rather than physical constraints.

Stage 6 - Physical Design

The logical system design from Stage 5 is now translated into a physical design based on the technical environment selected in Stage 4. In many areas physical design is dependent directly on technical issues specific to the chosen environment. Consequently SSADM is only able to provide generic guidelines in these areas. In this way it covers most but not all of the systems design phase.

SSADM provides no specific project management activities of its own, but it does require the presence of effective management procedures. At the end of most steps and stages SSADM will output a number of products for quality assurance and project control purposes. A structured project management method, such as the government standard PRINCE, is highly desirable but will not be discussed in detail in this book (for more information see Yeates, 1992). As part of the project management structure SSADM assumes that a Project Board will exist to control and agree the decisions of the project team. This board should ideally be made up of users and IS management.

Version 4+ of SSADM places more emphasis on tailoring and customisation than earlier versions. The intention is that organisations will adapt the default structural model and standard techniques of SSADM to suit the problem in hand. Clearly this will require careful management, particularly in checking that any modified steps provide the necessary inputs for subsequent SSADM steps.

1.5.2   Techniques

Many of the techniques used by SSADM are common to other structured methods, especially those used in the analysis phase. Several of them have been present in most versions of the method and are now well tried and tested. The main feature of SSADM's core techniques is their diagrammatic nature. There is a great deal of truth in the saying 'a picture paints a thousand words'. Diagrams are capable of representing information quickly, in a compact form, and also relatively unambiguously. No-one would suggest that the best way of planning or specifying a new building is by using textual reports; they would simply be too vague. The necessary precision is only available from diagrams, plans and models. It would also be very difficult for customers to assess the design of a new building without models and drawings. The same is true of information systems.

A full list of SSADM techniques can be found in Appendix F along with details of where they are used. The three major analysis techniques equate with the three SSADM views: Data Flow Modelling represents system processing; Logical Data Modelling represents system data; and Entity Behaviour Modelling represents the effect of time on data. These are all diagrammatic techniques that closely interrelate. It is a feature of most SSADM techniques that they cross-reference with each other to form a complete, consistent picture of the entire system under investigation.

Logical Data Modelling is applied throughout the life-cycle to provide the foundation of the new system; namely the data model. Entity Behaviour Modelling marks a change in emphasis from analysis of requirements to design of the system. Data Flow Modelling is a powerful technique for analysing processing but does not provide sufficient detail for use in process design. In Stage 3 we introduce a new technique, Function Definition, which transforms the results of Data Flow Modelling into a set of user defined functions. These functions are initially textual in nature but act as a basic unit of specification, to which we add greater detail following the application of further, more rigorous, techniques.

1.5.3   Products

Each step has a number of tasks associated with it, most of which lead to the creation or enhancement of standard SSADM products. At the end of an SSADM project the new system will be described by the sum of these products.

Products can be divided into three basic groups: Processing, Data and System-User (or Human-Computer) Interface. Clearly, to represent the system as a whole these groups must interlink and complement each other.

The ways in which they should inter-relate will be explained as each product is introduced in later chapters. At the end of every module we will carry out an 'assembly' step where all the products (except working documents) from the module will be checked for consistency and completeness.

1.6 The System Development Template

While we become engrossed in the step-by-step development we should never forget that an information system consists of three parts: an *external* shell through which users interact with the system; an *internal* design from whose physical presence users are shielded; and a *conceptual* model which represents the business requirements, and upon which the internal design is based.

This separation of concerns is known in SSADM as the Three-schema Specification Architecture (3-SSA). It is hoped that by keeping the specification - and as far as possible the implementation - of these three elements distinct, the final system will be more robust.

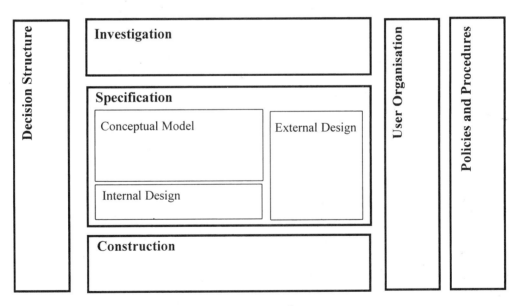

Figure 1.5 - The System Development Template

We can now visualise an SSADM project as one leading from investigation to specification to construction while influenced by the user organisation and the prevailing policies and procedures. Interleaved in all this there is a decision structure through which managerial choices are made. One way of representing all this schematically is depicted in Figure

1.5. The Three-schema Specification Architecture is represented in the Specification part of the template as the external design, conceptual model and internal design.

Whilst this book, for the sake of completeness, follows the default Structural Model of SSADM, it is intended that each project will define its own structural model, route map, or approach to systems development, using the System Development Template as a guide.

1.7 Non-SSADM Techniques

There are a number of general systems analysis techniques that SSADM will draw upon during a project, e.g. Capacity Planning, Cost/Benefit Analysis, Fact Finding. SSADM does not provide a set of precise step-by-step descriptions of these techniques, but does sometimes provide general guidance on their use or management. For detailed information on these areas the reader is advised to look to the bibliography in Appendix B, as it is not within the scope of this book to discuss them in any depth.

1.8 Computer Aided Software Engineering (CASE)

An awful lot has been written about the effectiveness (or otherwise) of CASE tools in supporting structured methods, so once again this book will not go into detail in this area.

Many people regard the use of CASE tools as essential to controlling and documenting large projects. SSADM has been promoted as an open method so there is a reasonable selection of CASE tools available for it.

The claims made in their favour by suppliers are often exaggerated, but most will provide a mix of the following features:

- Diagramming tools
- Diagram validation
- Automatic generation of first-cut low level diagrams
- Report production
- Code generation

The important thing to remember about CASE tools is that they do not carry out analysis and design for you, they merely support it by helping with diagram creation and amendment, and by providing an element of diagram consistency checking. We can draw an analogy with the production of a book. A word-processor will help you to write and to edit it. It will carry out spelling and grammar checks, generate indexes and contents pages and enable you to develop all manner of attractive layouts.

The one thing it will not do is to write the book for you, or even to teach you *how* to write it. The same is true of CASE tools: you do not need one to understand or apply SSADM, but you will find that they remove many of the administrative headaches associated with a typical IS development project.

In very small projects (less than one year of total effort) CASE tools may have a negative impact on productivity, as they can involve a lot of hard work in inputting required information. They may also be prohibitively expensive. However, there are a few inexpensive CASE tools on the market of relatively limited functionality, which will be useful in even the smallest of projects in enforcing rigour and providing high quality 'live' documentation.

1.9   Case Study

Finally, before starting on the text proper, readers are advised to take a brief look at the overview of the book's central case study in Appendix A.

2   Investigation of Current Environment

2.1   Introduction to Requirements Analysis Module

The requirements analysis module consists of two stages, undertaken in sequence:

- Stage 1: Investigation of Current Environment.
- Stage 2: Business Systems Options.

The overall objectives of the module are to gain a thorough understanding of the requirements of the new system, and to firmly establish the direction and viability of the rest of the project.

An Investigation of Current Environment involves applying several core SSADM techniques, and we will take this opportunity to introduce them gently and to become familiar with some basic concepts.

Once the Investigation of Current Environment is complete we will create and select a detailed Business System Option (BSO) to act as the basis for rigorous specification of the system. This BSO will consist of the list of user requirements that define the future system, a view of the computer processing needed to satisfy these user requirements, and a data model that supports this processing.

2.2   Stage 1 - Investigation of Current Environment

We begin the investigation with an analysis of current systems (if there are any) to drive the definition of requirements for the new system. Firstly the activities that take place in the system's environment must be understood. Then we will isolate those activities that depend on data and create a model of the processing involved. In the meantime a data model indicating how the data is connected will be developed. Towards the end of the stage we will use this data model to produce a platform-independent view of the future system's processing. Throughout we will be cross-referencing all products to ensure that we end up with a thorough list of supportable information system requirements.

We can usually get a good idea of a project's scope and complexity by familiarising ourselves with current services in the area under investigation. We achieve this by applying some of the most important and powerful analysis techniques from the SSADM toolbox, namely Business Activity

Modelling, Data Flow Modelling, and Logical Data Modelling. When performed with competence user confidence in the project team is also established.

As we document the current environment, we should uncover many of its major problems and shortfalls in support. We will document these, along with additional new requirements for the new system, using the technique of Requirements Definition.

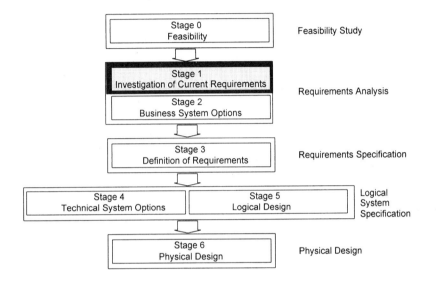

Figure 2.1 - The Stages of SSADM

No attempt is made at this point to model the required environment. This will follow in Stage 2 and (to a greater extent) Stage 3, when a detailed specification of the required system is created. For now we restrict ourselves to documenting the required system in the Requirements Catalogue.

2.3 Structure

Step 115 - Develop Business Activity Model

Any systems development that uses SSADM assumes that the project is triggered by a Project Initiation Document (PID). In practice this may often consist of a 'terms of reference' document supported by an agreement to proceed with the project. The terms of reference for the case study used throughout the book can be found in Appendix A.

The main purpose of Step 115 is to assess the scope of the project and confirm this scope with management. This is done by examining the terms of reference, and producing an understanding of the project environment using the technique of Business Activity Modelling.

If a feasibility or any other relevant studies have preceded the analysis, their results are examined, and overview current environment models created (if they are not already available).

The rest of the project is then planned including any customisation of SSADM steps or products.

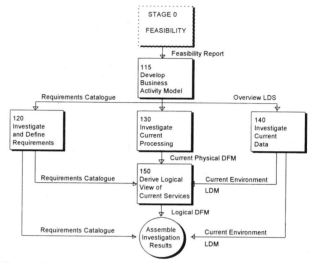

Figure 2.2 - Stage 1

Step 120 - Investigate and Define Requirements

The Requirements Catalogue is created or, if one exists from any preceding studies, expanded to form a detailed and comprehensive statement of system requirements.

This step is carried out in parallel with Steps 130 (Investigate Current Processing) and 140 (Investigate Current Data) which provide inputs to it based on problems or missing functionality in the current system.

Step 130 - Investigate Current Processing

The Business Activity Model (BAM) from Step 115 is transformed into a fully fledged Current Physical Data Flow Model (DFM) and decomposed to a level where all Elementary Processes have been identified and described.

Textual descriptions are produced for data flows and external entities, and a data catalogue is set up to describe data store contents.

Step 140 - Investigate Current Data

The data needs of the environment are reviewed and extended. A more rigorous analysis is carried out of entity definitions and relationships, and the Logical Data Model is cross-referenced with the DFM from Step 130.

Step 150 - Derive Logical View of Current Services

The Current Physical Data Flow Model from Step 130 is converted into a logical model of current services. This can then be used in Stage 3 to define the functionality which will be carried forward into the new system.

Assemble Investigation Results

The major products from Stage 1 will now provide a complete description of required services in a logical form. These are checked and reviewed with users, for input to Stage 2 - Business System Options.

2.4 Step 115 - Develop Business Activity Model

The main purpose of this step is to carry out a scoping exercise and to develop detailed project plans.

The step itself is a precursor to the detailed analysis which follows it. While developing the model which shows the activities pertaining to the working environment in which the new automated system is expected to reside, we become aware of the business events that trigger those activities and the business rules that have to be followed.

To get an understanding of the system environment, a model of the current business activities will be produced. This will lead to the identification of those activities that can be supported by an automated system.

Once we have an outline of the current position and an idea of the requirements for the new system we should be able to plan the rest of the project. This will involve allocating resources, estimating time scales, agreeing user representation, etc.

2.4.1 Fact Finding

Before we begin any kind of study we must have some information to analyse. There are many ways of gathering information which are well documented elsewhere (Yeates, Shields and Helmy, 1994). Fact-finding techniques are not considered part of core SSADM and will not be discussed in detail here.

However a few of the major techniques are worth mentioning briefly:

- **Interviews**. These will almost always form the backbone of any fact-finding exercise. Although the techniques below are useful there is no substitute for thorough detailed discussion with users and managers. It is only through well prepared, carefully targeted face-to-face questioning that we can get to the heart of the business problem. (For an in-depth treatment of systems analysis interviewing see James, 1989.)

- **Examination of Documentation from Previous Studies**. Terms of reference provide a start point, but other sources include: problem or change request logs; computer system descriptions; training guides; results of previous investigations.

- **Examination of Business Documentation**. The most important source of what information is actually needed is contained in the documents that float about as part of the day to day activities of the business. Sample documents and sample data values should be avidly collected and their content studied.

- **Questionnaires**. In some organisations these may be politically unacceptable. In any case they are only worthwhile as an initial fact-finding exercise as the results are always fairly limited in scope, due to the necessarily closed nature of the questions.

- **Observation of Operations**. This can be very time-consuming and tedious. However there is occasionally no other way to get at the minute details of operations. At the beginning of the project it is a good idea to visit the 'shop floor' as part of general familiarisation.

- **Workshops.** This way of gathering and clarifying information about business procedures whereby all the key participants of the system are gathered under one roof in the presence of two system analysis 'facilitators' is gaining in popularity.

- **Brainstorming Sessions.** There is nothing better for disentangling the issues raised by members of a system analysis team than putting them all under one roof and asking them to articulate their findings by 'thinking aloud'.

As soon as basic information is available SSADM techniques can be applied to begin forming a more precise picture of both current operations and new requirements.

2.4.2   Business Activity Modelling

Before we embark on an analysis of the activities that may be supported by a computerised information system we first have to understand those activities. We should always remember that the main purpose of performing systems analysis and design before constructing the system itself is to safeguard against delivering the wrong system to our users. There is nothing more unprofessional than delivering a system which gives a feeling to the users that this is not really what they expected. Business Activity

Modelling is the technique SSADM recommends as a start-off technique in our quest for delivering the right system to our users.

Business Activity Modelling is based on the Soft Systems Methodology ideas proposed by Checkland (1981,1990), but in SSADM we only use the technique to find out *what* is going on in the environment of the system under investigation. Considerations of *who* is involved in each activity, *when* is the activity performed and *why* are recorded and catered for, but the method assumes that there is no major conflict within the user community. The techniques that follow Business Activity Modelling deal in depth with *how* the system works.

SSADM is only concerned with building information systems where the information is in the form of distinct data items. The purpose then of the first step is to familiarise ourselves with the working environment in which our system will fit, with the distinct aim of isolating those activities that we feel will be aided by a computerised information system.

Like most of systems analysis, Business Activity Modelling is formalised common sense and is simplicity itself. We begin by finding out, at a pretty high level, what the people in the system's environment do. In the case of our case study, for example, a combination of observation, examination of business documents, a study of the terms of reference and, finally, interviews leads to the identification of the following activities: products that have to be bought are suggested; appropriate suppliers are identified; proposed purchase orders are recorded; information about product availability is received; alternative products are suggested for purchase; purchase orders are confirmed; invoices received, checked against deliveries and forwarded to Accounts; deliveries are arranged; delivery schedules are set up; deliveries are checked and, if accepted, placed in the delivery bay; delivered goods are allocated a stock location, removed from the delivery bay and placed in their proper place; stock records are updated after every delivery and every sale; stock lists are

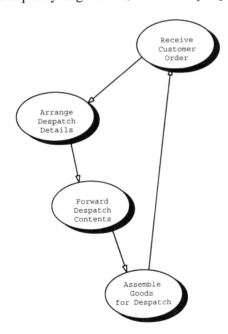

Figure 2.3 - Typical SRW activities

produced; customer orders are received, their despatch organised and forwarded to the despatch bay; ordered goods are assembled and despatched; customer order files are kept up to date; Sales and Marketing are kept informed of despatches.

As the activities increase it becomes convenient to represent each activity as a bubble and to show how these activities interact by joining them with arrows which indicate which activity has to precede which. Figure 2.3 depicts four activities suitably linked.

We then use our judgement to decide which of these activities we feel depend on data. Let us look at the activities of Figure 2.3; Receive Customer Order suggests the passive receipt of a customer order from Sales and Marketing, but closer scrutiny reveals that this is the time when the contents of the customer's order are recorded for future reference. The activity is therefore adjudged as data oriented; Arrange Despatch Details involves checking our stock files and arranging from which shelves stock has to be taken. Since the activity involves a consultation of our files we can think of it as *depending* on data and therefore classify it as data oriented; Forward Despatch Contents involves handing the despatch orders to the people who will assemble the order. It therefore is not data oriented; Assemble Goods for Despatch entails physically putting together a customer's order. It therefore is not a data oriented activity despite the fact that it *triggers* an update of the customer order files.

If we now mark the activities that we feel are data dependent with a bolder bubble we begin to get an idea of the system's boundary (see Figure 2.4).

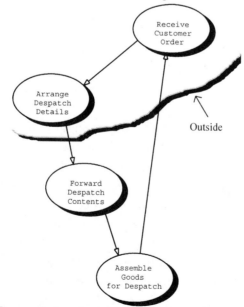

Figure 2.4 - Activities with boundary

When an activity inside the system boundary has no other activity triggering it, a little incoming thunderbolt can be used to show that information is arriving from somewhere else and we should be careful to capture it. Similarly, when an activity appears as a dead end it usually indicates that information is being sent out of the system. A little outgoing thunderbolt can be used to show this happening.

Performing this kind of more or less subjective analysis gives us a first shot at scoping the system. Figure 2.5 shows how the SRW system begins to shape up.

Inevitably, the boundary we have created is quite crude. What is important here is to agree that, for example, 'Update Stock Levels' is clearly inside our boundary while 'Store Goods in Depot' is a physical activity in which the information system plays no part (i.e. the information system we are investigating does not *place* the stock on a shelf, a human using a fork-lift truck does that).

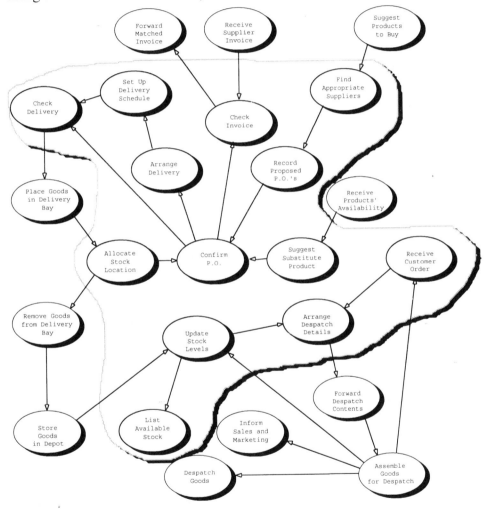

Figure 2.5 - The SRW Business Activity Model

When producing a Business Activity Model there is no need to be bogged down by unnecessary detail. An activity such as 'Find Available Fork-lift Truck' just prior to 'Store Goods in Depot' is clearly superfluous. We should avoid spending time on activity sequences which lie wholly outside the system. Similarly, common sense dictates that activities such as

'Find Pen', 'Open Stock File', 'Find Appropriate Stock', 'Strike Out Old Stock Level', 'Write-in New Stock Level', 'Close Stock Files' and 'Return Pen to Holder' should be resisted; 'Update Stock Levels' suffices.

The reason why we have chosen to place 'Suggest Products to Buy' outside our boundary may require some elucidation: In SRW Purchasers decide on the quantities of product that should be bought. They do this with the aid of the stock reports they regularly receive. This means that the stock system of each depot first becomes aware of what to purchase when one of the Purchasers sends a 'shopping list' to the P.O. Clerk. The P.O. Clerk has no authority to adjust or even suggest what should be bought. He or she simply *uses* the depot's files to find who supplies the products suggested by the Purchaser and raises the appropriate purchase orders. Since now an information system does not generate any information on its own, and since the activity of suggesting what to buy involves the creation of new data - the product quantities to be ordered - it follows that the said activity is outside our boundary. (We will have occasion to argue again about what lies inside and what outside our system as we refine our analysis. What we have to keep in mind is that we are seeking the boundary of an *information* system. Anything that adds information to the system is automatically recognised as lying outside the system since, as we have already observed, the information system cannot independently generate its own information.)

2.4.3 Work Practice Modelling

The technique of Business Activity Modelling is inextricably linked with the technique of Work Practice Modelling. The aim of Business Activity Modelling is to disentangle the data from the non-data oriented activities within the vicinity of the system. In doing so it clarifies which activities will remain unaffected by the system under investigation. As the analysis progresses the technique helps us communicate better with the users in order to mould together the future shape of their jobs.

This is done by studying the current working practices with a view of not missing them out of the future system. Let us look, for example, at the 'Forward Despatch Contents' activity which we have decided lies outside our system boundary. At first sight it appears superfluous and we could have decided not to show it on the BAM, linking instead Arrange Despatch Details directly to Assemble Goods for Despatch. The reason we chose to depict it is to remind management to delegate this responsibility if they decide that in future despatch details will be transmitted electronically to the despatch clerk. Should the people arranging the despatch details be responsible for checking that their instructions have been followed, or should the people assembling the customer's order be vigilant lest a despatch has been arranged?

The Work Practice Model begins with the set up of an organisation chart and identification of job titles within the area of concern. The organisation chart of SRW is given in Appendix A. The job titles that exist within the Warehousing and Purchasing areas are Purchaser, Stock Keeper, Goods In Clerk, Stock Clerk, Purchase Order Clerk, Despatch Clerk and Despatch Supervisor.

The Work Practice Model consists of the juxtaposition of the business activities with the job titles. It is heavily annotated with comments which will point to a better understanding of the organisation's working practices. Figure 2.6 contains a Work Practice Model for SRW where activities that lie inside the system's boundary are further annotated with a 'D' - for data.

Activity	D	Job Title	Comment
Suggest products to buy	D	Purchaser	The Purchasers' work is outside the system. Purchasers study stock lists and decide what should be bought. They send their suggestions to the P.O. Clerks
Find appropriate suppliers	D	P.O. Clerk	P.O. Clerks check the product files to find the suppliers of products. They then set-up a purchase order for each supplier
Record proposed purchase orders	D	P.O. Clerk	Two copies of each purchase order are filed. A copy is sent to the supplier
Receive products' availability		P.O. Clerk	Suppliers respond by informing SRW whether they can fulfil the whole order
Suggest substitute product	D	P.O. Clerk	The files are checked to see if any products can be replaced by similar ones. Currently this activity depends on the clerk's knowledge. It is hoped the new system will facilitate this activity
Confirm purchase order	D	P.O. Clerk	When it is clear that the supplier can satisfy the order, the order is confirmed
Receive supplier invoice		P.O. Clerk	Suppliers send invoices requesting payment
Check invoice	D	P.O. Clerk	Invoices are checked against delivered goods
Forward matched invoice		P.O. Clerk	If invoices are correct, they are sent to Accounts for payment
Arrange delivery	D	Stock Clerk	Delivery dates and times are agreed with suppliers
Set up delivery schedule	D	Stock Clerk	The Stock Clerk arranges so that SRW has enough people in place to unload the delivery trucks
Check delivery	D	Stock Keeper	Delivered goods are checked against purchase orders. Also, damaged goods are rejected
Place goods in delivery bay		Stock Keeper	Goods are physically placed temporarily in the delivery bay

Allocate stock location	D	Stock Clerk	A place in the depot is secured for each delivered product
Remove goods from delivery bay		Stock Keeper	Goods are physically removed from the delivery bay
Store goods in depot		Stock Keeper	Goods are physically placed in their allocated spots
Update stock levels	D	Stock Clerk	The Stock Keeper informs the Stock Clerk of the result of the delivery. Any adjustments to the planed stock allocations is recorded
List available stock	D	P.O. Clerk	At the request of a Purchaser, the P.O. Clerk produces a stock report which is sent to the Purchaser
Receive customer order	D	Desp. Clerk	Sales and Marketing forward customer orders to the depot. Two copies of each customer order are filed.
Arrange despatch details	D	Desp. Clerk	The Despatch Clerk checks the stock files and allocates the stock to be given to the customer
Forward despatch details		Desp. Clerk	The Despatch Clerk gives the despatch details to the Despatch Supervisor
Assemble goods for despatch		Desp. Super.	The Despatch Supervisor arranges for the physical assembly of the customer's order
Despatch goods		Desp. Super.	The fulfilled customer's order is despatched with a despatch note to the Customer
Inform Sales and Marketing		Desp. Clerk	The Despatch Supervisor sends the Despatch Clerk a 'matched despatch report'. The Despatch Clerk sends a matched customer order copy to Sales and Marketing

Figure 2.6 - A Work Practice Model

2.4.4 Create User Catalogue

Users take a central role within SSADM and so the identification of relevant users is quite an important task. Creating a User Catalogue (Figure 2.7) is a formal way of documenting the job titles and the business activities of each user. In essence, the User Catalogue is a summary of the Work Practice Model, arranged by job title.

The User Catalogue will later be used to help define the outward appearance of the new system (or at least its interface with users), but to start with its main purpose is to support the identification of users in the current environment.

User Catalogue	
Job Title	Responsibility (Job Activity)
Purchase Order Clerk	*Placing of Purchase Orders* (Record proposed purchase orders; Find appropriate suppliers; Receive products' availability; Suggest substitute product; Confirm purchase order; List available stock) *Matching Supplier Invoices* (Receive supplier invoice; Check invoice; Forward matched invoice)
Despatch Supervisor	*Despatching of Customer Orders* (Assemble goods for despatch; Despatch goods)

Figure 2.7 - A Section of the SRW User Catalogue

2.4.5   Produce Project Plan

When Business Activity Modelling is complete, an idea of the nature of the problem has been gauged. If the project has no firm plans, we should not proceed until the rest of the project is planned using the organisation's standard project management Policies and Procedures.

Particular attention should be paid to the involvement of users, and to gaining their commitment. SSADM products and activities to be used in the project should be identified and documented.

Project plans and the scope of the business area to be investigated are agreed with the project board, and we can now proceed to the detailed analysis of requirements.

2.4.6   Summary (Step 115)

The SSADM tasks carried out in Step 115 are:

Task

10   Identify and investigate the business activities pertaining to the area of investigation. Identify business rules and business events.

20   Identify the activities for which information support may be beneficial.

30   Ensure that the Business Activity Model identifies all the important aspects of the working environment. Identify who does what.

2.5   Step 120 - Investigate and Define Requirements

The main purpose of analysis is to identify the data oriented requirements of the new system. As we find each requirement we record it in the Requirements Catalogue. We will pay particular attention to defining measures of success for each Requirements Catalogue entry, so that the effectiveness of the final solution can be judged objectively. These will often take the form of testable non-functional requirements such as response times, service levels, etc.

We will carry out Steps 130 (Investigate Current Processing) and 140 (Investigate Current Data) in parallel with this step, so we should have a fairly constant flow of entries for the Requirements Catalogue.

Where there is no current system to be investigated we will obviously omit Steps 130 and 140, and the Requirements Catalogue will be the sole reference document for specifying the new system.

If we have not created a User Catalogue based on the current user activities, we will create one now based on user requirements.

2.5.1   Requirements Definition

As we produce the models of current processing and data we should keep our minds firmly fixed on the required system by asking questions about problems and shortfalls in support for the business area. Indeed our whole emphasis should be on the discovery of user requirements.

Users will usually identify a lot of problems with the current environment, many of which will be mentioned during our reviews of the development of the current system models. Problems often relate to:

- Restrictive operations. Many existing systems are unresponsive to changing requirements or exceptions to normal processing, often leading to systems being 'fiddled' in order to achieve the required results.
- Poor system quality. Systems developed over a number of years tend to have done so in a piecemeal fashion, leading to poor performance or clumsy procedures.
- Lack of system availability.
- Unreliability.
- Poor security measures.

As each requirement or problem is uncovered we need to define and document it. The technique for doing this is known as Requirements Definition.

Requirements can be classified in two ways:

1. Functional Requirements

Functional requirements deal with *what* the system should do or provide for users. They will detail what facilities are required and what activities the system should carry out. In other words they define the required functional support of the new system. The sorts of thing we need to record in this area are:

- Descriptions of required functions, e.g. to record receipt of new stock.
- Outlines of reports or on-line queries.
- Details of data to be held by the system.

2. Non-functional Requirements

Non-functional requirements detail constraints, targets or control mechanisms for the new system. The kinds of thing covered by this rather broad categorisation are:

- Required service levels, e.g. response times for on-line functions.
- Security and Access requirements
- Technical constraints, e.g. the system must make use of existing hardware only.
- Required interfacing with users and with other systems.
- Project constraints, e.g. system delivery date, cost limits.

In a sense non-functional requirements detail how well, or within what limits, a functional requirement should be satisfied. Non-functional requirements may apply to the system as a whole or to particular functional requirements.

It is important that functional requirements have measures of success included in their definition, to ensure that the requirements are actually met in full by any systems developed in the future. These may be in the form of related non-functional requirements (e.g. service levels) or subjective checks by responsible users.

Requirements Catalogue

As we identify requirements we will record them in the Requirements Catalogue (see Figure 2.8).

As well as a textual description the catalogue entry will include:

- A priority for the requirement, such as essential, desirable or nice to have.

System: SRW			
Source: *Goods In Mgr* Priority: *D* User Responsible: *F.Bloggs* Req. Id. *14*			
Functional/~~Non-Functional~~ Requirement: *To provide details of overdue deliveries.*			
non-functional considerations			
Description:	Target Value	Acceptable Range	Comments
Availability *Access*	*on-line 9.00 - 18.00 hr's Mon.-Sat.* *Goods-in-Mgr Clerk*	*response should be within 10 mins*	*early morning availability essential to clarify delivery clashes*
Benefits: *Will enable monitoring of supplier promptness and help in chasing up overdue deliveries.*			
Comments/Suggested solutions:			
Related Documents: *Interview notes No. 3, Function 14*			
Related Requirements: *No. 15, No. 16 (non-functional)*			
Resolution: *Part of all BSOs 1; accepted and followed through*			

Figure 2.8 - Sample Requirements Catalogue Entry

- Suggested solutions. Any ideas for solving the problem should be noted down as they are suggested. Too many good ideas are lost by neglecting to record them.
- The user responsible for signing off the requirement.
- Associated non-functional requirements.
- Related functional requirements. One requirement will often have an impact or dependence on another, or require common solutions, e.g. a requirement to report on overdue deliveries is closely related to and possibly a prerequisite for a requirement to enable on-line rescheduling of planned deliveries.
- Related project documents.

- Resolution of final solution. This may provide a textual description plus reference to other SSADM products which specify the solution.

In most projects there would also be project management information attached to the catalogue entry (as with all other SSADM-generated documents). This information (e.g. date of last amendment, version number) will be subject to standards as defined in the organisation's Policies and Procedures.

In addition to the detailed Requirements Catalogue entry, it is useful to set up a summary form, which provides just the requirement ID and a brief textual description (Figure 2.9).

Id	Description
14	List overdue deliveries
15	Facilitate rescheduling of overdue deliveries
16	Make use of existing PCs in stock office
17	Use product and supplier data created by the system in Sales and Marketing
18	Arrange delivery details
19	Support more precise locations for stock

Figure 2.9 - Sample Requirements Catalogue Summary

Some requirements are purely non-functional. In SRW, requirements 16 and 17 are purely non-functional.

Discussions with users will also reveal requirements for additional areas of support from the new system. For example, in SRW two problems were clearly identified: the whereabouts of stock is not pinpointed precisely enough and the despatch supervisor has to spend considerable time locating stock for despatch; the system can only handle one delivery per purchase order. Also, the problem owners wish to allow for inter-depot transfers and for the ability to record more than one supplier per product. These should be added to the Requirements Catalogue; we will be returning to them when we consider the new system a little later on.

Id	Description
19	Support more precise locations for stock
20	Allow for transfer of stock
21	Allow multiple delivery of purchase orders
22	Allow for more than one supplier per product

Figure 2.10 - Additional Requirements

Requirements Definition is an on-going activity which takes place throughout the project life cycle. Requirements are usually defined first at a high level and subsequently refined or expanded upon as the project progresses, so each catalogue entry is dynamic in nature and will probably be updated many times.

The Business Activity Model provides us with a good source of requirements. For each of these requirements an entry in the Requirements Catalogue is made. If the requirement leads to an update of business records, or if the requirement is for an enquiry that is vital to the system, a process on the Data Flow Model is dedicated to it. As this Data Flow Model is refined, new requirements will be identified which will, in turn, each give rise to a Requirement Catalogue entry.

For SRW, the on-going activity of requirement identification leads to the following requirements list:

Id	Description
1	Produce stock report
2	Record proposed purchase order
3	Confirm purchase order
4	Record customer order
5	Arrange despatch of customer orders
6	Provide delivery to despatch audit trail
7	Facilitate alternative product selection
8	Provide supplier performance monitoring
9	Record delivery data including rejections
10	Schedule deliveries (to nearest half hour)
11	Report on stocks nearing sell-by date
12	Provide possible stock-out warnings
13	Monitor supplier invoice
14	List overdue deliveries
15	Facilitate rescheduling of overdue deliveries
16	Make use of existing PCs in stock office
17	Use product and supplier data created by the system in Sales and Marketing
18	Arrange delivery details
19	Support more precise locations for stock
20	Allow for transfer of stock
21	Allow multiple delivery of purchase orders
22	Allow for more than one supplier per product
23	List un-allocated deliveries

Figure 2.11 - SRW Requirements Catalogue Summary

The Requirements Catalogue acts as a central reference document for all steps within the SSADM life cycle. Although it provides the definitive list of requirements it is insufficiently rigorous and far too textual to act as the complete specification of those requirements. In order to form a more precise picture, a range of further interdependent SSADM products will be developed, all based to some extent directly on the Requirements Catalogue entries.

The major purpose of the Requirements Catalogue is to document current problems and additional requirements. Therefore it is largely implicit that functional support provided by existing systems should be carried over to the new for any areas not specifically highlighted in the Requirements Catalogue.

2.5.2 Summary (Step 120)

The SSADM tasks carried out in Step 120 are:

Task

10   Identify areas where an information system will improve the work environment and describe appropriate requirements in the Requirements Catalogue.

20   Understand the activities of potential system users. Create a User Catalogue.

30   Use the Business Activity Model to identify areas which give rise to functional requirements. Record these in the Requirements Catalogue.

40   Identify with the users areas of additional functionality not currently available. Record these in the Requirements Catalogue.

50   Prioritise requirements where possible.

2.6   Step 130 - Investigate Current Processing

Step 130 is the step where the processing of the current system is modelled. The Business Activity Model of Step 115 indicates the data oriented human activities that take place in the environment that concerns us but is devoid of the detail required to build a computerised information system. In Step 130 we use the technique of Data Flow Modelling to obtain a more detailed model of all the system's data processes.

2.6.1 Data Flow Modelling

Data Flow Modelling is a widely used and mature analysis technique, and can be found in most structured methods. Data Flow Models (DFMs) are easy to understand and, with a little practice, reasonably quick and straightforward to develop. They consist of two parts: a set of Data Flow Diagrams (DFDs) and a set of associated textual descriptions. It is the DFDs that provide us with the truly effective analysis tool.

DFDs illustrate the way in which data (or information) is passed around the system, and how it is transformed and stored within the system. They have a number of points to recommend them; not least of which is their ability to represent both logical and physical views of a system's existing or required functionality. When used to show the information content of the data oriented business activities DFDs will provide a model that closely matches the users' perception of the current system. Their lack of ambiguity and ease of understanding therefore makes them a powerful communication tool.

Another great strength of DFDs is their hierarchical nature. The top level of the hierarchy (level 1) is used to show how the system as a whole operates, at a summary level. It will show the major flows of data or documents, the functional areas or high level processing of the system, and the principal data stores. The next level down will consist of a number of DFDs, each of which will break down or decompose one of the higher level processes to reveal its inner workings, i.e. its internal data flows, sub-processes, and data stores. The hierarchy can extend to an unlimited number of levels or decompositions, but in practice 2 or 3 levels are usually enough.

This hierarchical structure means that we can adopt a top-down approach to analysing processing that enables us to develop an understanding of the overall system, before delving deeper into lower levels of detail. We will stop the process of decomposition when we have reached a level where further decompositions are unlikely to improve our understanding. The other advantage of producing a hierarchy of diagrams is that we can present and review different parts of the model at appropriate levels of detail to different users in a way that reflects their area or level of knowledge and responsibility.

To start with our interest is really confined to the top-level DFD. We will first concentrate on the major functions of the system, i.e. those that our Business Activity Model suggests directly support the primary functions of the business area. A description of how we decompose DFDs will come later in this chapter. The key thing at this point is to understand that we do not need to capture every minute detail on our top-level DFD. The mechanisms for doing this will be introduced and applied later in the project.

Finally, before we look at DFD development in detail, always bear in mind that DFDs are an aid to understanding a system, not an end in themselves. It is very easy to become obsessed with the idea of producing the perfect DFD, and to regard it as a work of art. It is not; it is an analysis tool and will rarely be right first time. We should expect to amend it many times during the life of a project, as our understanding increases, and our willingness to alter DFDs is a sign of our flexibility and responsiveness.

DFD Concepts and Notation

Data Flow Diagrams use four main symbols:

1. External Entities

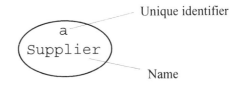

Figure 2.12 - External Entity

External Entities are people, organisations or other computer systems that act as sources of data to, or recipients of data from the system or area under investigation.

The same notation will be used for external entities in physical and logical DFDs. In physical DFDs an external entity will be any source or recipient of data that lies outside the physical system, whether that system is computerised or not. Consequently many of the people who actually input data into an existing computer system (or use output from it) will be considered internal to the physical system as a whole, i.e. actually part of the system itself (albeit a manual part) - as the analysis progresses and a clear differentiation between the system and its users takes shape, many of the people who have been perceived as part of the 'physical' system will end up as *external* to the 'logical' system.

For example SRW Purchasers decide on and provide details of orders to be placed with suppliers, but Purchase Order Clerks actually assemble and store the details for passing to the suppliers. In this instance the Purchaser is the external entity, i.e. the data source; while Purchase Order Clerks are considered to be, at least initially, within the boundary of the system.

The name given to an external entity refers to a *type* not an *occurrence* of the external entity. For example in the SRW system 'Supplier' is an external entity that acts as a recipient of Purchase Orders. It is a generic type; an occurrence of Supplier would be Heinz or Sharwoods.

2. Processes

Figure 2.13 - Process

Processes represent business activities carried out on and triggered by data. They should not be confused with computer programs. A process may sometimes equate directly with a program, but even then will be defined in user terms rather than in computer jargon. In other words it should reflect the business activity it supports.

DFDs normally only show processes that transform or change data in some way, rather than merely formatting it for report purposes. The exception to this is where the production of reports or queries forms a significant part of a system's functionality in the eyes of the users.

The name given to a process should be as brief as possible, but still convey its true purpose. Names such as 'Process' Delivery are too vague, after all the symbol tells us that we are 'processing' something; 'Check Delivery' is much more meaningful. The unique identifier should not be confused with a sequence number, it is not the purpose of DFDs to show the order of events.

In physical DFDs it is important to give the location of the business activity which triggers the process, even if this location refers to a large imprecise area such as 'Depot'. One of the properties of a physical process is that it takes place in a definable location or is carried out by a defined job holder (in which case the location will be a job title). If a process is always split into two distinct locations, then it is likely that we have two separate but dependent processes. Clearly physical locations will become more precise as we move down into lower levels of detail.

3. Data Stores

Data Stores are, as their name suggests, stores or holdings of data within the system. In physical DFDs we will use four types of data store:

- **D**: Computerised Data Store, i.e. a computer-held reference data file (D stands for Digitised).
- **M**: Manual Data Store, e.g. filing cabinet, record book
- **T(M)**: Manual Transient Data Store. This represents a temporary store where data is held until read *once*, and then removed or deleted, e.g. an in-tray or a mail box.
- **T**: Computerised Transient Data Store. A computerised temporary version of the above, e.g. a temporary sort file.

The name given to a data store should reflect its contents, and not just its storage mechanism. So we would never call a data store 'Filing Cabinet', as it gives no clue as to its content.

Figure 2.14 - Data Store

Figure 2.14 illustrates the SRW data store 'Purchase Orders'. This is a manual store consisting of copies of the paper-based purchase orders as sent to suppliers.

4. Data Flows

Data Flow arrows show the flows of data to, from and within the system.

They represent the inputs to and outputs from processes and data stores inside the system, and the information passing into and out of the system as a whole. Data Flows therefore act as links between other objects in a DFD.

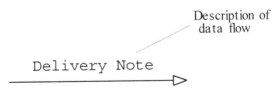

Figure 2.15 - Data Flow

Only certain objects can be directly connected by data flows:

- Two processes.
- A data store and a process.

- A process and an external entity.

We cannot connect a data store with another data store as this would imply that data magically floats around the system of its own accord. The truth is that some activity or process must take place to actually move the data. External entities cannot pass data directly to a data store as this would mean that they were inside the system boundary, and so not external entities at all. In some circumstances we might want to clarify a system by showing data flows between external entities, but these flows are strictly speaking outside the business area and so we will show them as dashed lines.

Flows may be either one-way or, rarely, two-way. Care must be taken that data flows only contain real data as required to support the business, i.e. do not contain system control messages or read requests. This is particularly important with two-way flows. When reading from a data store it is tempting to include a flow to the store containing the key of the required data; in fact only the flow from the store should be shown on the DFD as this represents the data that is of interest to the business activity.

All Data Flows should be labelled, and in documenting physical flows the label will often be the name of an actual document, e.g. Purchase Order Copy 1, Purchase Order Copy 2. Whatever name is chosen it should still give some clue as to its data contents.

By combining the different DFD objects we can build up a picture of how data is passed around and used in the system. For example, the DFD extract in Figure 2.16 illustrates the following business activities:

1. Suppliers send delivery notes to the Goods In section.
2. These are checked against the relevant purchase order.
3. Matched purchase orders are placed in a temporary file to await processing.

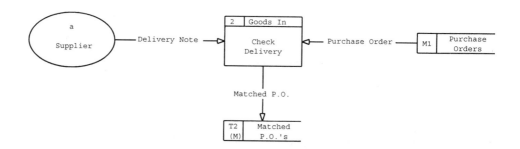

Figure 2.16 - A sample DFD section

Developing DFDs

In totally manual environments we begin with modelling *physical* flows of data within the current system, and only at an overview level.

With experience this can often be done quickly and with a great deal of accuracy straightaway from the results of information gathering. As you read through the textual summary the DFD is built up as each data flow, process and data store is identified.

For less experienced practitioners it can be helpful to use one or more of the intermediate techniques given below.

Regardless of how we produce them, it is essential that DFDs are developed and reviewed with users as we go along. In fact if possible we should have users present in the project team taking an active role in their initial production.

Context Diagrams

A Context Diagram is really a DFD that shows the entire system as a single process, with data flowing between it and the outside world as represented by external entities. Its main purpose is to help in fixing the boundary of the information system (and therefore the area under investigation) and to show its interaction with external entities.

The Business Activity Model will provide the first glimpse of the system boundary. We can now proceed with more care by identifying more clearly the persons, institutions or even other systems which will send or receive information from the system under investigation.

To develop a Context Diagram we carry out the following tasks:

(i) Identify all sources and recipients of data from the system, i.e. external entities.
(ii) Identify the *major* data flows to and from the external entities.
(iii) Convert each source or recipient into an external entity symbol.
(iv) Add the data flows between each external entity and a single box representing the entire system.

The best way of documenting the results of tasks (i) and (ii) is by using a table as in Figure 2.17.

Remember that to start with we are only interested in a level of detail sufficient to confirm the system boundary and project scope, and only with respect to *current* system operations.

External Entity	Source or Recipient (S or R)	Data Flow
Supplier	S	Delivery Note
	R	Purchase Order
	S	Delivery Details
	S	Invoice
Purchaser	S	Purchase Order Quantities
	R	Stock Record
	R	Rejected P.O. Copy #2
	R	Matched P.O. Copy #1
Customer	R	Despatch Note
Sales and Marketing	S	Customer Order
	R	Matched C.O. Copy #1
Accounts	R	Matched Invoice

Figure 2.17 - Identification of Flows Crossing the System Boundary

Using this table of sources and recipients we can draw the Context Diagram shown in Figure 2.18.

Notice that Purchaser appears twice on the diagram with a diagonal line through it. This line is used whenever an external entity is drawn more than once in any diagram to reduce clutter.

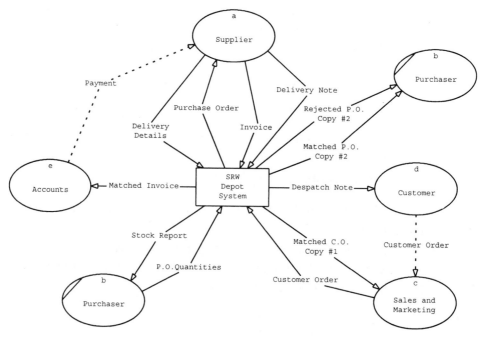

Figure 2.18 - Context Diagram (Current Physical Overview)

Of the external entities shown on Figure 2.18, some are more obvious than others. Customer and Supplier are clearly outside our system, since they lie totally outside the business; Accounts and Sales and Marketing lie inside the business but represent a different business area to the one we are investigating. They are therefore represented as external systems with which our system somehow communicates; Purchasers are on the brink and we considered placing them inside our system but they finally ended outside the system for reasons stated when we developed the Business Activity Model. (We have to be conscious that we are looking at the stock movements of goods within the SRW depots. The system we are developing becomes aware of possible new stock at the time a purchase order is set up. This purchase order is created within the system by the P.O. Clerk who works on the products recommended by Purchasers. The recommendation itself is not stored. This leads us to place Purchasers as external entities responsible for sending in a recommendation which the P.O. Clerk will turn into specific, *recorded* purchase orders.)

To aid communication with users, we sometimes show a flow of information between two external entities. These flows are shown on the diagram with a dashed line. In Figure 2.18 we have used this convention to show that customers send their orders to Sales and Marketing who in turn forward them to us.

As we go along with the analysis we will have occasion to add more external entities.

Document Flow Diagrams

Having defined the system boundary we can now move on to examine the flow of documents within the existing system using a Document Flow Diagram.

Document Flow Diagrams illustrate the flow of physical documents associated with the area under investigation. In this context documents may take the form of pieces of paper, conversations (usually over the telephone) or even data passed between computer systems.

To create a Document Flow Diagram we carry out the following tasks:

(i) Identify all recipients and sources of documents, whether inside or outside the system boundary.

(ii) Identify the documents which connect them.

(iii) Convert each source and recipient into an external entity symbol.

(iv) Add data flow arrows to represent each connecting document.

(v) Add the system boundary to exclude the external entities identified in the context diagram.

As with context diagrams, tasks (i) and (ii) are best documented in a table as shown in Figure 2.19.

Source	Document	Recipient
Purchaser	Purchase Order Quantities	Purchase Order Clerk
Stock Clerk	Stock Report	Purchaser
Sales and Marketing	Customer Order Estimate	Purchaser
Purchase Order Clerk	Purchase Order	Supplier
Supplier	Delivery Times	Purchase Order Clerk
Purchase Order Clerk	Purchase Order Copies x 2	Goods Receiving Clerk
Supplier	Delivery Note	Goods Receiving Clerk
Goods In Clerk	Matched Purchase Order Copy #1	Purchase Order Clerk
Goods In Clerk	Matched Purchase Order Copy #2	Stock Clerk
Goods In Clerk	Rejected Purchase Order x2	Purchase Order Clerk
Purchase Order Clerk	Rejected Purchase Order x1	Purchaser
Purchase Order Clerk	Purchase Order Amendment	Supplier
Stock Clerk	Matched Purchase Order Copy #2	Purchase Order Clerk
Stock Clerk	Stock Storage Report	Stock Keeper
Stock Clerk	Stock Report	Despatch Supervisor
Sales and Marketing	Customer Order	Despatch Clerk
Despatch Clerk	Despatch Report	Despatch Supervisor
Despatch Supervisor	Matched Despatch Report	Despatch Clerk
Despatch Clerk	Matched Customer Order Copy	Sales and Marketing
Despatch Clerk	Despatch Note	Customer
Despatch Clerk	Matched Customer Order Copy	Accounts
Supplier	Invoice	Purchase Order Clerk
Purchase Order Clerk	Invoice and Matched Purchase Order Copy	Accounts

Figure 2.19 - SRW Tasks

Using this table we can draw the document flow diagram shown in Figure 2.20 (with a system boundary transferred from the context diagram in Figure 2.18).

Converting Document Flow Diagrams to DFDs

To transform the Document Flow Diagram into a DFD we follow each document flow in turn, asking the following questions:

- What process generates this document flow?
- What process receives this document flow?
- Is the document stored by a process?
- Where is the document stored?
- Is the document created from stored data?
- What business activity triggers the process?

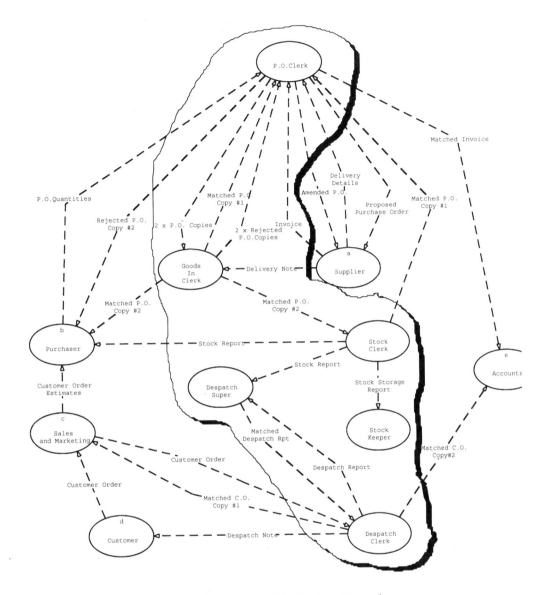

Figure 2.20 - Document Flow Diagram with System Boundary

Each time we identify the need for a process or a data store we will check to see if it has already been identified elsewhere in the diagram. If not we will add it to the emerging DFD. An understanding of the activities which give rise to each process helps keep the whole system development in context.

The best way to explain this is by using an example. So we will look at the flows between Sales and Marketing, Despatch Clerk and Despatch Supervisor (Figure 2.21).

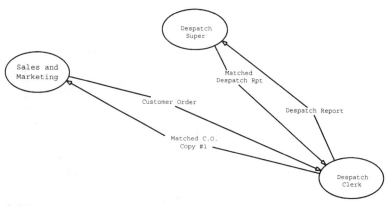

Figure 2.21

We start with the flow from Sales and Marketing toward the Despatch Clerk. Through the Business Activity Model and the Work Practice Model we notice that the Despatch Clerk, upon receiving the customer order consults the stock files, finds the stock to be used to fulfil the customer order, makes copies of the customer order and places those copies in the customer order files (Figure 2.22).

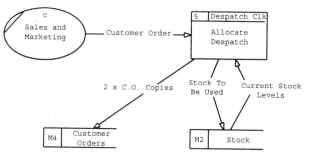

Figure 2.22

Moving to the document flow from the P.O. Clerk toward the Despatch Supervisor, we notice that the Despatch Supervisor *receives* despatch details in the form of a report and *assembles* the physical despatch. At first sight it appears that we have the situation depicted in Figure 2.23:

Figure 2.23

But, closer scrutiny reveals that the Despatch Supervisor simply assembles the despatch, annotates the despatch report and sends it back to the Despatch Clerk. This means that the Despatch Supervisor does not use any data store to record the assembly and despatch of the customer orders.

All the recording is done by the Despatch Clerk a little later on. We therefore see that the activity of assembling the despatch is not a proper *data* process, since all data processes *have* to use a data store. This leads us to the realisation that the 'assemble despatch' activity is *outside* the information system, as indeed we have already observed in the Business Activity Model. The relevant data flow section then becomes that of Figure 2.24. (It may take some time for novice analysts to appreciate what has happened here. When we produced the context diagram of Figure 2.18 we identified some fairly clear-cut external entities, but a closer look at each and every document flying about in the vicinity of the business area we are studying, coupled with the understanding we have gained from building the Business Activity Model, lead to the identification of an as yet undiscovered external entity; namely that of despatch supervisor.)

Figure 2.24

Once the despatch is assembled details are passed from the Despatch Supervisor back to the Despatch Clerk who matches them with the filed customer order copy and sends this back to Sales and Marketing. Details of the matched order are placed in the Customer Orders file (see Figure 2.25).

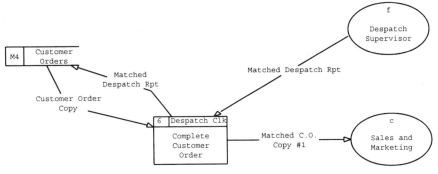

Figure 2.25

This now accounts for all of the document flows in Figure 2.20, and putting together the results of these transformations we get Figure 2.26.

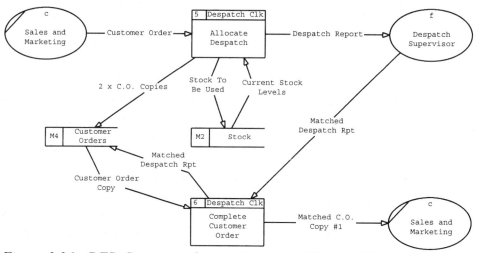

Figure 2.26 - DFD Corresponding to Document Flows of Figure 2.21

By transforming all of the flows in the Document Flow Diagram in this way, and combining the results, we can draw up a top-level DFD, as in Figure 2.27.

Notice that when a data store appears more than once on the diagram, we place a double bar at the left-hand end of its box. This serves a similar purpose to the diagonal line in an external entity box in helping to reduce clutter.

Although the main purpose of a DFD is to aid understanding of a system, it is important to make it as clear as possible by reducing the number of crossing lines. There is nothing more confusing than a DFD with data flow arrows intertwined with each other. Do not become obsessed with eliminating crossed lines, as it can be a time-consuming process when the DFD is likely to be amended frequently; just bear in mind that other people will need to understand the diagram easily. Another presentational guideline is to place data stores in the centre (as much as is possible), then surround them with processes and finally end up with the external entities on the edge of the diagram.

When we produce a first-cut DFD the chances of achieving the optimum grouping and breakdown of processes and flows straightaway are pretty slim. So be prepared to go through several iterations, merging or splitting processes, data stores and data flows, until they are all at the same general level of detail. Any objects that are combined at this stage will be expanded upon later when we decompose the top-level DFD into lower levels in the hierarchy. So as a guide try to keep the number of processes down to below ten or twelve. If there are many more than that it will be quite difficult to get an overall picture immediately.

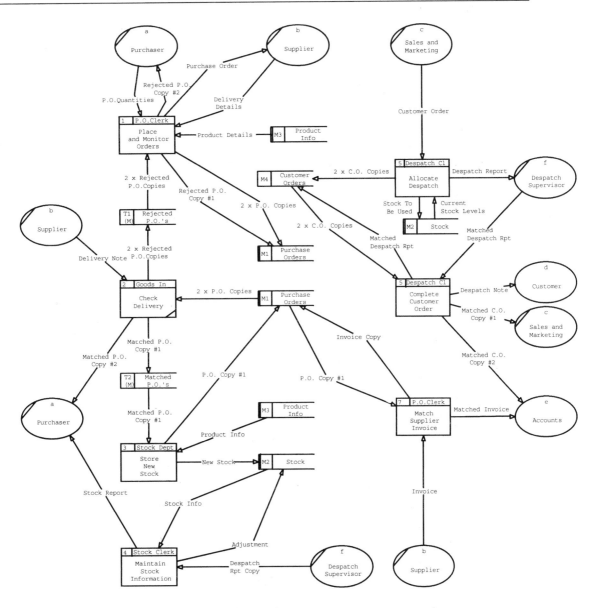

Figure 2.27 - Overview Current Physical DFD

For a given system, it is extremely unlikely that any two analysts will produce the same DFD, even if they both model the business with equal accuracy. DFDs are relatively unambiguous, but the breakdown and grouping of processes and data flows is very flexible, especially at the top level, and largely a matter of subjective judgement. The crucial test of a DFD's accuracy is whether it supports the functionality of the system. As long as users and analysts are happy that it does, it is 'correct', regardless of its artistic merits.

Overview DFDs such as that in Figure 2.27 are in some ways intentionally incomplete. For example in the SRW system there are processes carried out to maintain information about the depots themselves. We will be adding those as and when we identify them, usually with the help of the data model which is developed concurrently.

The current DFD helps in identifying areas that need further analysis. For example, a perusal of the DFD of Figure 2.27 indicates that process 3 (Store New Stock) seems to bounce data from one data store to another with no obvious external prompt. This means that something is amiss. We will be concentrating on this process a bit later on.

Also, data store M3 (Product Info) only has data coming out of it. Where does this data come from? Who is responsible for it? Is there a process that feeds this data store? Requirement 17 (use product and supplier data created by the system in Sales and Marketing) seems to give a hint of where the information in this data store comes from, but still leaves our questions unanswered. We will therefore be keeping an eye on this data store as we go along.

To an experienced analyst Document Flow Diagrams may appear a rather long-winded procedure, but for beginners, especially where the current system is heavily document based, they can be a very useful way of getting started. In some cases it may also be easier to produce the Document Flow Diagram first, and then use it to create the Context Diagram once the system boundary has been agreed.

Resource Flow Diagrams

For systems which are primarily concerned with managing or tracking the flow of physical goods, an alternative to the Document Flow Diagram is to begin with a Resource Flow Diagram. The procedure for developing Resource Flow Diagrams is basically the same as for Document Flow Diagrams except that our flows are of physical goods (e.g. stock, machine components, vehicles) rather than documents. The idea is that most of these goods or items will be accompanied by or associated with a flow of information about them, which can then be used as the basis for our first-cut DFD.

Physical Goods are represented by two additional DFD symbols:

1.   *Resource Flows*

Figure 2.28 - Resource Flow

2. Resource Store

Figure 2.29 - Resource Store

Resource Stores refer to areas where goods are stored and not to the goods themselves.

In the SRW system Resource Flows are relatively straightforward, and not extensive enough to provide a firm base for DFD development (the depot system is primarily an *information* system). However the process of Resource Flow Diagramming can be illustrated by examining the business activities concerned with the goods receiving procedures. Again we could begin with a list of sources and recipients as with Document Flow Diagramming, but resource flows and stores are frequently quite obvious, as in this example, and so can be drawn straightaway as in Figure 2.30 where we have combined aspects from many of our previous diagrams.

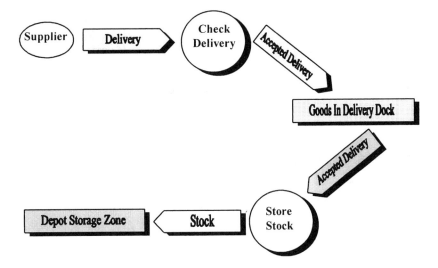

Figure 2.30 - A Resource Flow Diagram

Figure 2.30 tells us that suppliers make deliveries which are checked and, if accepted, are stored in the Goods In Delivery Dock. They are then removed and stored as Stock in a Depot Storage Zone.

Accompanying the Resource Flows in Figure 2.30 will be documents or data flows, which we now add to the diagram (Figure 2.31).

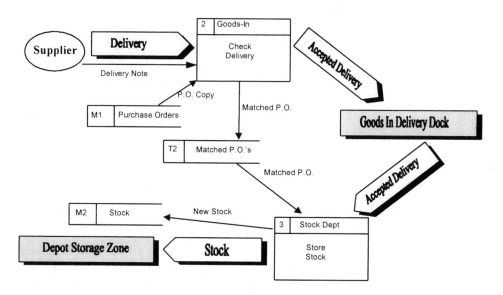

Figure 2.31 - Converting the Resource Flow of Figure 2.30 into a DFD

This now gives us a partial DFD for the SRW system. The names and numbers used may vary slightly but if we look closely at our level 1 DFD in Figure 2.27, we can see that the Resource Flow Diagram does actually confirm its accuracy in the delivery receipt area. If it would add to the understanding or acceptance of users we could annotate the level 1 physical DFD with resource flows and stores for presentations.

Only the context diagram and the current physical DFD are required for the purposes of documenting the processing side of things; all of the other diagrams we have discussed are essentially working documents, and are unlikely to be carried forward into subsequent steps.

Decomposing DFDs

The top-level (level 1) DFD provides us with an overview of required processing in the business area, but there is still a lot of information on the detailed workings of complex processes which is not shown.

Let us look, for example, at process number 1 of our overview DFD (see Figure 2.27). This process deals with the placement and monitoring of purchase orders. The name of this process alone indicates that at least two things are represented here: the 'placement' and the 'monitoring' of purchase orders. Further analysis suggests that, after receiving from a Purchaser a list of products that have to be ordered, the Purchase Order Clerk searches the product files to find the suppliers of the requested products; sets up purchase orders for each supplier; sends those purchase orders; receives notification from suppliers of whether they can fulfil the order; finds alternative substitute products when the supplier is out of stock; confirms the purchase order; arranges a delivery date; and forwards information about rejected deliveries back to the Purchaser.

We could now create level-two DFDs that illustrate the internal data flows, data stores and lower level processes of each individual process on the top-level DFD. These lower level processes could then be further decomposed into yet lower levels of DFD and so on, until we arrive at a full description of required processing.

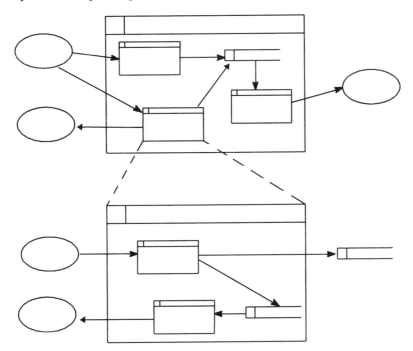

Figure 2.32 - DFD Decomposition

To start with we will decompose only the most complex processes to a level which helps us to understand the fundamental requirements of the new system. As the analysis progresses all processes will be decomposed until they reveal clearly the workings of the system.

Drawing Lower Level DFDs

We take the process box from the higher level DFD to form the boundary for the new DFD. The name and identifier of the parent process become the name and identifier of the lower level DFD (Figure 2.33).

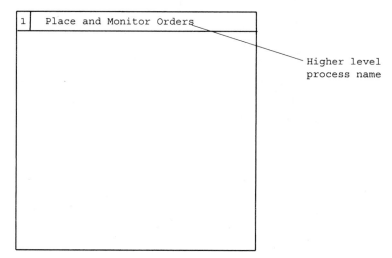

Figure 2.33 - Starting a Lower Level DFD

The sources and recipients of data for the DFD are those objects (external entities, data stores and other processes) which provided data for or received data from the process at the higher level (see Figure 2.34).

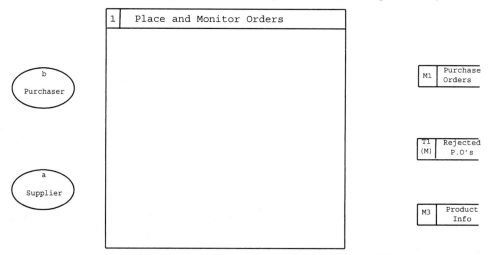

Figure 2.34 - Adding the External Entities and Process to retain consistency with the DFD of Figure 2.27

External entities and data stores may be decomposed at the lower level to provide a more detailed description of their role or contents. To maintain links between levels, the identifier of decomposed elements consists of the higher level identifier plus an alphabetic suffix (see Figure 2.35).

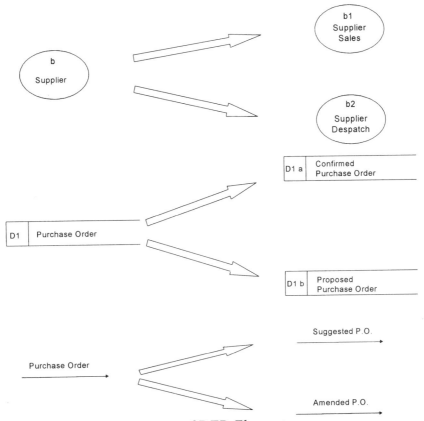

Figure 2.35 - The Decomposition of DFD Elements

Summary data flows may also be decomposed into several detail flows; but there must be *no* flows between objects at lower levels which are not represented at higher levels by at least a summary flow.

If any entirely new data flows, data sources or data recipients are uncovered while drawing low level DFDs, higher level DFDs must be amended to include them, as the objects communicating with the process must be consistent on all levels.

Processes *within* lower level DFDs are numbered by adding a numeric suffix to the identifier of the parent process (see Figure 2.36).

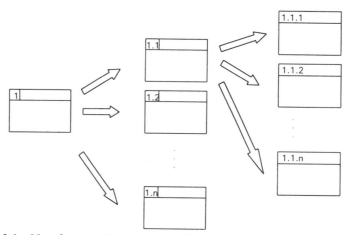

Figure 2.36 - Numbering Lower Level Processes

Data stores that are only used entirely *within* a lower level DFD are numbered by adding a numeric identifier to the identifier of the DFD (see Figure 2.37).

Figure 2.37 - Internal Data Store - The third digital data store that is solely used by process number two

Lower level DFDs are drawn in much the same way as the top-level DFD; by following data flows into the diagram and identifying receiving and generating processes, plus any associated data stores. In fact the only difference is that for the top level we follow flows into the system as a whole, while for other levels we follow flows into an individual process.

Inevitably, the detailed study of a process will lead to the identification of yet more data flows. For example, the 'Place and Monitor Orders' level 2 diagram contains flows, such as 'Product Availability', which are absent from our original level 1 overview DFD. To maintain consistency, the original level 1 diagram has to be adjusted by taking in the new level 2 insights. In fact, any useful CASE tool should do this, or at least warn of any inconsistencies between DFD levels.

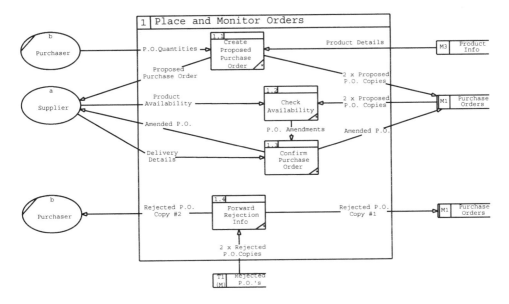

Figure 2.38 - Place Purchase Order DFD (level 2)

If a process is at a level where further decomposition would not reveal any additional requirements or system understanding we classify it as an Elementary Process, and mark its process box with an asterisk (Figure 2.39).

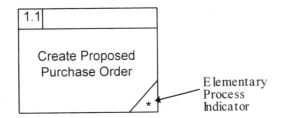

Figure 2.39 - Elementary Process

For each elementary process we will complete an Elementary Process Description (EPD), summarising its operations and activities as in Figure 2.40.

No textual description is necessary for higher level processes as they can always be described by the sum of the elementary processes that constitute them.

Elementary Process Description

Process ID: *1.1*

Process Name: *Create Proposed Purchase Order*

Description:

Purchase order details are received from purchasers for individual products. The Product files, which contain information about products and their suppliers, are read to determine the supplier for each product.

All the product orders for each supplier are batched together, and a single Proposed Purchase Order placed with them.

At this stage a Purchase Order is termed 'proposed', and will remain so until the supplier confirms that stock is available.

Note: In future, the system should allow for more than one supplier per product (see requirement 22). When this is so, the primary supplier of a product should be identified first.

Figure 2.40 - EPD

2.6.2 Create Current Physical Data Flow Model

The overview DFM will usually provide a good starting point for developing the full Current Physical DFM. We will begin by identifying any high level processes missing from the overview. For SRW this only involves adding processes to maintain the Supplier, Product and Depot files.

Once this is done we need to look for any additional data flows associated with the extra processes or which were left out of the overview model for reasons of clarity (such as routine amendment flows). We may also discover new data stores for inclusion on the top-level DFD, but it is more likely that lower level data flows will be found within lower level DFDs. Figure 2.41 illustrates the enlarged level 1 DFD for SRW.

We now examine each process on the level 1 DFD to check if it requires decomposition. Some level 1 processes will already be sufficiently well understood or straightforward for decomposition to be unnecessary, e.g. Allocate Despatch. For these processes we should complete their definition by filling out an Elementary Process Description (EPD).

Remember that for physical DFDs we are interested in documenting exactly how processes are actually carried out in the real world. It can be very tempting to omit or skim over details that seem to be due to 'trivial' physical constraints (such as batching up documents in an in-tray). This temptation should be strongly resisted. Missing out 'trivial' details will almost certainly confuse users, who will feel that the resulting diagrams are unrealistic, and could lead to important constraints being missed which should be documented in the Requirements Catalogue for inclusion in the new *physical* system much later in the project. When a good Business Activity Model is developed, it helps users see the transition between physical activities and data processes.

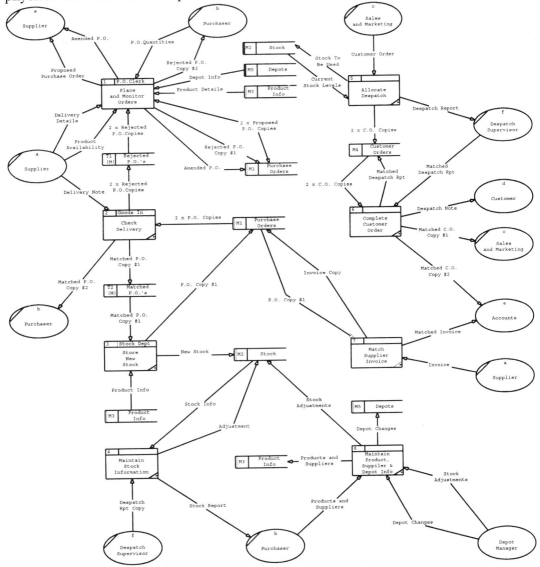

Figure 2.41 - Current Physical DFD (level 1)

If any of the level 2 DFDs are still unclear or their sub-processes complex, we may need to produce level 3 DFDs. Further levels (4 and below) are rarely needed. As a rule all processes at the same level of the hierarchy should be at equivalent levels of detail or complexity, and so require the same number of further decompositions. If we find that some of the high level processes need decomposing to more levels than the others, then we could consider splitting them up at the top-level. However, before we get caught up in excessive 'over modelling', we should once again bear in mind that the overriding aim of Data Flow Modelling is to reflect the user's perception of the system, and not to produce a pure model.

A few things to look out for when checking a DFM are:

- If any processes have more than 8 flows in or out there is likely to be a fair amount of activity going on inside it to handle these flows. So think about whether they would benefit from decomposition.
- If any processes have less than 4 flows in or out then they are probably at a reasonably low level already, so think twice about decomposing them.
- Processes that act as a 'dead end' for data flows (i.e. there are no flows out of them) are certainly incorrectly defined. Processes transform data, they do not store it, so there must always be a flow out to a data store, process or external entity.
- Processes that appear to generate data (i.e. there are no flows into them) are likewise incorrect.
- Data stores that have flows going into them (updates) but no flows out (reads) should be checked to see if they are actually used anywhere. It is possible that they are only used for reporting purposes, in which case the relevant processes may not be shown on the DFM.
- Data stores with no flows going into them should also be looked at closely. The only circumstances where this is valid are where the data store is maintained by another system (i.e. it is a reference only data store for the system under investigation).
- All data flows on the lowest level DFDs should be single direction flows.

Once we have decomposed the DFD hierarchy to its lowest level, the DFM is completed by adding the following textual descriptions:

- EPDs.
- External Entity Descriptions detailing the role and responsibilities of external entities (Figure 2.42).

External Entity Description		
ID	Name	Description
b	Purchaser	Originator of Purchase Order requirements following a review of stock levels and customer demand. (Also person responsible within SRW for the setting up and negotiating of products, product prices and suppliers, but this information is dealt with via Sales and Marketing who then inform the depot of products and their suppliers)

Figure 2.42 - Sample External Entity Description

- Input/Output Descriptions (I/O Descriptions) for bottom-level data flows that *cross the system boundary*. These detail the data items contained in each flow and will be used later in the project to define how the system communicates or interfaces with the outside world (i.e. to define dialogues with the system). The structure, with regard to optionality or repetition of data items, is recorded in comment form at this stage. Two of the I/O Descriptions for process 1 from Figure 2.38 are shown in Figure 2.43.

I/O Description				
From	To	Data Flow Name	Data Content	Comments
b	1.1	P. O. Quantities	Depot No. Product No. Qty Required Req-By Date Req-By Time Period	*The purchaser may state a date by when the product should be delivered or a time period, e.g. 3 weeks from now.*
1.1	a	Proposed Purchase Order	P.O. Number Supplier Name Supplier Address Depot Name Depot Address Req-By Date Product No. Product Name Qty Required Product Price	*Each Purchase Order will contain several lines (usually up to about 12).*

Figure 2.43 - Sample I/O Descriptions

Once the DFM is complete we should check that any problems identified by users regarding existing system support are fully recorded in the Requirements Catalogue. We can then proceed to translate the physical DFM into a logical DFM of current processing in order to identify its underlying functionality.

2.6.3   Summary (Step 130)

The SSADM tasks carried out in Step 130 are:

Task

10   If it is helpful draw a Document Flow Diagram, Resource Flow Diagrams or a Context Diagram for the current physical system.

20   Either use the above products or directly develop current physical Data Flow Diagrams.

30   Create Elementary Process Descriptions, External Entity Descriptions and I/O Descriptions for flows that cross the system boundary.

40   Update the Requirements Catalogue with any new processing requirements or current problems.

50   Ensure that the current physical Data Flow Diagram is consistent in terms of scope and terminology with the Business Activity Model.

2.7   Step 140 - Investigate Current Data

While it may seem more natural to begin the analysis with identifying the activities and processes of the current system, our ultimate aim is to provide a data model which will support the computerised processes of the future system.

In SSADM the vehicle for analysing the logical structure of an organisation's information is the Logical Data Model (LDM). A Logical Data Model is a way of graphically representing what that information is really all about, how it relates to other information and business concepts, and how business rules are applied to its use in the system. (The Logical Data Model is sometimes referred to as an Entity Relationship Diagram.)

The LDM is possibly the most important and ultimately the most rigorous product of an entire SSADM project. During Step 140 we will only model current data, so we must record any additional requirements for data in the Requirements Catalogue.

2.7.1   Logical Data Modelling

A physical DFD provides us with a model of how data is processed by a system. It also gives us an idea of how that data is actually stored, whether that is good or bad. It does not however tell us anything about the underlying meaning or structure of that data.

An organisation's data will be physically stored in many different places, e.g. paper files, computer files, temporary files (as represented by the various data stores in the physical DFDs). This data will almost inevitably contain duplications and compromises due to the physical restrictions of storage, processing or practicality. For example an actual purchase order will hold information about products (*product name, product number, product price*), suppliers (*supplier name, supplier address*), the order's heading (*purchase order number, purchase order date, depot name, depot address*) as well as the quantity of each product ordered (*quantity ordered*). While we may have a single physical grouping of data, what we actually have is information about several different things - products, suppliers, depots and purchase orders. In other words the underlying logical view is of a number of separate data groupings, each describing a different business concept or object. We will also find that information on, for example, products is physically held in many other places, such as on delivery notes, customer orders, invoices and despatch notes. This all leads to a confusing mess of duplication and interconnecting information which in turn leads to problems in maintaining data consistency and integrity.

Logical Data Modelling aims to unravel this mess by getting at the underlying picture of just what it is that the system actually holds data about, and exactly how this data truly interrelates.

Logical Data Models consist of two parts: a diagram called the Logical Data Structure (LDS); and a set of associated textual descriptions.

An LDM can be used to represent both the underlying data usage of current systems and the required data organisation of new systems. In Step 140 we will produce a LDM for the current system.

LDM Concepts and Notation

LDMs use four main concepts and symbols:

Entities

Any object or concept about which a system needs to hold information is known as an Entity Type (or entity for short).

(This must not be confused with an External Entity in Data Flow Modelling, although organisations will frequently need to hold data about many of these external entities and so they will also be represented by entity types.)

To be a valid entity we must wish to hold information on more than one *occurrence* of it. Entity occurrences are real world instances of an entity type. For example the entity type Supplier will have occurrences such as:

No 101
Quality Olive Producers
12 High Street etc.

No 102
Super-Deli Foods
Lake Industrial Estate etc.

In other words an entity type is a generic description or definition of an object, of which there will be a number of real world examples.

The symbol for an entity in an LDS is a round cornered rectangle containing the entity's name (which must be unique):

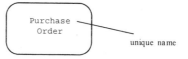

Figure 2.44 - Entity

An entity must have a number of properties to qualify as such:

(i)   There must be more than one occurrence of the entity.
(ii)   Each occurrence should be uniquely identifiable.
(iii)   There must be data that we want to hold about the entity.
(iv)   It should be of direct interest to the system.

Each item of information (or data) that we hold about an entity is known as an *attribute* or *data item*. Examples of attributes for Supplier might be *supplier number*, *supplier name*, *supplier address* and *supplier telephone no.*

Every entity in a system contains values for exactly the same attributes.

The detail of an entity's attributes is not formally included on the LDS itself. This is held in separate textual descriptions which will be discussed later. To start with we are concerned with identifying the major entities of the system. As the analysis progresses we will find more entities until a sound data model is achieved.

Relationships

Entities do not exist in isolation, but are related to other entities; in physical data structures these relationships are signified by physical links such as pointers or placement in the same file or document; in logical models relationships represent business associations or rules and *not* physical links.

Any entities which are related are linked by a line on the LDS. The line is labelled with the name of the relationship, and is named in both directions.

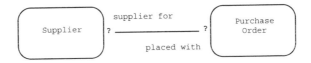

Figure 2.45 - Relationship

Figure 2.45 tells us that purchase orders are placed with suppliers. It does not tell us - yet - how many suppliers a purchase order can be placed with, or whether a purchase order can be created without a supplier being allocated. These are business rules which we add to an LDS by annotating the line with the relationship's *degree* and *optionality.*

Degree

The number of occurrences of each entity type participating in a given relationship is denoted by the degree or cardinality of that relationship, and illustrated on the LDS by adding 'crow's feet' to the relationship's line.

There are three types of degree, as shown in Figure 2.46.

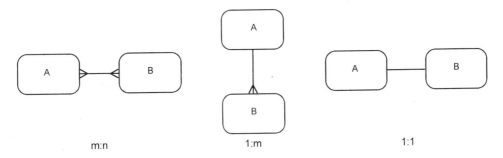

Figure 2.46 - Possible Relationship Degrees

Many to Many (m:n). This tells us that each occurrence of A is related to *one or more* occurrences of B, and each occurrence of B is related to *one or more* occurrences of A.

One to Many (1:m). This tells us that each occurrence of A is related to *one or more* occurrences of B, but each occurrence of B is related to *only one* occurrence of A.

One to One (1:1). This tells us that each occurrence of A is related to *only one* occurrence of B, and each occurrence of B is related to *only one* occurrence of A.

For example in Figure 2.47, each supplier can be the supplier for one or more purchase orders, but each purchase order can be placed with only one supplier (i.e. the relationship is 1:m). This reflects one of the business rules of SRW. If the rule was that each purchase order could be placed with more than one supplier, the relationship would be m:n.

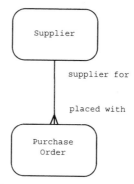

Figure 2.47 - Relationship with Degree

As we shall see in later sections relationships which are 1:1 or m:n are usually converted to 1:m on closer analysis; and indeed for many of the later design techniques of SSADM they must be. For now we are concerned with high level data usage only, so all types of relationship are acceptable.

Optionality

Each relationship is further annotated to show if it must exist for *all* occurrences of the participating entity types. If there can be occurrences of one entity that are not related to at least one occurrence of the other, then the relationship is said to be optional for that entity. The relationship line is then converted to a dashed line at its optional end (which could mean both ends if both entities are optional participants).

Suppliers do not necessarily have to be the supplier for any currently recorded purchase orders (they may have been in the past, but records of those orders have now been deleted). So supplier is an optional participant in the relationship.

However every purchase order must be placed with a supplier, so its participation is mandatory.

The diagram can now be redrawn as in Figure 2.48.

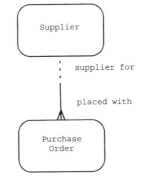

Figure 2.48 - Relationship with Optionality

The relationship now reads:

Each Supplier *may be* the supplier for one or more Purchase Orders;

and in the opposite direction:

Each Purchase Order *must be* placed with one Supplier.

Drawing the LDS

To start with we are only interested in producing a high level model of the current system's underlying data structure. The level of detail should be equivalent to that shown in the current physical DFD, i.e. sufficient to confirm the project's scope.

Due to its largely conceptual nature Logical Data Modelling can be one of the most intense activities of an SSADM project. In many projects the LDM is started by holding brainstorming sessions with small groups of analysts and users. It is quite possible that several overview data models will be created, all of which may support the information needs of the organisation. Analysts may have put a lot of effort into their creation and feel quite threatened when other team members propose alternatives. This presents quite a challenge to the management of modelling sessions, and procedures should be set up beforehand to deal with disputes.

As the analysis progresses the technique becomes more rigorous to ensure that the LDM represents all of the data used by or required for the system, and that it is logically correct. By that time the data model will conform to stringent rules and there will be no ambiguity as to its structure and contents.

Identifying Entities

Logical Data Modelling is a more rigorous technique than the relatively informal Data Flow Modelling and so provides one of the best ways of gaining a thorough understanding of current or required systems support.

With a little practice analysts often find that the best method of data modelling is to draw up possible LDSs almost instinctively, either directly from system documentation or interview results, or even during interviews themselves. Relationships are added as each entity is identified and then checked with users on the spot. This approach has a lot to recommend it, particularly at this level of detail or for small systems, as diagrams are produced and verified quickly.

Where a system is complex or unfamiliar to the analyst, a more systematic method is probably more suitable, especially for the novice. One such method, which at least has the advantage of safeguarding against missing the obvious, is described below.

To identify entities in the current environment we can begin by looking at our physical data stores to find out exactly what it is that they hold information about. If we take the customer order file and discuss it with users, we find that it not only contains details of each individual order, but of the customers themselves, i.e. *customer address, customer telephone number* etc., and so encompasses at least two entities, namely Customer and Customer Order. Continuing this for each data store gives us the following list of candidate entities:

Stock	Purchase Order
Supplier	Delivery
Product	Customer Order
Customer	Depot

There are no hard and fast rules for the spotting of candidate entities within each data store. Knowledge of the business area is the most useful aid to understanding the information usage and needs of a system.

However it does not really matter if the list is not correct first time, indeed it would be very surprising if it were. The whole process of Logical Data Modelling is, like so many other SSADM techniques, an iterative one, and there will be ample opportunity along the way to change and adjust the model.

Once the list has been drawn up we should verify it with key users during preliminary scoping interviews.

The key questions to ask of each entity are:

- Are any of the candidates merely attributes of another entity?
- Do any of the candidates represent a subset of occurrences of another entity?
- Do all of the entities have a unique identifier?

During this process we may discover new entities, merge existing entities or discard candidates as being outside the area of investigation.

Identifying Relationships

We now examine each entity in the list in turn to see if it is *directly* related, in a way which is of interest to the system, to any of the other entities. To check that all possible pairings of entities are considered it can be helpful to use an entity matrix as in Figure 2.49. Remember that we are looking for relationships or associations between entities as they currently exist, and not as we, or users, would wish them to. If we come across a relationship that is not supported in the way that we feel is best that is just too bad. It must be documented on the LDS as it is, but we will make a note of the 'better' relationship for use in the new system. An example of this will come a little later (between Purchase Order and Delivery).

By working through all of the cells in the matrix, putting a cross where a direct relationship exists between entities and leaving the cell blank where it does not, every possible pairing will be looked at. Each pairing need only be checked once, so the lower left-hand part of the matrix can be blocked out.

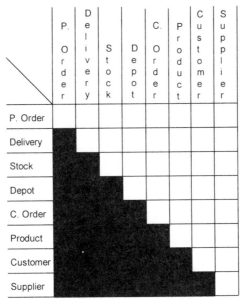

Figure 2.49 - Entity Matrix

Obviously this will not give us the full description of a relationship (as it provides no names, optionality or degree), but it will tell us where a potential relationship exists.

For the SRW system, as an example, we will look at the top line in detail (the Purchase Order Line):

1. Purchase Order - Purchase Order

There is no direct relationship between one Purchase Order occurrence and any other, so the cell is left blank.

2. Purchase Order - Delivery

Currently SRW have a rule, based on the limitations of their systems, that each Purchase Order must be delivered as a whole. If there are any items which are unavailable for delivery they will be cancelled (and possibly reordered). Each Delivery is checked and recorded against a single Purchase Order, so there is a clear direct relationship between the two entities.

3. Purchase Order - Stock

A Purchase Order will usually result in new stock being delivered. However no direct links are maintained between specific stocks of a product and the order responsible for their delivery, so no direct relationship exists between Purchase Order and Stock.

(As each purchase order is directly related to a delivery, and each delivery will in turn be related to the specific stocks it delivered, there is in fact an *indirect* relationship between Purchase Order and Stock via Delivery.)

4. Purchase Order - Depot

Each Purchase Order is placed by a specific depot, so a relationship exists.

5. Purchase Order - Customer Order

No direct relationship.

6. Purchase Order - Product

Each Purchase Order requests the delivery of quantities of products, so there is clearly a relationship.

7. Purchase Order - Customer

No direct relationship.

8. Purchase Order - Supplier

Each Purchase Order is placed with a single specified Supplier, so there is a direct relationship between the entities.

Putting the results of these decisions on the top line of the Entity Matrix gives us Figure 2.50.

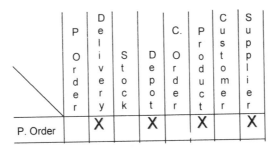

Figure 2.50 - Placing Relationships on the Entity Matrix

The rest of the grid is completed in a similar fashion (see Figure 2.51), by following the same procedure of examining each pairing.

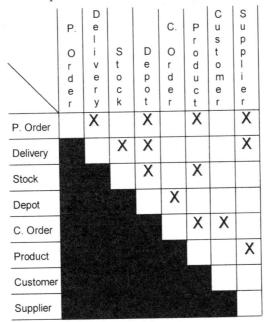
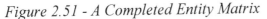

Figure 2.51 - A Completed Entity Matrix

One entity pairing that might cause some puzzlement is Stock - Supplier.

Although it is true that every stock of a product has been supplied by a particular supplier this relationship is actually maintained via the product entity: each stock is of a single product, which in turn is supplied by a single supplier; so we can trace the supplier of a specific stock through its product.

Describing Relationships

Having identified where we think relationships exist, we now consider their degree, optionality and names. We do this by identifying the business rules that apply to each entity pairing. The basic process is the same for all pairings, so we will look at just one example.

Stock - Delivery

We first consider the relationship from the Stock perspective: each Stock occurrence consists of a quantity of a single product in the same location, all of which was delivered on the same delivery. If we have a quantity of a given product, some of which was delivered in one delivery and some in another, then we will have more than one Stock. This is an example of one of SRW's business rules, and one which will continue in the new system. (For example, say we have in stock 100 cases of Greek yoghurt. It is extremely important to SRW to know if they belong to the same batch, and hence delivery, or not. If 30 of the above yoghurts were received last week and 70 this week they should be placed in different 'stocks' so that the older ones are despatched first. This SRW rule is important for all perishable goods since it would be foolish to mix together products with different 'sell by' dates.)

Thus each Stock occurrence is related to just one Delivery.

If we now look at the relationship from the Delivery perspective we note the following: each delivery of a product might contain too great a quantity to be stored in the same location, so could be split into two or more Stocks within the depot. (For example, if the largest physical space in SRW can hold up to 50 cases of yoghurt, a delivery of 70 such cases will be split into two, giving rise to two Stock occurrences.)

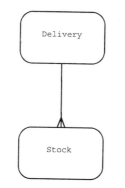

Figure 2.52

Thus each Delivery is related to one or more Stock occurrences (see Figure 2.52).

We now consider the optionality of the relationship: each Stock must have been delivered by a Delivery. So the relationship at the Stock end is mandatory. However a Delivery could be rejected by the depot, in which case it would be recorded but would not be related to any subsequent Stock occurrences. So the relationship is optional at the Delivery end (Figure 2.53).

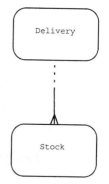

Figure 2.53

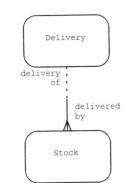

Choosing a name is often the hardest part of the procedure. It is important to name a relationship in both directions as it forces us to examine the true nature of the relationship, sometimes leading to the discovery of additional relationships or even entities. We should always try to choose phrases that accurately reflect the users' view of the relationship. In our example it is not too difficult to find reasonable names: delivery of and delivered by (see Figure 2.54).

Figure 2.54

The relationship now reads:

Each Stock must be delivered by one Delivery;

and from the other direction:

Each Delivery may be a delivery of one or more Stocks.

Continuing this process for all of the relationships identified on the matrix gives us a first-cut overview LDS for the current system (see Figure 2.55).

As with DFDs there are a few guidelines on LDS presentation which are worth mentioning. It makes the diagram easier to follow if we avoid crossing lines as much as possible. For 1:m relationships we should also aim to keep the entity at the '1' end above the entity at the 'm' end. Clearly there will be occasions when these two aims clash, so do not spend too much time on this.

The overview LDS provides us with a good basis for building a more complete model of current data. We begin the process of creating a detailed model by looking at this model and discussing it with users to check our understanding of the scope of current data and to see if there are any lower level entities which can be added immediately.

In the case of SRW this results in the addition of Product Type, Zone Type, Despatch, and Supplier Invoice. We 'discover' these four entities by various means:

The first two, Product Type and Zone Type, are discovered through the following train of thought: SRW clearly holds different types of product such as 'confectionery', 'wine', 'soft drink', 'canned food', 'ice cream' etc.; these product types are stored in different distinct areas or zones; each one of these zones is of a different type such as 'frozen', 'dry', 'bonded', 'pharmaceutical' etc. Each Zone Type can hold many product types, e.g., a 'dry' zone can hold 'biscuits', 'canned food', 'soft drink' etc.; but each Product Type may be assigned to only one Zone Type. Clearly, each SRW

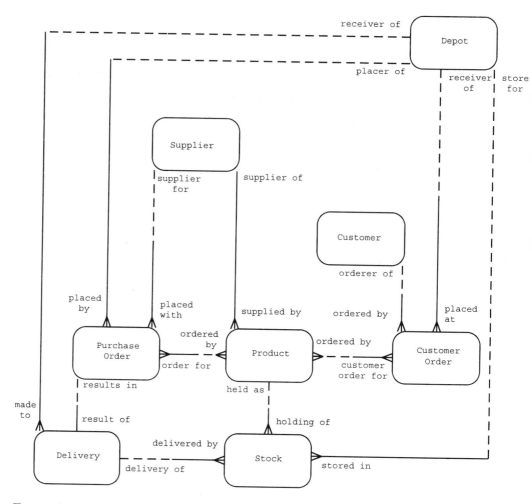

Figure 2.55 - Overview LDS (Current System)

depot contains many zones of various type, and each type of zone exists in more than one depot. Figure 2.56 shows these two newly 'discovered' entities and their relationship with Depot and Product.

The Despatch entity is more straightforward and should have been discovered earlier on. From the Business Activity Model we see that customer orders are put together and sent to the appropriate customers. Discussions with the despatch clerks reveal that many customer orders are bunched together in van loads. Each van load then becomes the responsibility of the van driver. A record is kept of the date and time of despatch. This information is held in the Despatch entity; each Despatch is therefore related to many customer orders.

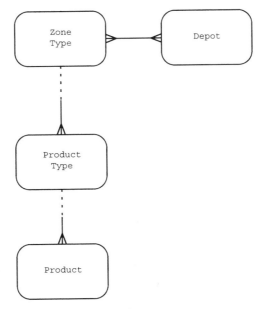

Figure 2.56 - The place of Zone Type and Product Type in the SRW LDS

Finally, discussions with the purchase order clerks reveal that a record of reconciled supplier invoices is also kept. This leads to the identification of the Supplier Invoice entity. Since SRW only accepts invoices of goods that have already been delivered and since it insists on one invoice per delivery, the Supplier Invoice entity has a 1:1 relationship with the Delivery entity. We will be returning to these two entities later on.

Before we go any further we must now introduce a few new concepts:

Identifiers

At this stage in our analysis we should be able to select at least one identifier for each entity type, i.e. an attribute that enables each occurrence of an entity to be uniquely identified, e.g. for Customer we could use *customer number*.

If an identifier cannot be found for an entity on the LDS, then it is highly unlikely that the entity is a correct one; it is far more likely to be a subset of another entity on the LDS.

Identifiers should be sought among the natural contents of each entity. Nevertheless, every now and then it is convenient to 'plant' a numeric identifier. Examples of such planted identifiers include driving licence numbers, bank account numbers, purchase order numbers, vehicle registration numbers etc. Numerical identifiers should not be indiscriminately planted on each and every entity encountered. As we will see this leads to impossibly cumbersome systems; it is also fundamentally wrong.

Master and Detail Entities

As mentioned earlier, most relationships are 1:m. The entity at the '1' end is known as the *master* and the entity at the 'm' end as the *detail* (Figure 2.57).

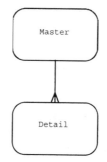

Figure 2.57 - Masters and Details

The terms master and detail refer only to an entity's role in a particular relationship; it is quite possible for an entity to be the master in one relationship and the detail in another, e.g. Product in the SRW current system LDS (Figure 2.58).

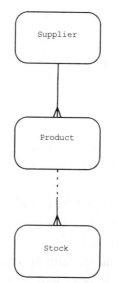

Figure 2.58 - Product is a Master of Stock but a Detail of Supplier

Logical Data Models are based on the principles of the relational data model (for a definitive discussion of relational databases see C. J. Date, 1995). Although we will not encounter formal relational data analysis techniques until much later in the project (in Stage 3), it will be helpful to look at a few relational concepts informally now.

Keys

Any attribute or set of attributes which together uniquely identify an entity is known as a *candidate key*. One of these candidates (there will often only be one) should be selected as the *primary key*. Whenever we require direct access to an entity, the primary key is used to identify which occurrence we are interested in. For example, if we needed to access the Supplier entity to find out a supplier's address, we would use the primary key of *supplier number* to identify the correct occurrence.

If we have a relationship between two entities we need to be able to associate the occurrences at one end with the related occurrences at the other. In a relational model (such as the LDM) we do this by including the primary key of the master in the set of attributes of the detail. The copy of the master's primary key in the detail entity is known as a *foreign key*. To illustrate this we will examine the relationship between Purchase Order and Supplier (Figure 2.59).

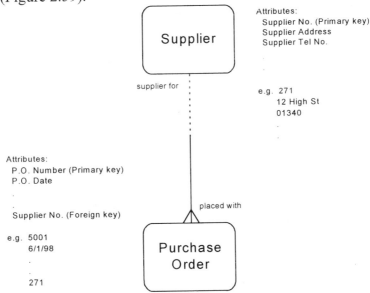

Figure 2.59 - Foreign Keys Enforce Relationships

To access all purchase orders placed with supplier number 271, we look for all occurrences of Purchase Order with a supplier number attribute value of 271. Coming in the opposite direction, to access the supplier for purchase order 5001, we look for the single occurrence of the Supplier entity whose primary key is equal to the supplier number given in the foreign key of purchase order number 5001, i.e. supplier number 271.

Primary Keys belong to one of three types:

(i)   A **Simple Key**, consisting of a single attribute;
(ii) A **Compound Key**, consisting of two or more foreign keys;
(iii) A **Hierarchic or Composite Key**, consisting of one or more foreign keys and a qualifying non-foreign key attribute.

The entities Purchase Order and Supplier, as shown in Figure 2.59, both contain simple keys.

(We will sometimes use the following convention, where the primary key is underlined and the foreign key preceded by a '*',

Supplier (*supplier number, supplier address, supplier tel. no.*)
Purchase Order(*P.O. number, P.O. date, *supplier number*)

to show the contents of each entity.)

We will be stumbling on compound and composite keys when we start resolving many-to-many relationships.

Resolving Many-to-Many Relationships

In our overview LDS for the current system we have several m:n relationships. These are fine for the purposes of presenting a high level summary of data usage, but must be resolved during more detailed analysis by replacing them with, at least, two 1:m relationships. The main reasons for this are:

- Many design techniques can only be carried out on hierarchical (i.e. master-detail) relationships which are hidden by m:n relationships.
- m:n relationships make navigation around the model very difficult or even impossible (and, although we are not really concerned with technical issues at this point, they cannot be implemented).
- m:n relationships almost invariably hide information about the participating entities or the relationships themselves.

To illustrate how to resolve them we will look at Zone Type and Depot which are related as follows:

Each Depot must be made up of one or more Zone Types.
Each Zone Type may be part of one or more Depot Zones.

The attributes that make up Depot are *depot number* and *depot address*, where *depot number* is a unique identifier which is assigned to each new SRW depot for identification purposes.

The attributes of Zone Type are *zone type code* and *zone type name*, where the *zone type code* is an abbreviation of the *zone type name*, e.g. 'fro' for 'frozen', 'bon' for 'bonded' etc.

So, for example, we might have the following cases:

Depot 101 has 3 'fro', 1 'bon' and 5 'dry' zone types;
Depot 102 has 1 'fro', 1 'bon', 2 'fru', 3 'dry' and 1 'pha' zone types;
Depot 103 has 2 'fro', 1 'fru', 1 'toi' and 3 'dry' zone types.

To make these associations we would have to set up great lists of foreign keys in both entities, of arbitrary length. As well as being against the rules of relational data modelling, this would cause a significant maintenance overhead, make navigation around the model very difficult and in any case would not be acceptable for many of the design techniques which follow.

So what we do is to create a *link entity* through which each depot is divided into many zones, each zone being of a specific type. This new entity, which we christen Depot Zone, is such that each of its occurrences identifies a particular zone of a depot and informs us of its zone type (see Figure 2.60).

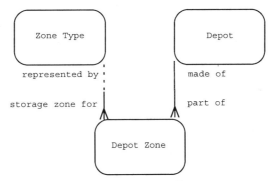

Figure 2.60 - Depot Zone links Zone Type to Depot

The primary key of Depot Zone is not straightforward. A first thought would be to choose a combination of the primary keys of Zone Type and Depot. This would have led to a compound key which would be fine if each depot could only have one of each kind of zone. But, as we have already observed, a depot may have more than one of each zone type - depot 101, for instance, has five distinct 'dry' zones.

Another guess would be to choose a simple key for Depot Zone by planting an arbitrary, unique counter. We would then have, say, Depot Zone 1001, 1002, 1003 etc. This would lead to

Depot Zone (*depot zone number*, *depot number, *zone type code)

Strictly speaking, this would work. Its main drawback is that all humans working in SRW will have to remember the meaning of these arbitrary numbers in order to avoid placing stock in the wrong zone. (Where is, for example, depot zone 1005? What does it hold?)

The final alternative is to choose a composite key for Depot Zone: The people working in an SRW depot refer to each zone as 'the bonded zone' if there is only one such zone, or 'bonded zone A', 'bonded zone B' when there are more such zones in the depot. Given that each employer of a depot automatically knows the depot's number, we see that the choice

Depot Zone (*depot number, * *zone type code*, *depot zone qualifier*)

manages the trick.

So the allocations given above would lead to the creation of 24 link entities, each identified by one of the following composite keys:

101/FRO/A	102/FRO/A	103/FRO/A
101/FRO/B	102/BON/A	103/FRO/B
101/FRO/C	102/FRU/A	103/FRU/A
101/BON/A	102/FRU/B	103/TOI/A
101/DRY/A	102/DRY/A	103/DRY/A
101/DRY/B	102/DRY/B	103/DRY/B
101/DRY/C	102/DRY/C	103/DRY/C
101/DRY/D	102/PHA/A	
101/DRY/E		

In effect the link entity acts as a list of associated entity occurrences. So if we want to know which Depot holds toiletries we just read through the list picking out all those that have TOI as part of their primary key.

A second example of a many-to-many relationship from the SRW LDS is the Product-Purchase Order relationship. This relationship as it stands is confusing. Product and Purchase Order are related because each purchase order contains many products that SRW are ordering. Furthermore, the quantity being ordered is also recorded, otherwise the order would be meaningless. If we now consider where to place the attribute that shows the amount of product ordered we will find that it does not fit naturally in either of these two entities.

But, if we look more closely at a sample purchase order of SRW (see Appendix A) we will discover that details of quantities and products are held in individual purchase order lines. So in this case we can choose a more natural link entity called Purchase Order Line (Figure 2.61).

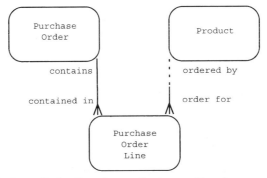

Figure 2.61 - P.O. Line links Purchase Order to Product

The key for Purchase Order Line could either be a combination of *purchase order number* and *product number,* or a combination of *purchase order number* and a unique line number within the Purchase Order (and with *product number* as a foreign key). As, from what the purchase order clerks of SRW have told us, it is possible for a purchase order to contain more than one line for the same product, the pair *purchase order number/product number* would not constitute a unique key; so we will adopt *purchase order number/purchase order line number* as the primary key.

A similar argument can be applied to the relationship between Customer Order and Product, giving us the link entity of Customer Order Line. However in this case SRW do not accept orders with the same product on two lines, so its key will be *customer order number/product number* - a compound key.

This whole process is known as resolving many-to-many relationships.

Resolving One-to-One Relationships

As with m:n relationships, 1:1 relationships are useful in overview LDSs to present a high level picture of data usage. However these too must now be resolved, either by merging the entities involved or by replacing the relationship with a 1:m (which a 1:1 relationship could be viewed as a special case of).

The problems associated with 1:1 relationships are less clear-cut than with m:n relationships:

- 1:1 relationships often obscure an underlying single entity.
- There may be a missing link entity.
- Later design techniques require all relationships to be master-detail.

In the SRW overview LDS there are two 1:1 relationships; between Delivery and Purchase Order, and between Invoice and Delivery.

Discussions with users reveal that deliveries are identified by the purchase order they are satisfying, and that the only information currently held about them details which parts of the purchase order they have successfully delivered. It is quite easy in this case to view Delivery as a logical extension (or conclusion) of a Purchase Order, so we will merge them and transfer all of Delivery's relationships to Purchase Order. To do this successfully, Purchase Order will contain attributes *delivery date* and *supplier's delivery reference* while Purchase Order Line will contain *quantity delivered*. (In the required system we will allow a purchase order to be delivered in parts **and** a delivery to contain products from many purchase orders. This means that not only the Delivery entity will reappear, but that it will have a m:n relationship with Purchase Order. Ambitious readers may wish to contemplate how to develop a data model that accommodates this general case yet only uses 1:m relationships.)

Closer inspection of the second 1:1 relationship of the overview LDS reveals that invoices actually contain invoice lines, each of which details the payment required for a single purchase order line. This means that we actually have two 1:1 relationships involving purchase orders and invoices (Figure 2.62).

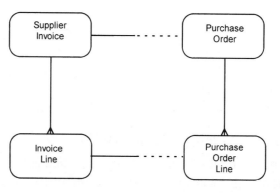

Figure 2.62 - Possible 1:1 Relationships from the SRW LDS

The information carried on invoice lines and purchase order lines describe very similar things, namely quantities of products - in the case of Purchase Order Lines of products ordered and delivered; in the case of Invoice Lines of products invoiced. So the two entities can be merged, with the *invoiced quantity* attribute made optional within Purchase Order Line, as it will have no value until after a delivery takes place (see Figure 2.63).

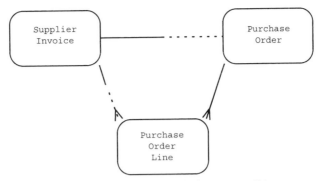

Figure 2.63 - Purchase Order Line 'absorbs' Invoice Line

It is sometimes impractical or illogical to merge entities, either because they describe very different (if related) objects, or because users are unhappy that important information is being obscured, as in the case of Invoice. In these situations the 1:1 relationship should be replaced with a 1:m, with the master end being the entity which is usually created first. In our Invoice/Purchase Order example the purchase order will always be created first, and so is declared the master (Figure 2.64). (Again, when we come to the required system we will allow an invoice to contain the products delivered as part of many purchase orders. This means that the relationship between Purchase Order and Invoice will be a m:n, but more importantly, it will be an indirect relationship through Delivery. Eager readers may wish to contemplate this situation before we meet it together.)

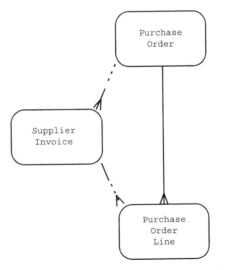

Figure 2.64 - Supplier Invoice becomes a Detail of Purchase Order

Applying all of these to the Overview LDS leads to the Current System LDS in Figure 2.65.

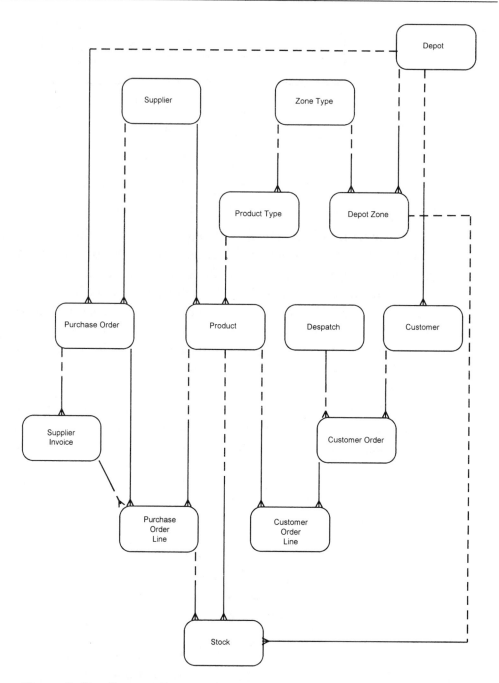

Figure 2.65 - Current Environment LDS

Removing Redundant Relationships

In some ways an LDS is a little like a route map: by following relationships around the LDS we can navigate between any pair of entities, and usually by a variety of routes. The shortest route is clearly via a direct relationship, but it is usually possible to travel indirectly via other entities.

One of our aims when drawing up an LDS should be to include only the minimum number of relationships needed to apply all of the business rules relating to data. Any unnecessary relationships are termed 'redundant', and will involve us in a maintenance overhead if implemented.

If we find an indirect relationship that enables us to navigate between exactly the same occurrences (and no others) of the two entities linked by a direct relationship, then that direct relationship is redundant. The fact that the route is longer is not important; the only thing that matters is that the business rule is preserved in our model.

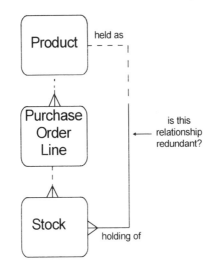

For example, if we take the entities Product, Purchase Order Line and Stock, we may wish to consider whether the relationship between Product and Stock shown in Figure 2.66, is redundant.

Figure 2.66 - Possible Redundancy

Clearly this relationship is also represented by the indirect relationship via Purchase Order Line, i.e. it can be deduced by linking Stock and Product via Purchase Order Line:

- Each Stock is present because of a Purchase Order Line which in turn must be for a specific Product. Hence we can establish which product constitutes any given stock.
- Each product may be part of one or more purchase order lines, each of which gives rise to one or more occurrences of Stock. Hence we can identify any stocks of a given product.

The direct relationship in Figure 2.66 would only duplicate this information and so is redundant.

The major difference between relationships and a route map is that each relationship carries with it a meaning, and so different 'routes' between entities will often have different meanings, thereby connecting different occurrences. When removing a redundant relationship we must always check that the entity occurrences it links are the same as those linked by the indirect relationship, i.e. that the deduced relationship is the same as the 'redundant' one, and that we are not losing important information.

Consider the subset of the SRW LDS in Figure 2.67.

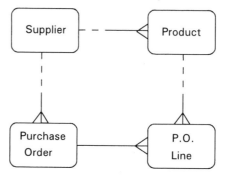

Figure 2.67 - Are any of the above Relationships Redundant?

Is the relationship between Supplier and Purchase Order redundant?

- For each supplier we can access all the products they supply, and from here we can identify all the purchase order lines that contain these products. Hence we can find all of the purchase orders for a given supplier.
- For each purchase order we can find all of the products on that order, and for each product we can identify the supplier. Hence we can find the supplier of any given purchase order.

So at first sight the Supplier/Purchase Order relationship may appear redundant. However, if we were to remove the relationship we would lose the information that each Purchase Order can and must be placed with only *one* supplier. Using the indirect relationship it would be possible for a purchase order to contain many lines, each line for a product of a different supplier. This would contravene an important business rule. Therefore, the relationship is NOT redundant.

Validating the LDM

Once we are fairly confident that our LDM is complete (that Entity Descriptions are sufficiently detailed and include the main attributes of each entity) it should be informally validated to ensure that it supports and is supported by the DFM (which is being developed in parallel).

Process Cross-reference

DFDs should support the processing of entity occurrences in the following ways:

- There must be at least one DFD process which records the creation of each entity.
- There must be at least one DFD process which records a value for each attribute.
- There must be at least one DFD process which records the deletion of each entity.

The only entities not subject to the above rules are those that are used for reference only, and which have been created by other systems (e.g. Product is created and maintained by the Sales and Marketing system).

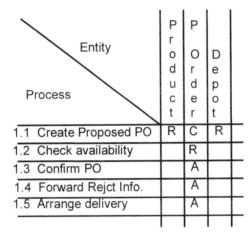

Process \ Entity	Product	Order	Depot
1.1 Create Proposed PO	R	C	R
1.2 Check availability		R	
1.3 Confirm PO		A	
1.4 Forward Rejct Info.		A	
1.5 Arrange delivery		A	

Figure 2.68 - Process/Entity Matrix (extract)

The correspondence of processes and entities can be checked by drawing a Process/Entity matrix (Figure 2.68), which lists entities along the top and elementary processes down the side. We then take each process in turn and examine any data flows going to data stores. These will represent updates to data (and therefore to entities). We should decide which entities are created, read, amended (updated), or deleted by the flow and mark the relevant cell in the Process/Entity matrix with a C, an R, an A (U), or a D. (The Process/Entity matrix is also known as a CRAD (CRUD) matrix.)

Each entity (that is not a reference only entity) should have at least one C and one D in its column. If there are any gaps the DFM should be checked for missing processes or data flows, and updated if necessary. For example, the Process/Entity portion in Figure 2.67 suggests that we have missed the process that is responsible for deleting a purchase order. We therefore proceed to enquire what mechanism does SRW use to archive old or obsolete purchase orders. This discussion with the users leads to the identification of process 1.6: 'Archive Old Order'. (Because deleting information from the system is quite a drastic measure we will be returning to it during Requirements Specification.)

Access Paths

We should also check that the LDM can provide access to all of the data items required by each elementary process. Most elementary processes will need to access a number of data items, which will be specified by some selection criteria. These items will often be represented by the attributes of more than one entity. We must now ensure that we can navigate around the relationships of the LDS, applying the selection criteria to filter out the entity occurrences we need to provide all of the necessary data. These navigations are called 'Access Paths'.

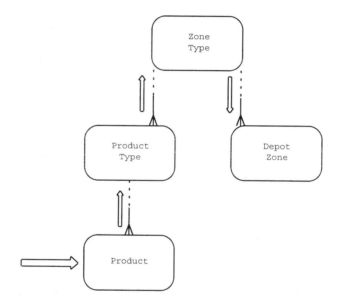

Figure 2.69 - Informal Access Path

For example, when we carry out the process 'Allocate Zone' we will need to find out which depot zone is allocated for the storage of our product within the relevant depot.

After some thought it becomes apparent that the entry point to the LDS is via the *product number* in the entity Product. We can then access its product type and then the zone type in which this product type fits. From here we can read through all the occurrences of Depot Zone for that zone type, until we find a depot zone which in turn is related to the relevant depot. We can show this informally by annotating the LDS as in Figure 2.69.

This is a fairly complicated access path; most will be very much simpler. But it does show that the required data can be accessed.

2.7.2   Summary (Step 140)

The SSADM tasks carried out in Step 140 are:

Task

10	Review and revise the overview LDM.
20	Define the major attributes of each entity.
30	Check that the LDM will support the Elementary Processes from the DFM.
40	Record any new data requirements or problems with current data in the Requirements Catalogue.

2.8   Step 150 - Derive Logical View of Current Services

In Step 130 we developed a detailed snapshot picture of the current system's processing, including all of its physical constraints and peculiarities. Many of these physical elements represent historical or administrative decisions which no longer apply, or which should not be carried forward into the new system. But at the heart of the DFM is a large amount of functionality that provides real active support for the business. It is very likely that our new system will be required to carry forward this support.

A physical DFM shows the current system in all its glory - good and bad. In Step 150 it is our task to convert the physical picture into a logical one, which reflects the underlying business functions of the existing system. We can then decide which elements will be retained in the new system, and add additional functionality (as specified in the Requirements Catalogue) to it to form a complete model of the required processing. We will carry out these latter activities in Stages 2 and 3; for now we are purely interested in deriving a logical DFM of current processing.

2.8.1   Logicalising Data Flow Models

If we have produced an effective Current Physical DFM, all of the detail we require on current processing will be available from the lowest level DFDs. It now 'merely' requires logicalising. We could start all over again with a top-down analysis of processing to produce a *logical* set of DFDs, but this would clearly make no sense at all as it would mean repeating a large amount of analysis. Instead we will work from the bottom-up, by removing the physical elements of elementary processes and bottom-level DFDs, and then reconstructing the hierarchy by logically re-grouping these transformed processes.

It is quite tempting to carry out a sort of intuitive logicalisation exercise, and this may work for experienced analysts. But for most people it is a much better idea to follow a methodical transformation, by considering each DFD object carefully.

Rationalising Data Stores

Data stores in a physical DFM reflect the way in which data is actually stored. In a logical DFM we replace these with logical data stores based on the organisation of data in the LDS.

To begin with it appears tempting to devote a single data store for each entity on the LDS. Unfortunately this could lead to an unmanageably large number of data stores, some of which would just represent link entities. It would also mean duplicating details of the data structure which are more properly documented in the LDS. To avoid these problems we will create logical data stores that represent *groups* of closely related entities (although some entities will stand out on their own and so remain the only entity represented by a data store).

As usual with most systems analysis there are no strict guidelines for grouping entities, but we can start by asking:

1. Are there any entities which can easily or naturally be described using a single phrase? (e.g. Depot, Depot Zone and Zone Type could be called Depot Information).
2. Are there any groups of related entities which are created at the same time? (e.g. Purchase Order and Purchase Order Line)
3. Are any groups of entities associated with the same major inputs or outputs? (e.g. Customer, Customer Order, Customer Order Line and Despatch)

At the end of the day we will probably create groupings by identifying entities which just 'feel right' together. Obviously what feels right to one person may not feel right to another, so there will be many different possibilities for grouping the LDS. One such way for the SRW LDS is shown in Figure 2.70.

To avoid data duplication the LDS must be divided into discrete groups such that:

- Each data store contains one or more related entities.
- Each entity is held entirely within a single data store (i.e. must not be duplicated or fragmented).

The only exceptions to this are decomposed data stores. Data stores on a physical DFD may be decomposed to clarify which parts of a data store a

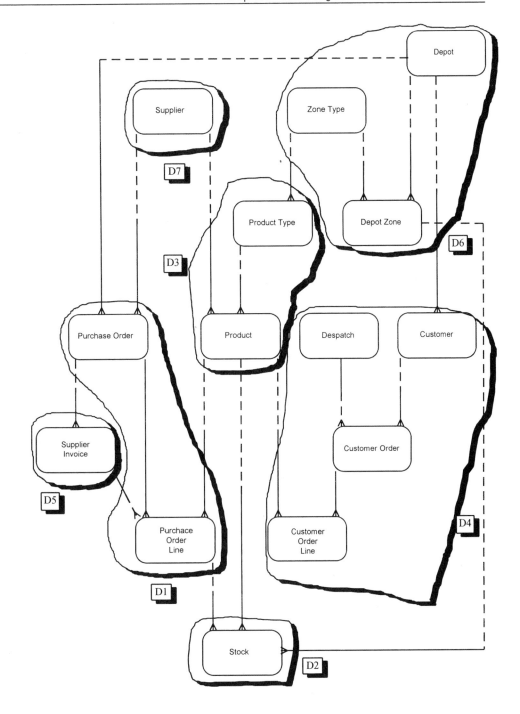

Figure 2.70 - Grouped LDS

process is accessing. If the decomposition is based on different subsets of data items then they may in fact be equivalent to different entities. Rationalising these data stores may mean that each decomposed data store is now equivalent to a single logical data store, so the decomposition is no longer necessary. However in cases where the decomposition was based on data item value or status it may still be valid, so there will be two logical data stores containing the same LDS extract.

We document the correspondence between logical data stores and entities using a Logical Data Store/Entity Cross-reference, as in Figure 2.71. The left-hand column lists the data stores, while the right-hand column shows the corresponding LDS subset. Each entity should appear only once. We do not show decomposed data stores on the cross-reference; just the parent data store, e.g. if we were to retain the value-based decomposition of Purchase Order into Firm and Provisional Purchase Orders, we would only show the parent Purchase Order data store.

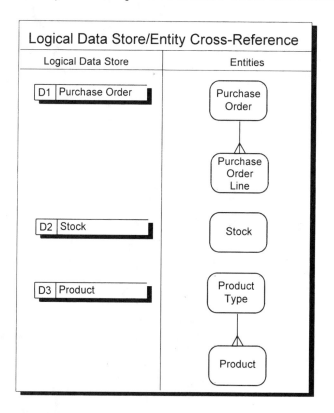

Figure 2.71 - A Section of the SRW Logical Data Store/Entity Cross-reference

The Logical Data Store/Entity Cross-reference is one of the most important documents of Analysis since it is the only means through which the consistency of our data and process models is enforced.

Removing Transient Data Stores

Transient data stores in physical DFDs almost always exist to satisfy some physical constraint. They either represent temporary halts in a data flow or a postponement in storing information. All transient data stores which represent a temporary halt should be removed from the logical DFD and replaced with a simple data flow. Transient data stores which represent a postponement in recording information have no meaning in an automated system, but have to be handled with a bit of care to ensure that the new system will preserve all healthy current working practices. To illustrate how to handle transient data stores we will consider the 'Store New Stock' process in Figure 2.72. (Remember that this process sticks out like a sore thumb in the DFDs of figures 2.27 and 2.41. We will now demonstrate how the process of logicalisation can clarify certain aspects of the current DFD which may have escaped us until now.)

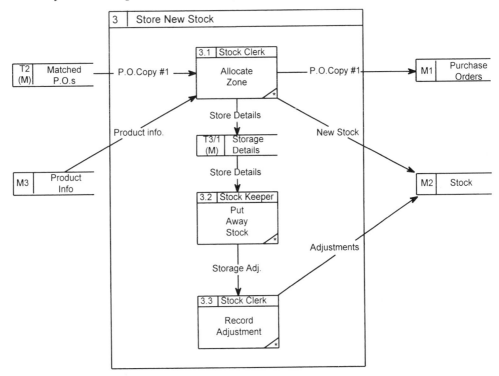

Figure 2.72 - Store New Stock contains Transient Data Stores

The internal transient data store represents the activity whereby the Stock Clerk writes the storing instructions on a piece of paper which is placed in a tray to be collected by the stock keeper. It therefore only represents a delay in action and is, logically, superfluous. Its removal gives us Figure 2.73. (Note that the removal of this data store does not lead to any loss of information; the 'New Stock' data flow contains the relevant storage details.)

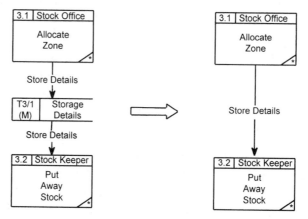

Figure 2.73 - Transient Data Stores may become Direct Data Flows

The removal of the second transient data store T2(M) which lies outside the process (see Figures 2.27 and 2.72) is slightly trickier to handle. This is because it contains information about products that have been successfully delivered. We need to make sure that this information has been recorded before we dismiss the transient data store. When goods are delivered and SRW accepts them, the acceptance has to be recorded in the appropriate place. If we now recollect, purchase orders and deliveries are linked in a 1:1 relationship which led us to merge delivery information in the Purchase Order and Purchase Order Line entities of the LDS. According now to the Logical Data Store/ Entity Cross Reference, these two entities have ended up in the 'Purchase Orders' data store. We therefore have to make sure that the 'Check Delivery' process which is responsible for accepting deliveries does show a data flow into that data store. If it does, the 'Matched P.O.'s' transient data store is superfluous and can be replaced by a data flow. If it doesn't, and indeed it doesn't in our DFD of Figure 2.27, we have to adjust the DFD before replacing the transient data store with a data flow. We will return to this point a bit further on.

Rationalising Elementary Processes

Processes in a physical DFM will accurately describe what is being done with the information in a system, but will also reflect the way in which activities are physically organised. In particular they will provide details of the location of processes, and reflect organisational structures and job responsibilities.

The purpose of a logical DFM is to describe the underlying logical processing; in effect to represent the ideal organisation of data processing activities that would occur if no physical constraints existed.

Transforming physical processes into logical processes is an iterative activity, involving discipline in identifying purely physical elements of processing. There are no strict rules or tasks which we can apply to rationalising processes, but SSADM does offer a fairly comprehensive set of guidelines:

- Remove details of the location of a process since location only indicates a physical constraint. (While removing details of locations from processes we will often find that the organisational structure or job holder concerned is actually altering the data that is input to the physical process. In these cases the location will become an external entity. In this way the activity of logicalisation firms up on the system boundary -see Figure 2.74.

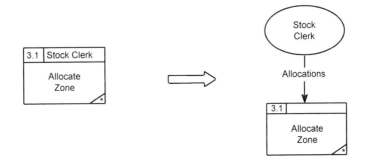

Figure 2.74 - Locations may become External Entities

- Merge any process that merely re-formats or re-arranges data (e.g. it indicates a sort or a batching process) with the process that triggers it.

- Check that each process actually transforms data, and does not just report on it. Reporting requirements should be documented in the Requirements Catalogue, unless they form a major part of the system's functionality, in which case they will remain as elementary processes.

- Try to combine processes that *always* occur together in sequence. In particular look for processes linked by a single data flow, which only occur separately due to their physical locations (Figure 2.75).

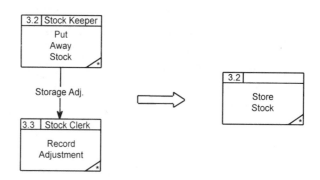

Figure 2.75 - Processes that always occur together are combined

- Combine processes which are duplicated in the physical DFM. Again, this will usually occur for reasons of physical location, or overlapping job responsibilities.

- Where more than one process contains a common activity, create an elementary process description for the duplicate processing and cross-reference with all processes which use it, e.g. complex calculations are frequently carried out as part of several processes.

- If a process contains an element of human judgement or subjective decision making, this element is represented by data flows to and from an external entity. The same applies to processes which require a user to check the results of a system instruction (Figure 2.76).

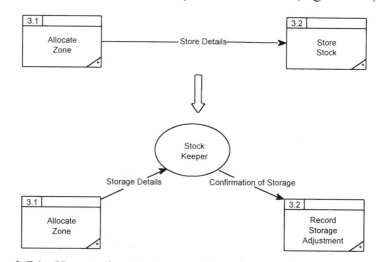

Figure 2.76 - Human decisions are reflected through External Entities

In Figure 2.76 we have also taken the opportunity of renaming process 3.2. We chose to do so because the original name has a physical connotation which may obscure the information content in which we are interested; the new name is more precise in information terms.

• Data flows into the system which clearly act as a trigger for a set of processing will ideally be received by a dedicated process.

• Data flows are totally stripped of any physical connotations. For example, data flow 'P.O. Copy #1' which is used by process 3.1 - Allocate Zone - contains information of goods that have been received. We therefore strip this flow of its 'paper copy' connotations by renaming the flow 'Accepted Delivery Details'.

• All data stores are shown as digitised to reflect that they represent groupings of entities which are, after all, 'logical' and therefore totally stripped of any physical connotations.

Putting together the above transformations we arrive at the logicalised version of Store New Stock in Figure 2.77. Notice that we have concentrated solely on this process and left the transient data store T1 which links processes 2 and 3 unaffected for the time being.

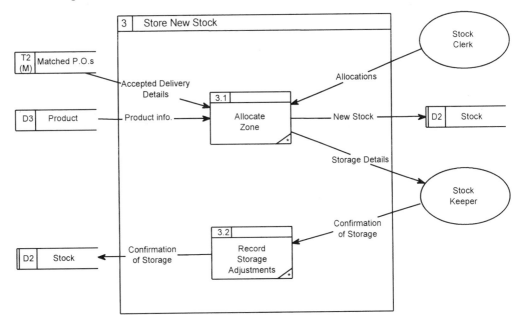

Figure 2.77 - Logicalised version of Figure 2.73

In rationalising bottom-level processes we are only concerned with processing that is to be carried forward into the new computer system. So we should remove any purely human activities and replace them with external entities. Indeed we did this, albeit informally, when we produced the BAM. The reader only has to compare the relevant section of the BAM of Figure 2.5 with Figure 2.77 to see that we have ended up with processes and external entities which correspond almost directly with the activities which have ended inside the system boundary. The main reason for not relying solely on the BAM and relying instead on logicalisation to prune the current DFD is that the BAM, due to its informal nature, has to be handled by an experienced team. Nevertheless, it is quite possible, and indeed recommended in small projects, to move from producing a BAM directly to an LDM and a logical DFM, totally bypassing the current DFM.

The logicalisation of the 'Store New Stock' process has led to a change in work practices which should not escape the astute system analyst: Whereas in the Business Activity Model and in Figure 2.72 the stock keeper informs the stock clerk of any stock allocation adjustments and the stock clerk updates the files, in the proposed new system it is the stock keeper who records, directly, any storage adjustments.

Rebuilding the DFM Hierarchy

It is likely that some or all of the original boundaries of the lowest level DFDs (and thus of high level processes) were determined by physical factors, such as location. These factors are no longer relevant, so we will now regroup our logicalised elementary processes to form new low level DFDs based on logical considerations. We will then use these to define higher level processes which will in turn reflect a more logical view of functionality.

Possibly the most effective way of starting this is to combine all of the lowest level DFDs into one very large DFD, in which every process is elementary. This should be fairly straight forward as each DFD will show which others it interfaces with around its border. We can then draw new boundaries around logically related processes to form new bottom-level DFDs. The problem with this is that the 'big' DFD will often be too large or cumbersome to draw. So we will usually end up by examining the bottom-level processes in their separate, but interlinked, diagrams.

However, these are purely matters of presentational convenience, and whichever way we choose to approach it our main task is to establish new logical groupings of elementary processes. Groupings can be difficult to define, and are usually based on subjective views of functionality. Once again strict rules are difficult to apply; it is far more a matter of experience and judgement. However to help us there are three basic classes of grouping to look for:

1. Functional Groupings

The most important thing when grouping processes is to reflect the users' perception of functional areas. Current systems may already be organised along functional lines, at least in part, so we should be able to carry some groupings forward from the physical DFM. We may also have identified some functional areas during Business Activity Modelling.

Obvious functional areas for SRW include: Purchase Order Placing; Stock Receiving; Customer Order Despatch.

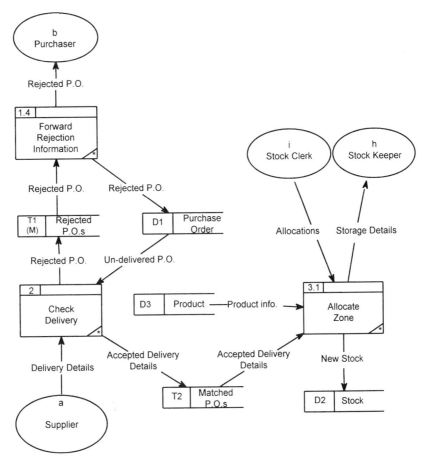

Figure 2.78 - Logicalising a Section of the SRW DFD of Figure 2.41

In some cases high level physical processes will have been linked by flows running through a transient data store, e.g. process 2 - Check Delivery - which is linked to process 1 - Place and Monitor Orders - and process 3 - Store New Stock - in the SRW DFD of Figure 2.41. With the removal of the interceding data stores these processes will end up being linked directly by data flows, which implies a close functional relationship. More often than not these processes will now be merged. In the case of

SRW, the following picture emerges when we remove the transient data stores and strip down to elementary process level the vicinity concerned with the arrival of new stock (see Figure 2.78).

Following our earlier discussions, we will dismiss the transient data stores after we make sure that we don't lose any of the delivery information contained in them:

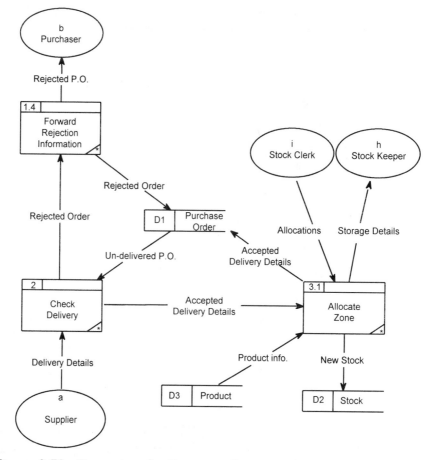

Figure 2.79 - Removing the Transient Data Stores of Figure 2.78

The diagram of Figure 2.79 shows two direct links between processes. We first deal with the link between processes 2 and 1.4. What task is process 1.4 performing? It forwards information about rejected goods back to the purchaser who originated the order while keeping a record of the rejection. But that task can be handled by a data flow from process 2 directly into data store D1. Process 1.4 therefore only adds to the bureaucracy of the organisation and we can, after consultation with the users, remove it totally. (This will of course have repercussions on the working practices of SRW because now the people checking a delivery are responsible for forwarding relevant rejection information to the purchasers, not the people who set up the purchase orders. But note that, due to the versatility of the new system, everybody concerned can have access to this information because we *have* recorded it in the system - see exercise 2.23.)

Turning now to the data flow between processes 2 and 3.1, we find that things are slightly more involved. We detect this from the fact that process 3.1 - Allocate Zone - involves a second trigger from the stock clerk which results in an update of the Stock data store. Here we ask ourselves whether there is a time lapse between accepting a delivery in the delivery bay and actually deciding where to store it. Consultations with the users reveals that such a lapse does indeed exist; zone allocation takes place independently and what the stock clerks really want is information about recently arrived goods. We solve this 'problem' by allowing access by the stock clerks to the Purchase Orders data store (see Figure 2.80).

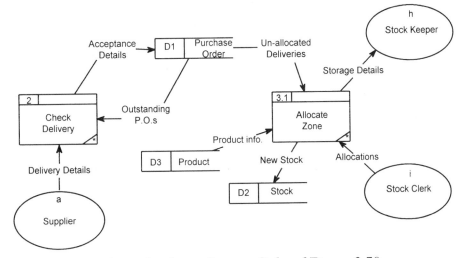

Figure 2.80 - Resolving the direct Process links of Figure 2.79

(The final remark above actually means that a new requirement to 'provide information of unallocated deliveries' has to be added to our Requirements Catalogue.)

The above discussion indicates that there is a close functional proximity between the 'Store New Stock' and 'Check Delivery' processes on the level 1 DFD in Figure 2.41. We can therefore consider grouping them to form a new level 1 process called, say, 'Receive New Stock' (see Figure 2.81). Note also how the Goods In people become an external entity to indicate that it is they who decide what to accept or reject.

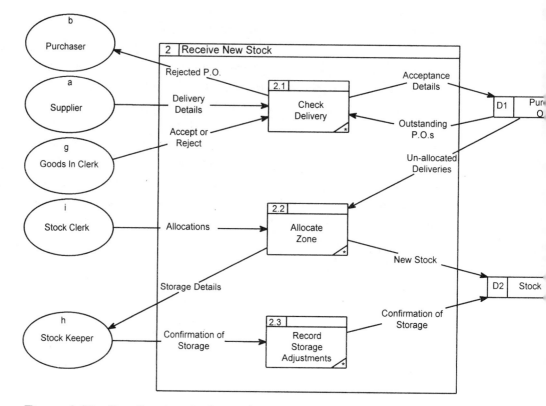

Figure 2.81 - Readjusting the logicalised Processes of Figure 2.41

(Figure 2.81 involves the processes of Figure 2.78 which, due to merging, appear with new identifiers. Readers should take some time to follow the remanifestations of the processes involved lest they perceive that some prestidigitation has taken place - see exercise 2.25)

Close functional relationships between processes are also sometimes indicated by interaction with the same groups of external entities.

2. Process Type Groupings

Processes often fall into distinct types:

- Those that support the business functions of the system.
- Those that maintain system information or control. In the SRW system there are processes within each functional area concerned only with archiving (i.e. the removal of data from the system to some sort of back-up, such as a tape library). So we could group all of these together in a low level DFD called Housekeeping.

3. Data Access Groupings

If functional or process type groupings prove difficult to identify, we may find it useful to group together processes that access the same or similar data. Indeed, for systems whose main purpose is the maintenance of reference data this may be equivalent to grouping processes along functional lines.

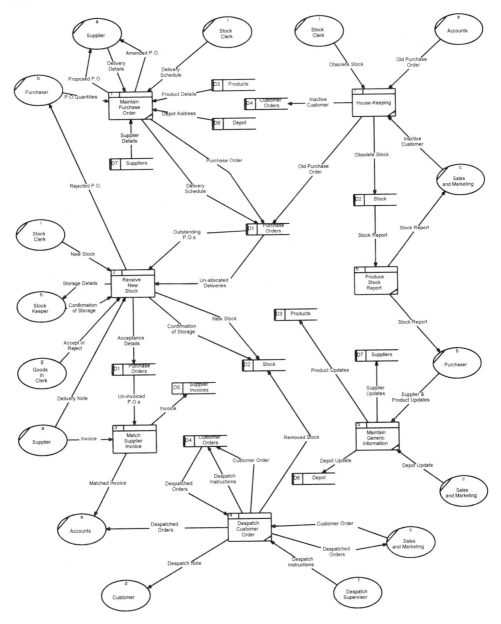

Figure 2.82 Logical DFD (Showing Current Services)

Probably the easiest way to identify which processes access which entities is to draw up a Process/Entity matrix such as the one in Figure 2.68. We could then group together processes that have entries (either create, read, amend or delete) for a similar set of entities. If we find that a process could belong to more than one grouping then we should place it in the one that contains its most important data accesses (creates and deletes rather than reads).

In general, process groupings should be based on functionality, and only for those processes which do not clearly fall into neat functional areas should we look for process type and then data access groupings.

Rebuilding the hierarchy for SRW leads to the level 1 DFD shown in Figure 2.82.

2.8.2   Completing the Logical DFM

Once we have drawn all of the DFDs and verified them with users and against the LDM, we should update the EPDs, External Entity Descriptions and I/O Descriptions to reflect the new logical model.

Many of the problems associated with physical constraints in the current system will in effect 'disappear' with logicalisation. However some will still be applicable to the new system, e.g. legal requirements to use particular forms or carry out duplicate manual processing. We should record any physical constraints that are still valid in the Requirements Catalogue.

2.8.3   Summary (Step 150)

The SSADM tasks carried out in Step 150 are:

Task

10   Rationalise the data stores in such a way that no entity is split between data stores.

20   Rationalise the processes on the lowest level DFDs and rebuild the hierarchy from the bottom up.

30   Complete the Data Flow Modelling documentation by producing, where appropriate, new Elementary Process Descriptions, I/O Descriptions, and External Entity Descriptions.

40   Study the elementary processes to ensure that they are supported by the current environment's Logical Data Model.

50   Update the Requirements Catalogue with possible new requirements and with physical constraints that will still apply in the new system.

2.9   Assemble Investigation Results

We must now check the main products of the investigation for completeness and consistency. As with all assembly steps, no specific quality control procedures are laid down by SSADM; these are assumed to be part of the organisation's project management Policies and Procedures.

The current physical DFM is considered to be a working document which is superseded by the current logical DFM. The products to be checked are therefore:

- Context Diagram.
- Logical Data Flow Model.
- Current Environment LDM.
- Logical Data Store/Entity Cross-reference.
- Requirements Catalogue.
- User Catalogue.

We should pay particular attention to the Requirements Catalogue, and its review with users, as this will drive the development of BSOs and any subsequent detailed specification of requirements.

2.10   Requirements Analysis Exercises

2.1 *(Business Activity Modelling)* Produce a Business Activity Model for the current manual system described below:

Fresco is a ticket agency, dealing in concert and theatre tickets. All of their business is conducted over the telephone, with customers ringing up to request tickets for a wide variety of performances.

Concert and theatre venues provide Fresco with a constant stream of information on forthcoming events, which is then used by Fresco's manager to compile a fixture list for use by the sales staff in responding to customer calls. The manager will also select a number of events for which Fresco will purchase tickets in advance of customer requests (e.g. for popular events). Details of these 'pre-purchase' orders as they are known are passed to the post clerk who is responsible for placing orders with each venue. The post clerk sends out each order with its payment attached. Once tickets are received the post clerk files them in the tickets file.

When customers ring the sales team their ticket requests are checked against the ticket file. If pre-purchased tickets are available they are put in an envelope marked with the customer's name and filed at the back of the ticket file. If not, the sales team fill out a ticket request form and put it in a desk tray for collection by the post clerk, who will then place an order with the appropriate venue in the same way as for pre-purchased tickets.

Details of the customer and the tickets are passed to the payments section for invoicing (by the sales team for pre-purchased tickets and by the post clerk for new tickets). The payments section will then send an invoice to the customer, and await payment if the customer is paying by post or accept payment immediately for credit card holders. A copy of the invoice is placed in the invoice file for matching with payments, and once paid a further copy is placed in a tray labelled 'despatch list' for collection by the post clerk.

The post clerk collects paid invoice copies three times a day, and retrieves the appropriate tickets from the ticket file for despatch to customers.

2.2 *(Data Flow Modelling)* Produce an overview physical DFD for the Fresco system of exercise 2.1.

2.3 *(Logical Data Modelling)* Produce an overview LDS for the following system:

Natlib is a small private library specialising in natural history books. They have a collection of titles available for loan by registered readers, free of charge.

Each reader is allowed to borrow up to eight books at a time. Loans are to be recorded against particular book copies, rather than their title, as Natlib may have several copies of any given book.

When all copies of a book are already out on loan a reader may wish to place a reservation for it. Each reservation is recorded against a book title. When a copy of the title is subsequently returned Natlib will place it on one side, record which copy is to satisfy the reservation, and notify the reader that it is ready for collection.

2.4 *(Business Activity Modelling)* Produce a Business Activity Model for Natlib (as described above), using the following additional information:

The new system will cover functions in several areas: reader registration; book registration; book loans; book reservations; book returns; and issue of loan reminders.

When readers borrow a book their status is checked to see if they have already reached their loan limit or have any outstanding overdue loans or fines, in which case they will not be allowed to borrow any more books until they have taken appropriate action.

New loans will be recorded and details of their 'due for return' date given to the reader. Overdue loans will be monitored and up to three reminders sent to the reader. Each time a reminder is sent its date will be recorded against the reader, whose status will then be updated.

When readers reserve a book the title will be checked to ensure that it is currently held by Natlib, and if so the reservation will be recorded.

When a reader returns a book its return date will be recorded against the loan record and its condition (if it has changed) against its copy record. For overdue returns and damaged copies the librarian will levy a fine against the reader and record its amount (and any subsequent) payment on the loan record. If payment is not made in full, the reader's status will be updated.

Each return will be checked against outstanding reservations. If the title is reserved the book copy will be placed on one side, the reservation will be updated with details of which copy has been returned and the appropriate reader will be notified.

The actual purchase of new books will not be covered by the new system as it already functions well. However the system will need to record details of new titles, as sent in by book suppliers and publishers, and of new copies as they are registered by the librarians at Natlib.

2.5 *(Data Flow Modelling)* Produce a Data Flow Diagram from your Business Activity Model of exercise 2.4.

2.6 *(Data Flow Modelling)* Decompose all processes of your Data Flow Diagram from exercise 2.5. How has it affected your original answer to exercise 2.5?

2.7 *(Requirements Definition)* Produce a list of requirements from your models of exercises 2.4-2.6.

2.8 *(Logical Data Modelling)* Produce an overview LDS for the following scenario:

Treebanks is an exclusive racquet sports club. Members join the club to play particular sports, e.g. tennis, squash, badminton. They may also (in addition) become members of teams, each of which is dedicated to single sport.

A file is kept on each member detailing which sports they have signed up for, and which teams they belong to.

Each playing court at Treebanks is designed for a specific sport, and playing sessions can be booked by either a team or by an individual member.

Bookings are recorded on a booking sheet, which is divided into one hour sessions. A booking may also be made for Treebanks equipment to be used on court, e.g. racquets, balls. Each piece of equipment is labelled with a unique number and some, such as umpiring chairs, are tied to particular courts. An index card file is used to keep track of equipment, and when a piece of equipment is booked its number is added to the booking sheet and its index card updated.

Each session belongs to a specific price band (at the moment there are six of them), according to its time, day of the week, etc. These bands are regularly changed.

2.9 *(Logical Data Modelling)* Suggest keys and other attributes for each of your entities from exercise 2.8.

2.10 *(Method)* Suggest situations where you would consider not using the Data Flow Modelling technique.

2.11 *(Business Activity Modelling)* Set up a Business Activity Model for the activities apparent in the following scenario:

An educational institute runs short courses. Each course is run many times during the year. Once a month the institution's courses are advertised in the local paper. If enough students show an interested in a course, then a lecturer and a substitute lecturer are allocated to it. The role of the substitute lecturer is to replace the main lecturer when that person is unable to teach a particular session. At the end of a course students are presented with a Certificate of Attendance which acts as proof of the fact that the student has attended the course. Prior to the start of a course, a class list is printed out and given to the main lecturer.

2.12 *(Logical Data Modelling)* Produce a Logical Data Model for the scenario of question 2.11.

2.13 *(Data Flow Modelling)* Produce a *logical* Data Flow Model of the scenario of question 2.11 as supported by the data model of question 2.12 .

2.14 *(Logical Data Modelling)* Suppose that the educational institute of question 2.11 wishes to tighten its control over its distribution of its Certificates of Attendance by actually recording the students who are present in each session. How would the data model you created in question 2.12 be affected by this new requirement given that all the institute's courses consist of exactly 10 two-hour sessions and that a student does not receive a Certificate of Attendance if he or she has not attended at least seven sessions of a course?

2.15 *(Logical Data Modelling)* Further suppose that the educational institute of questions 2.11 and 2.14 offers assessment at the end of each course. This assessment takes the form of a written test. If students score more that 50% on this test they are awarded a Certificate. This Certificate states the course taken, its level, the mark attained by the student and the day of the award. Adjust your data model of question 2.14 to accommodate these new requirements.

2.16 *(Logical Data Modelling)* How would your data model of question 2.15 change if the courses of the educational institute are not of the same size and duration?

2.17 *(Requirements Definition)* Provide a list of requirements that are supported by your data model of question 2.16. Clearly state which requirements are simply maintaining the functionality of the description of question 2.11 and which are additional to it.

2.18 *(Data Flow Modelling)* Produce a Data Flow Model for the system described by the requirements of question 2.17.

2.19 *(Logical Data Modelling)* Produce a Logical Data Model for the following scenario:

Markalot is a new university which has caught on to the fact that if it sets easy assessments all students will get high marks and the Government will reward it for this achievement. Evidently the University, despite its mission statement that refers profusely to 'quality', does not care much about the worthlessness of its degrees. Nor do its students who are, remarkably, requested to pay high fees for the 'education' they get. You have been employed by Markalot as a systems analyst to design a system for the efficient recording of student assessments. The main objective of the system is to be able to identify the lecturer who has allocated the highest marks during an academic year. Typically, a Markalot student enlists for taught modules. At the start of an academic year each taught module is allocated to a lecturer who becomes responsible for teaching and assessing the module. For each module 100 multiple choice questions are set. Students are asked to sit one exam per module. Each exam for a module lasts one hour and consists of 25 of these questions randomly chosen by the system. Students are expected to input their answers directly on the system which should be able to output an 'instant' result as soon as the exam is finished. After each exam, the 5 questions which students find the most demanding are marked as 'not to be used again' and replaced by 5 fresh questions. When students score over 50% they pass the module. If they score between 30% and 49% they are allowed a reassessment next time the exam is run. To enter this reassessed exam they have to pay an examination fee. The date they make the payment is recorded. When students score less than 30% in an exam they are forced to redo, and pay for, the whole module next time it is offered. At the end of each exam students get a transcript of their attempt which shows their answers as well as the correct answers to the questions.

2.20 *(Data Flow Modelling)* Produce a Data Flow Model for the scenario of question 2.19 which acknowledges the data model you produced for it.

2.21 *(Requirements Definition)* Produce a list of requirements that conforms to the scenario and your answers to questions 2.19 and 2.20.

2.22 *(CASE tool and DFD levelling exercise)* The level 1 DFD depicted in Figure 2.41 contains seven elementary processes. This suggests that the diagram could be levelled otherwise. By bunching together processes 2 & 3, 5 & 6, and 4, 7 & 8 setup a new level 1 DFD made up of 4 processes. Progress your new level 1 processes to elementary level. Which depiction of the system do you prefer?

2.23 *(Work Practice Modelling)* Study the text concerning Figures 2.78 and 2.79. Refer to the Work Practice Model to see whose jobs will be affected. Adjust the WPM to reflect the changes introduced by logicalisation.

2.24 *(logicalisation)* Using the Data Store/Entity Cross Reference of Figure 2.70, produce a logical DFM section that represents the current physical processes 4 - Maintain Stock Information -, 5 - Allocate Despatch -, and 6 - Complete Customer Order -, as seen in Figure 2.41. Does your answer match with process 4 - Despatch Customer Order - of Figure 2.82?

2.25 *(version control)* Trying to follow what happens to each current physical process, data flow and data store during logicalisation is a project management nightmare (which probably suggests that a situation has to be quite complicated before we decide to produce a full current physical followed by a full logical DFM). Produce a list of all current physical elementary processes implicit in Figure 2.41 and correlate them with the elementary processes of an equivalent list for the logical DFM of Figure 2.82.

2.26 *(traceability)* For each requirement in the requirement catalogue summary of Figure 2.11, show the logical elementary process which is dedicated to it. Are there any elementary processes which do not answer the needs of a specific functional requirement? Should there be any?

2.27 *(Business Activity Modelling)* Produce a Business Activity Model for the following scenario:

Bodgett & Son are a building firm of medium size, working for a single central office. They carry out most kinds of general building work and have expanded greatly in recent years. They are in the process of developing new systems to handle their administration tasks, and have already computerised the accounts area. The next area of investigation is the estimating and management of building work, or 'jobs'.

All work carried out by Bodgett & Son is preceded by a formal estimate, carried out by an outside surveyor or, for smaller jobs, an employee.

When an estimate request is received from a prospective customer the admin. section assess the likely size of the job and select either a surveyor from their standard list of acceptable surveyors, or a suitable Bodgett employee. The surveyor list is kept up to date by the admin. section from changes supplied by Bodgett's manager. Surveyors are contacted to check that they are available at the time requested by the customer and entered onto a booking sheet. At the end of each day a member of admin. will use the booking sheet to draw up booking letters to send out to surveyors.

Surveyors (or employees) return the completed estimate to admin. who then prepare a formal estimate letter for the customer. Large pieces of building work may be subdivided into a number of smaller jobs. Details of the estimate and jobs are filed in the estimates file.

Customers will usually send back a slip at the bottom of their estimate detailing their acceptance or rejection of some or all of the estimate. The estimate file is then updated by admin., and any acceptance forms placed in a tray for processing later in the day by the job administrator.

The job administrator then picks up the acceptance forms and retrieves the relevant estimate details from the estimate file. Details of work already booked for Bodgett are held in the job file. These details are checked by the job administrator and the newly accepted estimates are scheduled around these existing jobs. Most jobs will at this point be subdivided into a number of much smaller tasks. The job administrator will create a materials order line for any building supplies that are needed for a task, and attach these to the task details for order placement by the order clerk at the start of the next working day. There may be more than one order line for any given task.

All new job and estimate details are then placed at the front of the job file and labelled as ready for ordering. The customer is then notified by the job administrator of the provisional start and finish date for their work.

The order clerk checks the beginning of the job file each morning and groups together materials orders for placement with suppliers. Copies of each order are then placed in an orders file at the store room entrance. The job file is marked as 'order placed'. As materials are received the order copies are updated until they have been fully satisfied. The job file is then updated to show which tasks have materials ready for them. When the materials for the last task in a job are ready the job itself is marked as 'ready'.

Each material is supplied by only one specialist supplier.

The staff office maintain a list of employees and what skills each one has. This list is constantly updated as the manager hires new employees. Each day the job file is checked and the jobs that are ready are compared with the employee list. Each task record is matched with a single employee and annotated with when the employee is free to carry out the work. One employee will be designated as job supervisor. When all tasks have been allocated the staff office will know the firm start and finish dates for the job and the customer is notified.

The job supervisor will monitor the progress of each job and keep the job file updated. It may be necessary to change the Start and Finish dates for a job, in which case it is the responsibility of the supervisor to notify the customer.

Once the job is finished the job supervisor will fill out a completion notice and send copies to the customer and to the accounts section, and will attach a further copy to the job file.

2.28 *(Logical Data Modelling)* Produce a Logical Data Structure for the current environment depicted in exercise 2.27.

2.29 *(Data Flow Modelling)* Produce a Current Physical level 1 DFD for Bodgett & Son.

2.30 *(Data Flow Modelling)* Decompose process 1 - Estimate Job - from the suggested solution to exercise 2.29.

2.31 *(logicalisation)* Logicalise the DFD produced in exercise 2.29.

3   Business System Options

3.1   Stage 2 - BSOs

The purpose of Stage 2 is to agree the functionality of the new system. In Stage 1 we produced a detailed description of the business problem in the form of current system models and a comprehensive statement of user requirements. Our task in Stage 2 is to develop possible system solutions to this business problem, and to evaluate their impact and benefits. There will inevitably be several options for satisfying any set of user requirements. The final selection will be made by assessing the relative merits of the alternatives options, and adopting the one that most closely matches the ideal requirements of the business while still giving reasonable returns. This may involve dropping some of the less important requirements if they cannot be cost justified.

Stage 2 provides a major decision point for the project. In Business System Options we are interested in narrowing down the area of study to just those requirements that can be cost justified and deciding on the shape of the system that we will be specifying in detail in Stage 3.

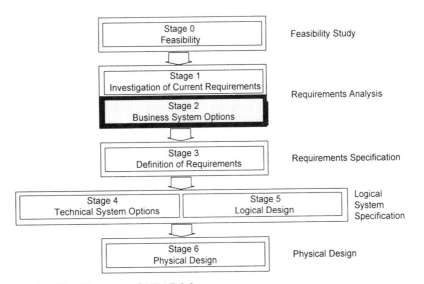

Figure 3.1 - The Stages of SSADM

A precise definition of BSOs is difficult to give as they will vary in content from project to project. However, they will all attempt to do the same thing, and that is to describe a potential computerised information system. This description will be largely textual, but may be supplemented by diagrams such as DFDs and LDSs. BSOs should contain details of *what* the system will do, rather than *how* it will do it, i.e. the functionality of the future system.

The main aim is to fix the requirements of the new system. After the project board has made its choice, no new requirements will be contemplated until the end of the SSADM cycle. If after the end of Stage 2 any new requirements are discovered, and these requirements are vital to the success of the business, apart from suggesting that the Requirements Analysis was shoddy, the project has to come to a halt and an Exception Report requesting an executive decision in accordance to the Policies and Procedures of the organisation has to be drawn up. In other words, the requirements that are chosen during BSO effectively constitute a contract against which the future system will be judged.

BSO sits firmly inside the Decision Structure of the development template.

3.2   Structure

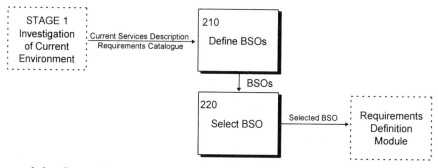

Figure 3.2 - Stage 2

Step 210 - Define BSOs

A number of BSOs are outlined, each satisfying at least the minimum system requirements. These are then shortlisted to about two or three options to be fleshed out, and supported by cost/benefit and impact analyses.

Step 220 - Select BSO

The detailed BSOs are presented to the project board and a single, possibly hybrid, option is selected. This final BSO is documented in detail and agreed as the basis for system specification in Stage 3.

The project board may find none of the proposed options acceptable, and request the development of new options before selection is made. In this way we may get iterations of Steps 210 and 220. Figure 3.3 shows the process of choosing a business option with all the likely iterations included:

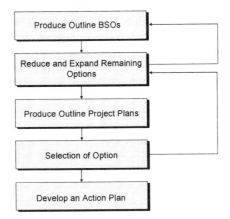

Figure 3.3 - Choosing a Business Option is an Iterative Process

3.3   Step 210 - Define Business System Options

Rather than a series of precise techniques, SSADM only offers a set of guidelines and suggested procedures for this step. The actual activities involved in defining possible system solutions (e.g. cost/benefit analysis) are those of general systems analysis and will be highly dependent on circumstance and organisational standards as defined in the organisation's Policies and Procedures. These activities will not be discussed in any great detail here (for further information see Appendix B, Selected Reading).

3.3.1   Establish Minimum Requirements

Each BSO must satisfy at least the minimum requirements of the new system. At this stage the Requirements Catalogue will contain a large number of very detailed entries, each of which will have been individually prioritised. To grade and sort all of these by priority and to list every requirement satisfied by each BSO would be extremely cumbersome and rather confusing as a basis for discussions with users. It is more useful to divide requirements into functional areas, each with its own overall priority. The set of minimum requirements for the new system can then be expressed as a list of functional areas to be covered by all BSOs.

The SRW business area we are investigating can be split into three sub-systems; one that keeps a record of purchase orders, one that monitors the storage of stock, and one that deals with customer orders.

For each subsystem we can define an option which retains the current functionality; where the paper-based system is exactly replaced by a computerised version of itself; and an option that adds to each subsystem the new functionality as dictated by the Requirements Catalogue. This line of thought gives us six disjoint options, none of which constitutes a reasonable minimum for SRW. (If SRW had no IT experience, or if the technology to be used happened to be innovative, we would consider one of these options as our minimum recommendation which would act as a pilot for future enhancements.)

It soon becomes clear that an option that does not cater for the computerisation of at least the current purchase order and storage functionality is not worth the effort and would not be cost effective. The minimum BSO then becomes the one defined by the following list of functional requirements:

Id	Description
1	Produce stock report
2	Record proposed purchase order
3	Confirm purchase order
9	Record delivery data including rejections
10	Schedule deliveries (to nearest half hour)
11	Report on stocks nearing sell-by date
12	Provide possible stock-out warnings
13	Monitor supplier invoice
14	List overdue deliveries
15	Facilitate rescheduling of overdue deliveries
18	Arrange delivery details

Figure 3.4 - The Minimum Functional Requirements

3.3.2   Develop Skeleton BSOs

We will develop a range of up to six skeleton BSOs, in largely textual form, varying in functionality from a BSO that satisfies just the minimum requirements to one that satisfies all requirements. Each BSO description should include the following non-functional details:

- Approximate cost of the option.
- Development time scale.
- Known technical constraints. Although BSOs should be largely logical in nature, there may be restrictions imposed by technical strategies or limitations that are impossible to dismiss, as they will limit the *functional* possibilities of any new system.
- Organisation of the system. This will include information on the required type of access to the system (e.g. on-line or off-line), interfaces with other systems and the distribution of the system. No

attempt should be made to specify the technical environment for the new system (as BSOs are primarily logical in nature, dealing as they do with functionality), but any non-functional requirements that will definitely need to be considered later in evaluating Technical System Options should be noted in the Requirements Catalogue.

- Approximate data and transaction volumes.
- Training requirements.
- Major benefits to the business.
- Impact on the organisation and other existing systems.

It is useful to relate these details to individual functional areas within the BSOs, so that the relative merits of each of those areas can be discussed.

In SRW, business options would include the minimum; the minimum plus handling of transfers between depots; the minimum plus the current customer orders, i.e., the full current functionality; the full current functionality plus transfers; and an option encompassing all requirements, including the provision of a complete delivery-to-despatch audit trail - requirement 6.

It is convenient to present options in a grid which clearly shows the constituent requirements of each option (see Figure 3.5)

Id	Requirement	BSO1	BSO2	BSO3	BSO4	BSO5
1	Produce stock report	X	X	X	X	X
2	Record proposed purchase order	X	X	X	X	X
3	Confirm purchase order	X	X	X	X	X
4	Record customer order			X	X	X
5	Arrange despatch of customer orders			X	X	X
6	Provide delivery to despatch audit trail					X
7	Facilitate alternative product selection					X
8	Provide supplier performance monitoring					X
9	Record delivery data including rejections	X	X	X	X	X
10	Schedule deliveries (to nearest half hour)	X	X	X	X	X
11	Report on stocks nearing sell-by date	X	X	X	X	X
12	Provide possible stock-out warnings	X	X	X	X	X
13	Monitor supplier invoice	X	X	X	X	X
14	List overdue deliveries	X	X	X	X	X
15	Facilitate rescheduling of overdue deliveries	X	X	X	X	X
16	Make use of existing PCs in stock office					
17	Use Sales and Marketing data					
18	Arrange delivery details	X	X	X	X	X
19	Support more precise locations for stock					X
20	Allow for transfer of stock		X		X	X
21	Allow multiple delivery of purchase orders					X
22	Allow for more than one supplier per product					X
23	List un-allocated deliveries					X

Figure 3.5 - The Business Systems Options

Requirements 16 and 17 are non-functional requirements that effect all BSOs.

3.3.3 Produce Shortlist of Options

Hopefully none of the skeleton options will be entirely out of line with the wishes of users, partly because our investigation of requirements should mean we have a fair idea of what will be acceptable. For the same reason there are unlikely to be large variations in the options at this point, so to continue with as many as six will mean a lot of effort for little return.

It is important to resist any temptation to reduce the list to a single 'obvious' option, as this will frequently be unduly influenced by the current system. Instead we will discuss differences between all of the options with users, with the aim of reducing the list to just two or three. The most important factors in eliminating options are likely to be in the areas of cost/benefit, development time scales and relative priorities.

In the case of SRW it was clear that management were committed to the system so there was no point going on with the less ambitious BSO1 and BSO2. Further sounding-out indicated that the transfer of stock was considered a very important aspect of the new system, thus eliminating BSO3 from further consideration.

3.3.4 Fully Define Options

Once we have narrowed the list down, we need to flesh out the remaining options. Remember that our aim is not only to describe the functionality and organisation of the proposed system, but to provide information that will enable the option to be assessed by the project board. The resulting BSO descriptions must be largely textual in nature but any differences in functional support and system boundary can be emphasised by using DFDs and LDSs.

The shortlisted BSOs will be much more detailed than the skeleton BSOs, and in particular will require greater attention to the following:

- **Cost/Benefit Analysis.** This will necessarily be fairly approximate at this stage, as the technical environment is unknown and the system has yet to be specified in detail.

- **Impact Analysis.** The proposed system is certain to have an impact on the working practices and business organisation (e.g. it may create or eliminate jobs, or change existing job descriptions). An outline impact analysis, even an informal one, will be essential for users in evaluating a BSO.

- **System Development and Integration Plans.** Each option will require a different development strategy, and may possibly lead to large-scale re-planning of the project. Any problems with integrating the new system with existing systems should be highlighted.

We must always take care when developing BSOs that the finished product is easily understandable to users, as it is they who will make the final decision on the system solution.

Supplementary DFMs and LDMs

The Data Flow Model we have built and the Logical Data Model that supports it depict the current system only. This means that the repercussions of the requirements that lead to new functionality may not be yet clearly understood, both in terms of current work practices and in terms of development effort required. It is therefore vital to ensure that new requirements are isolated and studied carefully. For SRW, three such requirements are the following:

7	Facilitate alternative product selection
20	Allow for transfer of stock
21	Allow multiple delivery of purchase orders

They all require an interesting data modelling solution which extends the notions we have already covered. (In order not to mix business system option issues with data modelling issues we will be presenting the data modelling repercussions of these three requirements in the next chapter.)

During BSO we may wish to provide an extra chunk of DFM or LDM which may help in the understanding of these requirements. If this is done, we have the extra bonus of being able to provide a better estimate of development costs.

Function Point Analysis

Function Point Analysis provides a neat way of using the models we have already created to calculate a verifiable estimate of the future system's development costs. The main premise behind Mk II Function Point Analysis (Drummond, 1992) is that the time and effort needed to design, construct, test and implement a process, any process, depends on the number of inputs to that process, the number of outputs from that process, and the number of entities that need to be visited to conclude that process.

When the analysis has been done in the manner suggested by the default structure of SSADM, most user requirements map directly to an elementary process; this elementary process has data flows going in and/or out of it, each containing a documented number of data items which we can count; it also uses a number of data stores which contain a number of entities as shown on the Data Store/Entity Cross-Reference. We can therefore use a spreadsheet to add all the inputs, all the outputs and all the entity accesses of *all* the requirements in the Requirements Catalogue. This gives us N_i, N_o, and N_e, the system's total number of inputs, outputs and entity visits respectively. We use these values to ascertain the system's worth in 'unadjusted function points' using the formula

$$UFP = 0.58 * N_i + 0.26 * N_o + 1.66 * N_e$$

We then calculate the 'size' of the system by multiplying UFP by a 'technical complexity factor' TCF

$$S = TCF * UFP$$

The TCF factor ranges from 0.65 for systems which are built by experienced teams using tested technology, to just over 1 when new methods, platforms or technology are to be used.

With S in hand, the time in weeks needed for the whole development is given by

$$Weeks = 2.22 * \sqrt{S}$$

while the effort required to develop an on-line system is

$$Effort = S / p$$

where the productivity p is found from the table in Figure 3.6.

For off-line systems the effort is increased by 50%.

The number of people required to complete the job is given by

$$H = \frac{0.044 * Effort}{Weeks}$$

System Size (S)	Productivity for a development using 3GL (p)	Productivity in a 4GL environment (p)
50	.099	.158
100	.106	.169
150	.111	.178
200	.116	.185
250	.118	.189
300	.119	.191
350	.119	.190
400	.117	.187
450	.113	.181
500	.109	.174
600	.098	.156
700	.085	.137
800	.074	.118
900	.065	.104
1000	.058	.093
1100	.055	.088
1200	.054	.087

Figure 3.6 - Industry Average Productivity Values

This last formula can also be used in conjunction with the table in Figure 3.7 to estimate the number of people who have to be involved in every SSADM module and beyond.

	Effort	Elapsed Time
Requirements Analysis	11%	20%
Requirements Specification	11%	15%
Logical System Specification	5%	5%
Physical Design	10%	10%
Code and Unit Testing	46%	25%
System Test	12%	15%
Implementation	5%	10%

Figure 3.7 - Industry Average Percentages per Development Module

All the weightings of Function Point Analysis given above correspond to industry averages. Each development team can use these as an estimate or as a comparison of their performance when compared against the industry's averages.

3.3.5   Summary (Step 210)

The SSADM tasks carried out in Step 210 are:

Task

10	Establish minimum requirements for the new system.
20	Produce up to six outline BSOs.
30	Discuss the outline BSOs with users, and produce a shortlist of two or three options. Add more detail to the shortlisted options, supplemented with DFMs and LDMs if they are helpful.
40	Study the impact each option has on the data model.
50	Carry out a cost/benefit and impact analysis for each BSO.

3.4 Step 220 - Select Business System Option

We now present the BSOs defined in Step 210 to the project board or user representative body. The activities involved in preparing and carrying out the presentation will be dictated by the internal standards of the organisation and the circumstances of the project. For example, if the project team represents an external software house, the presentation may well take the form of a sales session, whereas if the team is an internal one the format of the presentation will probably follow organisation guidelines.

Whatever the circumstances, our overall aim will be to explain each option clearly, placing emphasis on its relative strengths and weaknesses, to a level that will enable management to select a single BSO as the basis for the rest of the project.

In practice the board may decide to adopt a hybrid BSO, combining features of two or more of the original BSOs. They may also generate new ideas leading to a repeat of Step 210, and the definition of completely new BSOs, although if our analysis has been thorough this should be unlikely.

BSO presentation also provides the project board with an opportunity to reassess the viability of the project as a whole, and possibly to cancel it. This will be especially true if a formal Feasibility Study was not undertaken.

We should record the results of the presentation in detail, paying special attention to the reasons for selection of the chosen option. We must ensure that the selected BSO is fully documented, as it will provide the basis for the rest of the project and for the final system. This will already have been done if one of the proposed BSOs is selected without change, but if the selected BSO is a hybrid then a fair amount of definition work may be required.

3.4.1   Presenting the Business System Options

During the presentation of the two remaining options, discussion focused primarily on requirements 6 and 8.

It was felt that requirement 8 which deals with the monitoring of supplier performance was a bit loose. Management was not yet clear how to measure this performance and it was felt that an ill thought report might lead to wrong conclusions. The requirement was therefore dropped.

With regard to requirement 6 which leads to an audit trail from delivery to despatch, reservations were raised as to its consequences. Keeping information on which delivery was responsible for each individual stock of a product would mean additional costs in maintaining data and in supporting extra processing. More importantly, it would also mean additional stock keeping activities to ensure that stocks of the same product, possibly in the same physical zone, but resulting from different deliveries were always kept apart. The tracing of deliveries will mean that any contaminated or sub-standard stocks linked to a particular delivery can be identified and withdrawn. For products with more than one supplier (this will be possible with the new system), the relevant supplier involved can then be identified. The data model in its present form can handle this.

If though the audit trail is to continue so that each individual customer of a stock has to be identified, then current working practices have to become much more precise. The data model has to also be adjusted so that a relationship between a customer order line and stock is maintained (see Exercise 3.5). Because of the effect the audit trail of each customer order would have on the working practices, it was felt that the audit trail should only involve deliveries and stock.

This discussion then led to the proposition that maybe all the activities relating to customer orders should be put on hold until such time when more thought would have been put into integrating a complete audit trail. It was then accepted that requirements 4 and 5 which deal with customer orders would be dropped.

Discussion then shifted to the area of Supplier and Product information. This information can be accessed from the system currently maintained by Sales and Marketing. To save the cost and time involved in full integration, the depot system could maintain its own versions of the relevant information, updated automatically each morning from the system in Sales and Marketing. Once created the depot system would regard this data as reference data and use it as read only. Alternatively, full integration with the Supplier and Product system could be considered. This will mean less duplication of data across the business. It will also remove the restriction of a timed daily batch run that could cause problems, and allow depots to access up-to-the-minute supplier and product information.

The following features were considered and formally included in the specifications:

- On-line access to all information, including facilities for ad-hoc queries.
- Security mechanisms and access controls.
- Automation of routine operations, such as zone allocation.

It was clear that the major objectives associated with cost savings, extra services and improved efficiency are satisfied by both options. There will be savings in staff as many operations will be automated, and it is expected that most paper filing will be eliminated.

Security is improved with the introduction of data back-ups and access controls.

Stock keeping activities will not be greatly impacted except that, with the introduction of automatic zone allocation, smaller zones will be introduced leading to more precise stock storing instructions.

Most of the data will be held centrally, with workstations in all of the depot offices and in the Purchasing and Sales and Marketing divisions. Any reports or queries still based on paper will be printed locally, with the exception of stock listings for the Purchasing and Sales divisions which will be produced centrally.

Purchase order details will be entered into the system on-line by the Purchasing division, and Customer orders by the Sales and Marketing division. All subsequent processing and inputs will be carried out in the individual depots.

The management at SRW decide to stand by their decision to back a full development, satisfying all requirements with the exception of requirements 4, 5 and 8. They feel that the features of the new system can be cost justified and that the development time scales are acceptable. The organisational impact is in line with their wishes, and staff whose jobs are automated or eliminated will be re-deployed.

3.4.2 Documenting the Selected Business System Option

The business system option chosen by SRW is BSO5 without customer orders and supplier monitoring. This choice also affects requirement 6 which is appropriately rephrased in the list of opted for requirements depicted in Figure 3.8.

Id	Requirement
1	Produce stock report
2	Record proposed purchase order
3	Confirm purchase order
6	Provide delivery to stock audit trail
7	Facilitate alternative product selection
9	Record delivery data including rejections
10	Schedule deliveries (to nearest half hour)
11	Report on stocks nearing sell-by date
12	Provide possible stock-out warnings
13	Monitor supplier invoice
14	List overdue deliveries
15	Facilitate rescheduling of overdue deliveries
16	Make use of existing PCs in stock office
17	Use Sales and Marketing data
18	Arrange delivery details
19	Support more precise locations for stock
20	Allow for transfer of stock
21	Allow multiple delivery of purchase orders
22	Allow for more than one supplier per product
23	List un-allocated deliveries

Figure 3.8 - The chosen Business Systems Option

3.4.3 Summary (Step 220)

The SSADM tasks carried out in Step 220 are:

Task

10   Present the Business System Options to the project board and assist the decision-making process.

20   Document the selected Business System Option. Include rationale for selection of option and rejection of others.

3.5 Business System Options Exercises

3.1 *(Business System Options)* Use Function Point Analysis to estimate the manpower and time needed to complete the SRW warehousing system.

3.2 *(Business System Options)* Perform Function Point Analysis on the following data to show that two people working half a year would be enough to complete this project. You may assume this is a straightforward project for an on-line system to be done in a 3GL environment:

	Requirement	inputs	outputs	entity accesses
A1	☞ℳ◻•◻☺ℳ•◻	10	2	4
A2	✌☺⯃◪☺&⯃Ⅴ	10	3	6
A3	ℳ◻◻◯ℳ◻&⯃	1	25	1
A4	☺ℳℳ◻ℳ•◻◯ℳ◻•◻	10	10	9
A5	☼ℳℳ◻◻♎ℳ	4	10	5
A6	✄◻◻◻⯃◯ℳℳ	26	9	2
A7	☼ℳℳ◻◻♎•◻ℳ&	5	11	8
A8	✄ℳ◻Ⅴ⯃ℳ•☺♎	14	4	5
A9	☝ℳ◻◯ℳ◻ℳ◻ℳ◯ℳ	22	7	4
A10	♟ℳ•◻ℳ☺◯ℳ•	6	6	4
A11	☺✗✗ℳ••◻◻◻	9	9	7
A12	✌⯃◻ℳℳ◻◻◻♎ℳ	3	24	5

3.3 *(Business System Options)* For the requirements in Exercise 3.2 show that one person working for four weeks with a second person working for two weeks would complete the Requirements Specification of this project. Also show that Coding and Unit Testing would require about four programmers working for around six weeks.

3.4 *(Business System Options)* Use Function Point Analysis on the data of Exercise 3.2 to estimate the manpower and people needed to complete the rest of the life-cycle phases depicted in Figure 3.7. Is your answer identical to that you obtained for Exercise 3.2? Should it be?

3.5 *(Logical Data Modelling)* Produce a Logical Data Model for a system that will be able to trace a product dispatched to a customer all the way back to the supplier's delivery that brought the product to SRW as well as the original purchase order that gave rise to the delivery.

4 Requirements Specification

4.1 Stage 3 - Definition of Requirements

Our aim in Stage 3 is to produce a detailed and rigorous specification of system requirements. The statement of requirements from Stage 1 and the selected BSO from Stage 2 provide the inputs to Requirements Specification, but in themselves do not specify the new system in enough detail. By the end of Stage 3 we will have started to move into the area of system design, in that the overall shape and structure of the new system will be fully documented. Our objective is to provide sufficient detail for the logical design of dialogues and internal processing of the new system to take place.

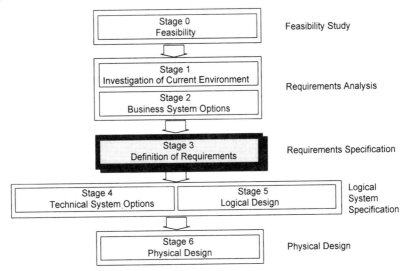

Figure 4.1 - The stages of SSADM

In many ways Stage 3 is the engine room of SSADM. It marks the point at which we move firmly from investigation and analysis to specification and external design, and uses some of the most powerful of SSADM's standard techniques. This is a very long chapter, but deservedly so. It is one of the most intensive and time-consuming stages to complete, and involves the introduction and explanation of some of the most rigorous of SSADM's techniques.

Throughout Stage 3 the Requirements Catalogue remains at the centre of the method, as a central repository of functional and non-functional requirements, and continues to be updated with refined or deduced requirements. The Logical Data Model is extended and enhanced using the technique of Relational Data Analysis, and will continue to provide the definitive view of the system's data requirements and business rules.

A DFM is an invaluable aid for investigating system processing and for communicating with users. However, it is less useful as the basis for specification and design of systems. So, from the middle of Stage 3 we will use the concept of a 'function' to tie together more detailed and rigorous models of processing elements. This does not mean that the DFM is forgotten but once we have updated it to reflect the selected BSO it will act more as an overall central reference than as a driving force of the method.

It is also in Stage 3 that we introduce the 'third view' of SSADM, representing the effects of events (and therefore time) on data.

4.2 Structure

Stage 3 consists of eight highly interdependent steps (Figure 4.2).

Step 310 - Define Required System Processing

The Logical Data Flow Model from Stage 1 is updated and extended to reflect the selected BSO. This involves translating the processing requirements identified in the Requirements Catalogue into Data Flow Diagrams.

Step 320 - Develop Required Data Model

The current LDM is also updated using the Requirements Catalogue. Entity Descriptions are fully completed and the LDM is validated against the required DFM.

Step 330 - Derive System Functions

The required DFM is used to draw up an initial set of functions. Function Definition is used to specify units of processing carried out in response to real world events or enquiry triggers, and to define the structure of system/user interfaces.

Step 335 - Develop User Job Specifications

The job of each user is defined and a Work Practice Model is created to show how the system affects each user.

Step 340 - Enhance Required Data Model

The technique of Relational Data Analysis is used to analyse data input to and output from the system. The resulting relational data models are then used to validate and enhance the LDM.

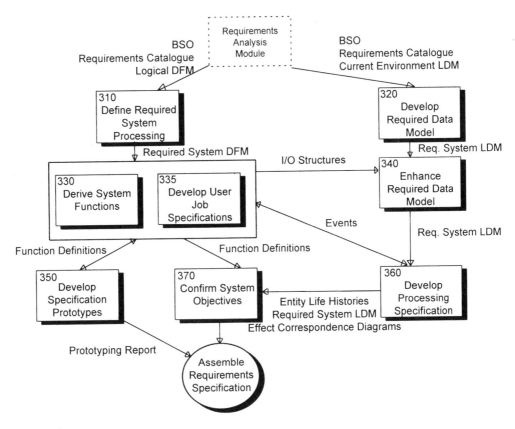

Figure 4.2 - Stage 3

Step 350 - Develop Specification Prototypes

SSADM uses prototyping to verify that user requirements are correctly understood, rather than to incrementally develop the final system. Critical system dialogues are prototyped and the results fed back into Function Definition and the Requirements Catalogue.

Step 360 - Develop Processing Specification

The techniques of Entity Behaviour Modelling and Conceptual Process Modelling are used to specify update processing in detail, and to model its effects on the LDM. SSADM views processing as a set of responses to real world *events*. Events and their effects are rigorously examined, leading to updates of the LDM, Function Definitions and the fleshing out of processes previously only outlined in the DFM.

Step 370 - Confirm System Objectives

The requirements specification is reviewed to ensure that it fully satisfies all relevant entries in the Requirements Catalogue. Particular attention is paid to the satisfaction of all non-functional requirements.

Assemble Requirements Specification

The products of Stage 3 are checked for completeness and consistency, and the Requirements Specification is published.

4.3 Step 310 - Define Required System Processing

This step is carried out at the same time as Step 320 (in which the required LDM is developed). The Logical DFM from Step 150 provides us with a picture of the underlying functionality of the current system. In Step 310 we will amend or enhance this model to produce a Required System DFM. We will do this by carrying forward those elements of the Logical DFM which are to be retained in the new system, and by adding new processing as detailed in the Requirements Catalogue (and included in the selected BSO). We will also use the User Catalogue to define User Roles in the new system. This will effectively provide us with a logicalised view of the users of the required system.

4.3.1 Requirements Definition

We begin by annotating the Requirements Catalogue to show which requirements are to be implemented by the new system. BSO selection may result in some of the requirements being dropped. We should make sure that the reasoning behind their withdrawal is added to the relevant Requirements Catalogue entries.

4.3.2 Required System Data Flow Modelling

We now take the updated Requirements Catalogue and amend the DFM to create the Required System DFM. Although the DFM will not be used in specifying the new system, it will be maintained as a means of placing the system design in context, and of describing how functions fit together at a high level. To transform the Logical DFM we take the following steps:

(i) Remove any processing which will not be required in the new system, e.g. all processes which deal with customer orders.

(ii) Add level 1 processes and data stores (based on the LDS extensions which are being applied in parallel) to support new business activities, e.g. Transfer Stock, Schedule Delivery.

(iii) Amend or develop lower level DFDs to reflect changes in processing, such as new level 1 processes, new or amended support

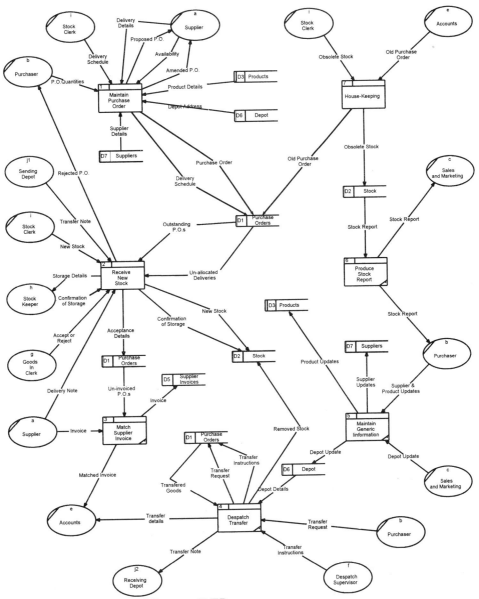

Figure 4.3 - Required System DFD

for existing activities, processes to maintain new entities, and changes to process groupings.

(iv) Amend the level 1 DFD to reflect lower level changes.

(v) Complete I/O Descriptions, External Entity Descriptions and EPDs for any new elements of the system, and update existing descriptions to reflect any changes.

(vi) Annotate the Requirements Catalogue with details of how the Required System DFM satisfies requirements.

Figure 4.3 shows the required level 1 DFD for SRW.

In Figure 4.3 we have kept all the housekeeping processes even though the responsibility for many of them lies with other sub-systems within the company. We have done so to remind ourselves of these responsibilities which arose during the BSO discussions. We will be returning to them in Step 335 when we scrutinise the working practices taking place in the vicinity of the new system.

The contents of the required DFM's data stores are dictated by the Data Store/Entity Cross-Reference of Figure 4.15. This is an important point worth repeating: the flows in and out of data stores contain data items which should be contained in those data stores; but the contents of each data store is defined through the content of the entities it encompasses, as shown in the Data Store/Entity Cross-Reference; meaning that we cannot finalise the DFM before we finalise the LDM; and that we cannot finalise the LDM before finalising the DFM. We therefore see once again that Logical Data Modelling and Data Flow Modelling, if the latter is performed, go hand in hand, cross-checking and validating each other.

4.3.3 Identifying Events

While developing the Required System DFM it is worth thinking ahead to Function Definition and event identification.

Functions consist of units of processing carried out in response to real world events, such as requesting stock transfers, or receiving deliveries. This processing may encompass more than one Elementary Process on the DFM. We should attempt to develop the DFM in such a way that it is possible to identify which Elementary Processes, when taken together, will handle the effects of an event, from input to output.

Events in DFMs (other than time based events, such as the end of a tax year) are represented by data flows into the system. So when creating the Required System DFM, we can try to make events and associated processing easy to identify in Function Definition by:

- Ensuring that each Elementary Process is *driven* by a single major data flow. If we find that a process is driven by two flows, then each of the flows should be a trigger for mutually exclusive executions of the process.
- Minimising the number of inter-process data flows. Too many directly linked processes will lead to difficulties in identifying

discrete units of processing, and usually indicate that Elementary Processes should be merged.

Once the Required System DFM is complete, we should validate it against the Required System LDM (which is developed in parallel) by creating or extending the Logical Data Store/Entity Cross-Reference, and by checking that Elementary Processes exist to create and delete every entity (using a Process/Entity Matrix if necessary).

4.3.4 User Roles

The User Catalogue developed in Stage 1 represents a physical view of the current system with respect to the tasks and activities of users.

We now look for user *roles* in the new system, which will consist of groups of job holders who will carry out the same tasks, and therefore require the same access to the system. If an organisation is well structured most job titles will correspond to a single user role, and each user role will correspond to a single job title.

An extract from the user role form for SRW reveals that some tasks in the new system will be carried out by more than one type of user but that by and large each user has a definable role of their own (Figure 4.4).

User Role	Job Title	Activity
Delivery Scheduler	Stock Clerk	Book Delivery Update Delivery Maintain Schedule Overdue Delivery Query Check Available Time Slots Delivery Query Book Transfer
Goods In Clerk	Goods In Clerk	Amend Delivery
Stock Clerk	Stock Clerk	Add New Stock Remove Obsolete Stock Allocate Stock Location
Stock Keeper	Stock Clerk Stock Keeper Goods In Clerk	Confirm Stock Location Amend Stock Location

Figure 4.4 - User Roles

When we start to develop dialogues (between users and the system) in later steps, we will use this list to identify which functions each user role will require access to. Each required access will indicate the need for a dialogue. By creating dialogues for each role, and then assigning these roles to individual users, we can limit users access to just those functions that they need and are authorised to carry out.

The identification of User Roles marks the point where the influence the new computerised system will have on current working practices starts to manifest itself. The business activities that were earmarked as lying inside the system boundary have given rise to DFM processes which in turn will give rise to user functions dedicated to each user role. The working practices of these users will therefore be altered because of the system's existence. In some cases the responsibilities of users may shift from one to another. We have already seen evidence of such a responsibility shift when discussing the implications of who should be responsible for informing purchasers about order rejections. We will be returning to this responsibility shift in Step 335, a step dedicated to the development of job specifications.

Strictly speaking, the external entities of the required system DFM should consist of the system's User Roles.

4.3.4 Summary (Step 310)

The SSADM tasks carried out in Step 310 are:

Task

10 Update the Requirements Catalogue to reflect the BSO selection made in Step 220.

20 Update the level 1 DFD to include additional processing required in the new system. Exclude processing which is outside the new system as a result of BSO selection.

30 Update lower level processes, and cross-reference the updates with relevant Requirements Catalogue entries; Update Elementary Process, I/O and External Entity Descriptions as necessary.

40 Verify that the logical data stores are consistent with the entities on the Required System LDM, using a Logical Data Store/Entity Cross-Reference, and that they can support all data flows to and from them.

50 Create User Roles and check that they are consistent with external entities and data flows on the DFM. Validate the User Roles by mapping them onto the relevant business activities.

4.4   Step 320 - Develop Required Data Model

This step is carried out at the same time as Step 310 (in which the required DFM is developed). The LDM from Step 140 is amended to reflect the selected BSO. Any additional processing introduced to the current system is studied and the data needed to support it is modelled. The resulting data store/entity cross-reference becomes the link between the required DFM and the LDM.

4.4.1   Required System Logical Data Modelling

The Required System LDM forms the backbone of the requirements specification and of the subsequent logical design. It will be constantly referenced and adjusted as specification progresses, using the results of detailed low level analysis and design techniques.

In Step 320 we conclude the top-down analysis of data by transforming the Current Environment LDM into the Required System LDM. We do this by examining the Requirements Catalogue to identify what elements of the data model should be removed and what new elements have to be added to support new functionality.

Removing Redundant Elements

The selected BSO may apply to only part of the current system, in which case we would need to remove those parts of the LDM which are not required for the new system. Where the business activities to be covered by the required system include those of the existing system, it is unlikely that any elements of the current system LDM would be redundant in the Required System LDM (with the exception of relationships which may become redundant as a result of adding new entities, and hence new indirect relationships). In the case of SRW, the entities Customer, Customer Order, Customer Order Line and Despatch are removed for reasons given at the time of selecting the BSO.

Adding New Elements

It is far more likely that the transformation of the current into the Required System LDM will result in additional entities and relationships. There are a few additions to the SRW model worth looking at. Some can be handled with the concepts we know already and some will force the introduction of a few new concepts.

The SRW Requirements Catalogue specifies that a Purchase Order will be allowed to result in several deliveries, and that a Purchase Order Line (P.O.L.) may itself be split over more than one delivery. We can model this requirement by creating an entity Delivery, distinct from Purchase Order. Each Delivery can then be viewed as containing a number of Delivery Lines, each of which, according to the prevailing business rules, will be the result of just one Purchase Order Line (Figure 4.5).

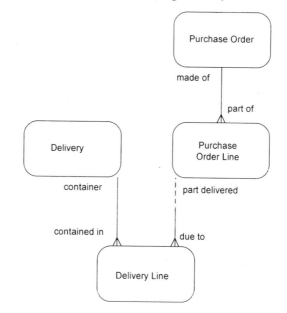

Figure 4.5 - Data Model supporting several deliveries per P.O.L.

An indirect relationship between Purchase Order and Delivery is maintained through Purchase Order Line and Delivery Line (and is effectively a m:n).

The re-appearance of the Delivery and Delivery Line entities resurrects the arguments that led to Figures 2.53-2.55. The relationship therefore that allows the system to provide a delivery to stock audit trail, as requested by requirement 6, is that shown in Figure 4.6.

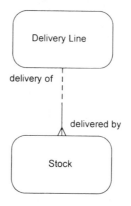

Figure 4.6 - Each Stock is the result of a Delivery Line

Mutually Exclusive Relationships

The new system is required to support transfers of stock between depots. Each time a transfer takes place it may include quantities of more than one product. One way of modelling this situation is to have two new entities, Transfer and Transfer Line, where each transfer line relates to a single product, in much the same way as a purchase order line does.

Each transfer line will take away (or reduce) quantities of stocks from one depot and deliver new stocks to another depot. Therefore we have two parallel relationships between the entities Transfer Line and Stock: one indicating the stocks being reduced; and one the stocks being created (Figure 4.7).

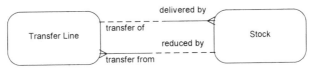

Figure 4.7 - The Relationship between Transfer Line and Stock

Each Stock is certainly delivered by something, but not necessarily a Transfer. So while a Stock occurrence may or may not be delivered by a Transfer, it must be delivered by either a Transfer or a Delivery. This is an example of ***mutually exclusive*** relationships.

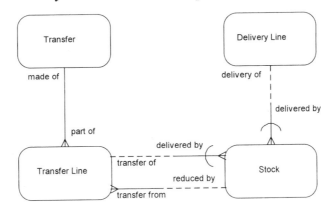

Figure 4.8 - A Mutually Exclusive Relationship

Where two or more relationships are mutually exclusive we show this on the LDS by adding small arcs to the affected relationship lines at the relevant end (see Figure 4.8). If one or other of the relationships *must* exist, but not both, we make the relationship lines mandatory (i.e. solid). If one or other of the relationships *may* exist, but not both, we make the relationship lines optional (i.e. dashed). If we have a large number of mutually exclusive relationships it can get difficult to identify which relationships are covered by the same set of arcs. In this situation we would label each member of a set with an identifier (e.g. a lower case letter).

Entity Sub-types

When a transfer is received by a depot it is treated in exactly the same way as a delivery from an external supplier. Also, the paperwork involved to setup a transfer request is not dissimilar to the setting-up of a normal purchase order. It therefore seems reasonable to consider each transfer request as just another type of purchase order. While thinking in this manner it soon becomes clear that the introduction of inter-depot transfers simply introduces the notion of 'internal' and 'external' purchase orders. We represent this idea on the LDS by extending the entity notation to include sub-types as demonstrated in Figure 4.9:

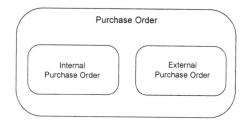

Figure 4.9 - Entity Sub-types

In Figure 4.9, 'Purchase Order' is the super-type while 'External Purchase Order' and 'Internal Purchase Order' are sub-types.

Sub-types share the key of the super-type as well as any common attributes. In other words, sub-types do not have a separate key that distinguishes them from each other.

In SRW, an internal purchase order stands for a transfer between two depots while an external purchase order is a transaction between a depot and a supplier. In data modelling terms, this means that an External Purchase Order contains *supplier number* as a foreign key while an Internal Purchase Order contains the *depot number* of the 'sending' depot. This is graphically illustrated in Figure 4.10:

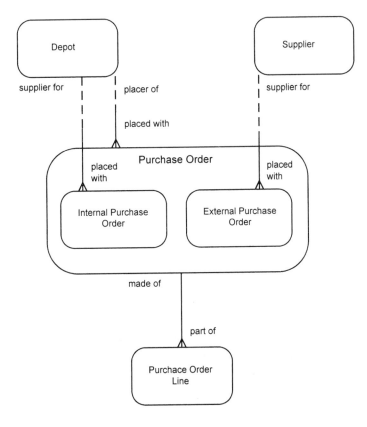

Figure 4.10 - Entity Sub-types

Entity Aspects

Sometimes an entity needs to be modelled in more than one sub-system. When such an entity is identified, the term 'aspect' is used for the entity in each sub-system. For example, the SRW sub-system we are dealing with contains the entity Supplier Invoice. This entity is recorded in our system because it is the stock people who receive an invoice for reconciliation. From the DFD we see that we only record the invoice in our system and never do anything about it. As far as we are concerned, it is the Accounts people who will retrieve the invoice we have reconciled and arrange for its payment. This means that for us a Supplier Invoice is something to reconcile while for Accounts it is something to arrange payment for. If we were to unify the two systems we should be aware of the different behaviours of the entity in each relevant sub-system.

Aspects in different sub-systems need to be co-ordinated. For example, Accounts should not pay for an invoice if we, at Stock Control, have not reconciled it against delivered and accepted goods.

Aspects are denoted by a dash after the entity name, as shown in Figure 4.11

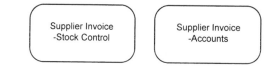

Figure 4.11 - Entity Aspects

It is possible to show different aspects of an entity as linked to one 'basic' aspect via one-to-one relationships.

Strictly speaking, every entity is the aspect the system we are building has of the real life entity being modelled.

Pig's Ears

When ordering a product it is possible that a supplier will not have sufficient stocks itself to satisfy the order. Requirement 7 stipulates that the new system should identify alternative products which can be substituted for the unavailable one in the order. This means that each product could be related to a number of alternative substitute products. This is an example of a recursive relationship, where an entity is related to itself. It is also sometimes called a 'pig's ear', due to its appearance (see Figure 4.12).

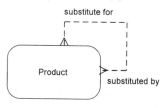

Figure 4.12 - Pig's Ear

However this is a m:n relationship which must now be resolved. The method for doing so is precisely the same as we would use if the entities at each end were different, i.e. by using a link entity (see the Product Substitute entity in Figure 4.13).

As we add each data related entry in the Requirements Catalogue to the LDS, we should update the entry with a cross-reference to relevant entities or relationships.

The completed LDS for SRW is shown in Figure 4.13.

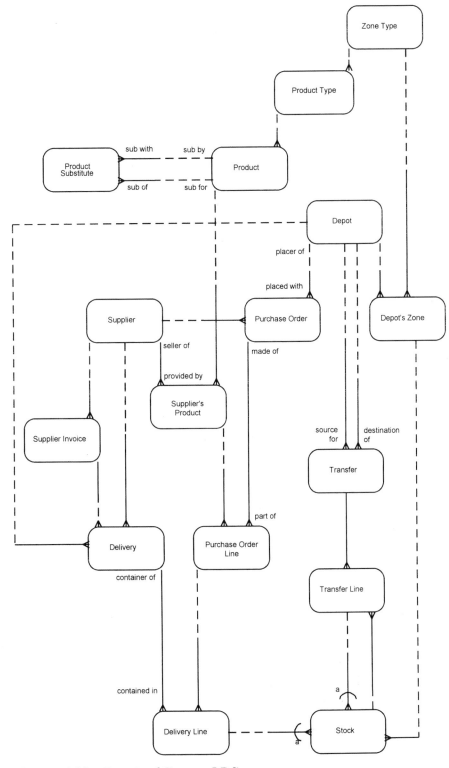

Figure 4.13 - Required System LDS

Complete LDM Documentation

Each entity on the LDS is defined through its contents and its relationships. It is therefore vital that the contents of each entity are explicitly stated. If a CASE tool is at hand this can be done more or less effortlessly. In the absence of a decent CASE tool an Entity Description form such as that depicted in Figure 4.14 should be raised.

Entity Description				
Entity Name *Purchase Order*				
Description *A request for purchase and delivery of goods from a single supplier.*				
Attribute			Primary Key	Foreign Key
Purchase Order Number			*Yes*	
Purchase Order Date				
Supplier Number				*Yes*
Depot Number				*Yes*
Purchase Order Status				
must/may be	either /or	Link Phrase	one & only one /one or more	Entity Name
must be		*placed with*	*one & only one*	*Supplier*
must be		*placed by*	*one & only one*	*Depot*
must		*contain*	*one or more*	*P.O. Line*
Entity Volumes: Max. *15000* Min. *6000*			Average *10000*	
User Role			Access	
P.O. Clerk			*Read, Create, Delete, Modify*	
Despatch Scheduler			*Read*	
Purchaser			*Read, Create*	
Growth Rate: *15% per year*				
Archiving *Purchase Orders should be archived to tape six months after the last related line has been delivered or cancelled.*				

Figure 4.14 - Entity Description

The kinds of thing we might include in Entity Descriptions are:

- A description of the entity.
- Attribute Names. In Stage 1 we will have noted only the most significant attributes - we now document all known attributes.
- Primary and Foreign Keys.
- Relationship details.
- Volumes. Approximate values for the average, maximum and minimum number of occurrences.

- User Access. Details of which user roles have access to the entity, and of what type (i.e. Create, Read, etc.).
- Growth Rate.
- Archiving Instructions. Details of when occurrences should be archived or deleted.

Many of these details will already exist as non-functional requirements in the Requirements Catalogue.

The contents of an entity description are normally the subject of installation standards as prescribed by the prevailing Policies and Procedures. In some organisations only brief descriptions will be required, while in others they may run to several pages for each entity and include descriptions of relationships and details of each individual attribute.

Alternatively attributes can be defined in detail in a Data Catalogue made up of Attribute Descriptions. Each Attribute Description will usually contain:

- A description of the attribute.
- Cross-references. Each attribute should be cross-referenced with other forms that refer to it. We are mainly interested here in which entity or entities contain the attribute, but we could also cross-reference with I/O Descriptions, etc.
- Grouped Domain. A domain is a set of values which may validly be taken by an attribute, e.g. Product Quantity has the domain Integer, Delivery Slot has the domain Time. If a domain is shared by a number of attributes it is called a Grouped Domain.
- Length.
- Mandatory or Optional. Each attribute may be mandatory or optional within an entity occurrence. If it is mandatory we could specify a default value.
- Derivation. An attribute may result directly from input to the system or be derived from input or other attributes.
- Validation. If appropriate we can add details of validation checks for the attribute.
- User Role Access.

The data model is complete when the contents of each entity are clearly understood. The attributes of all the Stock Control entities of Figure 4.13 follow:

DELIVERY
Delivery Number
*Supplier Number
*Invoice Number
*Depot Number
Delivery Date
Delivery Start Time
Delivery End Time

DELIVERY LINE
*Delivery Number
*Purchase Order Number
*Product Number
Quantity Due
Quantity Delivered
Quantity Accepted

DEPOT
Depot Number
Depot Name
Depot Address
Depot Tel. No.

DEPOT'S ZONE
*Depot Number
*Zone Type Code
Depot Zone Letter

PRODUCT
Product Number
*Product Type Code
Product Name

PRODUCT SUBSTITUTE
*Product Number [substitute]
*Product Number [substituted]

PRODUCT TYPE
Product Type Code
*Zone Type Code
Product Type Name

PURCHASE ORDER
*Purchase Order Number
*Depot Number
*Supplier Number
Purchase Order Date
Purchase Order Status

PURCHASE ORDER LINE
*Purchase Order Number
*Product Number
*Supplier Number
Quantity Required
Quantity Confirmed
Unit Price
Req-By Date
Req-By Time-Period

STOCK
Stock Id
*Delivery Number
*Purchase Order Number
*Product Number
*Depot Number
*Zone Type Code
*Depot Zone Letter
*Transfer Number
*Stock Id [Transferred]
Quantity Stocked
Quantity Reserved
Sell-by Date
Use-by Date
Batch No.

SUPPLIER
Supplier Number
Supplier Name
Supplier Address
Supplier Tel. No.
Supplier Contact Name

SUPPLIER INVOICE
*Supplier Number
Invoice Number
Invoice Date

SUPPLIER'S PRODUCT
*Supplier Number
*Product Number
Latest Price
Main Y/N?
P/S Reference

TRANSFER
Transfer Number
*Depot Number [From]
*Depot Number [To]
Transfer Date

TRANSFER LINE
*Transfer Number
*Stock Id
Quantity Transferred

ZONE TYPE
Zone Type Code
Zone Type Name

In the above list, primary keys are underlined and foreign keys are preceded by a star '*'. This means that a primary key made of more than one attribute is a compound key if it is made solely of foreign keys, otherwise it is a composite key. For example, Supplier's Product has a compound key while Supplier Invoice has a composite key made up of the supplier's key and the invoice number used by the supplier (the assumption here being that while we cannot guarantee that the invoice numbers allocated by suppliers are unique across all suppliers, we can expect that suppliers do not duplicate their own invoice numbers).

The key of Purchase Order Line may need some elaboration. The Purchase Order Line entity 'inherits' two foreign keys, *purchase order number* from Purchase Order and the *product number, supplier number* pair from Supplier's Product. It would therefore seem plausible to use the contents of these two foreign keys, made of three data items, as the compound key of Purchase Order Line. But, more careful consideration reveals that the pair of *purchase order number* and *product number* suffices, the *supplier number* being superfluous in pinpointing a particular purchase order line. Since keys should be minimal, we have opted for this pair as the key of Purchase Order Line.

Finally, a data store/entity Cross-Reference is defined (see Figure 4.15). This dictates the contents of the Data Flow Model's data stores, leading to the level 1 DFD presented in Figure 4.3.

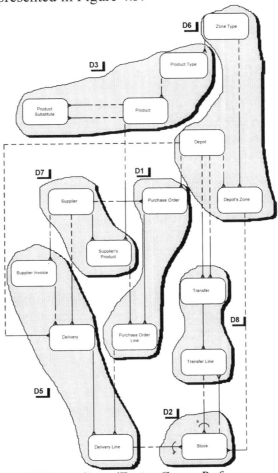

Figure 4.15 - The SRW Data Store/Entity Cross-Reference

4.4.2 Summary (Step 320)

The SSADM tasks carried out in Step 320 are:

Task

10   Update the LDM to include additional data requirements in the new system. Exclude elements of the LDM which are outside the new system as a result of BSO selection. Complete the documentation of entities, including the definition of all attributes. Cross-reference all changes with relevant Requirements Catalogue entries.

20   Check that the LDM will support the elementary processes in the Required System DFM.

30   Update the LDM with appropriate non-functional requirements from the Requirements Catalogue.

4.5   Step 330 - Derive System Functions

Up to this point the major vehicle for documenting system processing has been the DFM. Data Flow Diagrams are excellent for presenting 'snapshots' of how a system works, and how its components link together. However they only describe processing in outline, and by their snapshot nature provide a static view of activities. For example, they do not give any indication of human-computer interface structures, process sequencing, iteration or optionality, or of enquiries.

From Step 330 the specification of processing will revolve around the definition of Functions. We will initially identify update functions by looking at the elementary processes in our Required System DFM, and enquiry functions from the Requirements Catalogue (in consultation with users). We then continue to develop them iteratively until all the necessary components are available for physical design and implementation to take place.

Function Definitions are not formal models of processing. They act more as a co-ordinating concept or cross-reference for other products, which collectively define a function. Function Definitions are principally concerned with establishing the external design of the system. They play a minimal role in conceptual modelling for which they act as input.

4.5.1   Concepts

Function

We can define the concept of a Function in several ways, which together give a good idea of what a Function actually is:

- A Function is a set of processing that users wish to carry out at the same time.
- A Function is a set of processing designed to handle the effects of an event (or group of events) on the system.
- A Function is the basic unit of processing for input to Physical Design (where programs will be specified to implement it).

Each Function may encompass several individual update or enquiry processes, each of which responds to a particular event or trigger, but will usually cover just one.

Types of Function

We classify Functions in three ways:

- **Enquiry or Update.** Update functions may include enquiry elements, but their main purpose will be to update system data.
- **On-Line or Off-Line.** It is possible for functions to include both types of processing. We will need to decide which part of the processing is most significant in order to classify it properly.
- **User or System Initiated.** Every function must be triggered in some way. If the trigger is a real world event there will be a resultant data flow across the system boundary, it is *user initiated.* If the trigger is an internal event such as a date being reached or a stock balance falling below a certain value, there will be no flow across the system boundary, so the function is *system initiated.*

Components of a Function

SSADM uses the concept of 'the Universal Function Model' to describe the standard components of a function (Figure 4.16).

The UFM provides a model of all of the components that go to make up a function. We will now begin the process of specifying these components, and as the project progresses we will gradually add more and more detail until the function is completely defined.

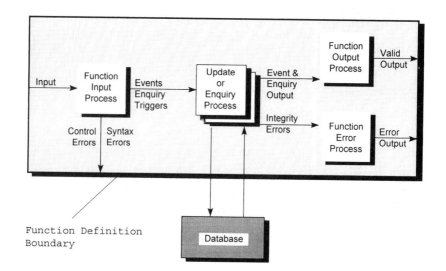

Figure 4.16 - Universal Function Model

In Step 330 we will define the following components of a function:

- **Input.**
- **Valid Output.** At this stage both inputs and outputs are made up of *logical* data items (i.e. data items input to, or generated from, LDM attributes), so will not include system control or validation items such as:
    - error messages
    - page numbers
    - current dates
    - user login numbers
- **Events or Enquiry Triggers.** Many events and enquiry triggers will not be discovered or fully understood until we carry out Entity Behaviour Modelling in Step 360, so function definition will interface closely with Step 360.
- **The Function Definition Boundary** (and textual description of the function).

We add the other function components during Stages 5 and 6:

Stage 5 -   Input and Valid Output (further definition)
             Event and Enquiry Output
             Update Processes
             Enquiry Processes
             Integrity Errors

Stage 6 -   Syntax and Control Errors
             I/O Processes
             Error Outputs

4.5.2   Defining Functions

Functions are initially identified by examining the Requirements Catalogue for enquiries, and the Required System DFM for updates, and establishing which events or enquiries the users wish to be processed together.

Identifying Update Functions

Each *major* data flow which crosses the system boundary should correspond to at least one event. So we can identify an initial set of functions by taking the Required System DFM and following each of these data flows into and through the bottom-level processes, tracing all of its data items until they have been either stored or output. We can then identify all of the processes involved in handling the flow (and hence the events) and ring them to form a single function.

For example, by tracing the data flows P.O. Quantities (representing the event Request Purchase Order) and Availability (representing the event Confirm Order) into the level 1 process Monitor Purchase Order we can create initial functions 1 and 2, as in Figure 4.17. On occasion, when the DFM contains processes that trigger each other, functions may cover more than one Elementary Process.

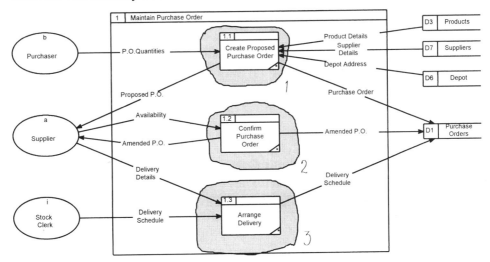

Figure 4.17 - Identify Functions from the DFD

More frequently, each function will correspond to a single Elementary Process, particularly if we tied each process to a distinct driving (or triggering) data flow and kept inter-process data flows to a minimum during DFM development.

Once all input data flows have been traced, we may be left with some processes which have not yet been allocated to a function. Assuming that these do not represent processes which have been incorrectly modelled, they will represent system-initiated processing. In the SRW system process 6, Produce Stock Report, is such a time-initiated process.

Once we have allocated all processes and traced all data flows, the events handled by each function must be identified. Many functions will process a single event type, but it is quite permissible for a function to handle batches of different event types which are input in a single data flow. This is especially true for off-line functions where input frequently consists of large amounts of data from different, and often unsorted, forms.

It is also possible to define a function which handles events input via more than one data flow; in which case each execution of the function must be triggered by one or other of the flows, but not both.

Identifying Enquiry Functions

Enquiry functions (other than those which form a major part of the systems functionality) will be documented in the Requirements Catalogue, rather than the Required System DFM. Each enquiry entry in the Requirements Catalogue will initially be identified as a function in its own right. One such enquiry function from the SRW system is the Stock Nearing Sell-by Date Report. This is a direct response to requirement 11 which, being a requirement for an enquiry on which the functionality of the system does not depend, has not ended up in our required System DFM.

Later on we may merge enquiries or add them to the definition of update functions.

Confirming Functions

We should discuss the initial set of functions with users, to verify that they represent the way in which they require processing to be organised. We may find that users wish to split up a function, because they will need to carry out different parts of the function independently, or that they want to combine them to form bigger functions.

The users of the SRW system estimate that in about 15% of cases they will need to amend existing deliveries while arranging new deliveries with a supplier. To cater for these occasions we can create two functions in response to elementary process 1.3: one to arrange a delivery for the first time and one to amend an existing delivery. Alternatively, we can retain one function which, when activated will prompt the user to state whether they wish to arrange a fresh delivery or amend one that has been arranged earlier.

Although we should attempt to satisfy as many of the users' requirements as possible it is important not to get carried away with defining composite functions that will hardly ever be used.

If the way in which the function is to be used is in doubt, the function should be submitted for more rigorous study as we will show in the following sections.

Documenting Functions

Once functions have been defined and confirmed with users we can begin their documentation. Descriptions of each function will be continually expanded as the project progresses, but even at this point we can provide quite a lot of detail:

- **Name and Identifier**. Function names and identifiers should be unique within the project, and if possible names should differ from those of the constituent elementary processes.
- **Type**. Update or Enquiry, On-Line or Off-Line, System or User initiated.
- **Description**. For functions which cover just one Elementary Process or one Requirements Catalogue enquiry the description will probably be very similar to the EPD or Requirements Catalogue entry.
- **Business Events, Activities and System Events.** As we will explain a bit further on, a business event is something that happens which triggers a series of user activities. Some of these activities will require the services of the system. Each activity that leads to an update of system's data leads to the recognition of a system event. We have used the BAM to record activities, and the DFM to identify major system events. We will be using Entity Behaviour Modelling to identify more system events in Step 360.
- **User Roles.** The set of users for whom the function is designed.
- **Error Handling**. This will be very informal at this point, as error processing will not be fully defined until much later. However it is worth noting any high level requirements for future consideration.

- **Constituent DFD Processes.** When the function has been identified through the DFM, the relevant elementary processes are listed.

Function Definition	
Function Name *Book Delivery*	Function Id: *3*
Function Type Update/On-Line/User	
Function Description *Suppliers contact the depot to arrange delivery of goods contained on one or more Purchase Orders. An enquiry will be made to check on free delivery time slots for the suppliers preferred delivery date, if the goods are not to be added to an existing delivery.* *The delivery is then confirmed for a slot and the relevant Purchase Order Lines (or parts of) are assigned. Suppliers have to state the Purchase Order Line they wish to deliver. The system confirms that the products are indeed expected and we record the quantity expected.*	
Business Events *Delivery Arrangement, Delivery Amendment*	
Activities *Arrange Delivery, Set Up Delivery Schedule*	
System Events *New Delivery Schedule, Updated Delivery Schedule*	
User Roles *Delivery Scheduler*	
Error Handling *The transaction will be terminated if the goods to be delivered do not match the outstanding Purchase Orders.*	
DFD Processes *1.3 (Arrange delivery)*	
I/O Structures *3.1*	
I/O Descriptions *a - 1.3, 1.3 - d1, i - 1.3*	
Requirements Catalogue Ref. *10*	
Related Functions *None*	
Enquiries *Check Available Slots*	
Common Processing	

Figure 4.18 - A Paper Based Function Definition

- **I/O Structures.** This refers to the diagram described in the next section, which details the structure of the interface between the function and a user.
- **I/O Descriptions** for data flows into and out of the function, and which cross the system boundary.
- **Requirements Catalogue Reference.** A most important entry. A function that cannot trace its inclusion back to a requirement that has made it through Stage 2 is not part of the system.

- **Related Functions.** Functions which are commonly carried out together, but which are still distinct from each other, should be cross-referenced.
- **Enquiries.** If an enquiry is only ever carried out as part of an update function then that enquiry element will be modelled separately but still lie within the update function's definition. For example, the function Book Delivery will often involve an enquiry to determine which delivery slots are free. If there were other occasions when we needed to carry out this enquiry we would define it as a function in its own right. In this case there are not, and so it will be included in the definition of Book Delivery.
- **Common Processing.** EPDs relating to common processing which is below the level of an event will remain and be cross-referenced to appropriate function definitions. This section is completed during Physical Design.

In a similar way to the Requirements Catalogue, we may find it useful to set up a Function Summary (see Figure 4.19). Although not an official SSADM document, it can be invaluable as a quick reference.

Id	Name	Description
1	Propose Purchase Order	Details of required quantities of individual products are entered on-line in batches throughout the day. These product orders are batched (by off-line processing) by supplier and proposed Purchase Orders created.
2	Confirm Purchase Order	Suppliers provide details of stock availability for proposed Purchase Orders. Purchase Order Lines which can be satisfied are confirmed. For those which cannot an alternative supplier is selected and a new Proposed Purchase Order created.

Figure 4.19 - Function Summary

4.5.3 Specifying User Interfaces

Functions are units of work that users wish to carry out using the new system. To do so they will need to hold a dialogue with the system, i.e. to interface with each function. We now turn our attention to specifying the structure of these interfaces. As we have seen we will classify functions as *primarily* on-line or off-line, but in fact they may contain both kinds of interface, e.g. where we enter data on-line into a function, which then generates a report or form off-line.

Most update functions will already have a number of I/O Descriptions associated with them, as identified from the Required System DFM. These provide a list of all data items input to the function and of the major data items output from the function, thus providing us with a limited view of the user interface. However this view contains two major omissions:

1. System Responses

Output elements of I/O Descriptions only contain those data items which make up the final output from the function, and so omit any outputs designed to verify or confirm user input, i.e. system responses. We can illustrate this by looking at the function Propose Purchase Order (Function 1 Figure 4.17). The I/O Descriptions for this function are given in Figure 4.20.

I/O Description				
From	To	Data Flow Name	Data Content	Comments
b	1.1	P.O. Quantities	Depot Number Product Number Qty Required Req-By Date Req-By Time-Period	The purchaser may state a date by when the product should be delivered or a time-period, e.g. 3 weeks from now.
1.1	a	Proposed Purchase Order	P.O. Number Supplier Number Supplier Name Supplier Address Depot Name Depot Address Req-By Date Product Number P/S Reference Product Name Qty Required Product Price	Each Purchase Order will contain several lines (usually up to about 12). Product No is the unique number of a product, e.g. the bar code P/S Reference is the reference number suppliers use for that product.

Figure 4.20 - I/O Description

This would indicate that no output is received by the purchaser, i.e. that the purchaser inputs a group of data items (on-line) without response from the system, which ultimately results in the output of proposed purchase orders (off-line). In fact, when a purchaser inputs a product number the system will respond by displaying the product name so that the purchaser can verify that the product number is correct.

This kind of response is not part of the required final output of the process, but merely acts as an input confirmation. For this reason it is not included in the DFM, but it *will* be documented as part of a Function Definition.

2. Interface Structure

Looking again at the I/O descriptions in Figure 4.20, we can see that inputs and outputs are shown as separate unstructured groups of data items, with occasional comments that certain sub-groups will be repeated within the overall group (e.g. *product number, quantity required* etc. in I/O Description 1.1-a). This would imply that we input a continuous stream of data which results in a continuous stream of output data.

However, in reality users will require input and output data to be inter-leaved, with some data items being repeated or omitted.

For example let us take the on-line interface between users and the function Propose Purchase Order, represented at the moment by I/O Description b-1.1.

Purchasers will enter data in batches throughout the day, for a range of products and for all depots. For each depot, a depot number will be entered, followed by a series of product requirements for that depot, each of which will be confirmed by the output of relevant product details.

This textual description is not sufficiently precise or rigorous enough to act as a specification of the users' required interface, but it does point to the need to model the structure, as well as the content, of such interfaces. We do this by using I/O Structures.

4.5.4   I/O Structures

An I/O Structure consists of an I/O Structure Diagram, and an accompanying I/O Structure Description.

I/O Structure Diagrams

I/O Structure Diagrams use a notation based on that of Jackson Structured Programming (JSP), to show the sequence, optionality and iteration of data items crossing the system boundary, i.e. the user interface. Each function will have at least one I/O Structure, and in cases where there are on-line and off-line components will usually have at least two (one for each type of interface).

I/O Structure Notation

We will explain the notation of I/O Structure Diagrams using an example: The Propose Purchase Order function is made of two parts. First, purchasers suggest products to be procured by individual depots. Then, overnight, all the suggestions are reorganised and the system produces proposed purchase orders. Clearly, purchasers work on-line while the production of each proposed purchase order is done off-line. The function therefore consists of two parts, one on-line and one off-line. The *on-line* interface for Propose Purchase Order (described above) has the I/O Structure Diagram shown in Figure 4.21.

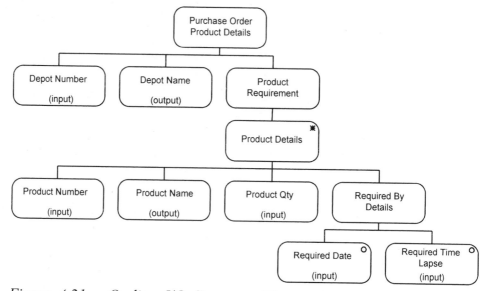

Figure 4.21 - On-line I/O Structure Diagram component for Propose Purchase Order

The top box contains the name of the I/O Structure. We should try to choose a name which describes the contents of the interface.

The other boxes fall into two groups:

- **I/O Structure Elements.** These are the bottom boxes or 'end leaves' (i.e. those that have no other boxes below them) of the structure, and represent actual groups of data items. Each element is labelled as either input or output and will only include logical data items (not system control messages, operator id's, etc.).
- **Structure Boxes.** These are all of the intermediate boxes (between the top box and the end-leaves). They are used to illustrate how the data items are structured within the interface.

I/O Structure Descriptions

For each I/O Structure Diagram we complete an I/O Structure Description detailing the contents of the I/O Structure Elements. For elements that consist of a single data item this is a trivial exercise, but usually each element represents more than one data item.

We complete the documentation of I/O Structures by assigning a unique numeric identifier to each I/O Structure (preferably consisting of the function identifier, plus a unique suffix), and adding this to the Function Definition.

I/O Structure Description		
I/O Structure Name Purchase Order Product Details		Id
I/O Structure Element	**Data Item**	**Comments**
Depot Number	Depot Number	The depot's identifier is entered
Depot Name	Depot Name	Each depot has a name that betrays its geographical location
Product Number	Product No	
Product Name	Product Name	The product's name is output to provide a visual check
Product Qty	Quantity Required	
Required Date	Req-By Date	
Required Time Lapse	Req-By Time-Period	

Figure 4.22 - The I/O Structure Description of the on-line I/O Structure Diagram for Propose Purchase Order

Sequence

The sequence of the boxes of an I/O Structure Diagram is read from left to right. So in Figure 4.21 Depot Number (input) is followed by Depot Name (output) which is followed by what is hanging under the 'Product Requirement' structure box.

Selections

Some parts of an interface will be mutually exclusive, i.e. we input (or output) one element or another, but not both. This is referred to as a selection. Selections are denoted by a small circle in the upper right-hand corner of the box, as in the section of Figure 4.21 depicted in Figure 4.23.

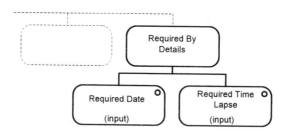

Figure 4.23 - Selection

Figure 4.23 tells us that we input *either* the contents of the Required Date element *or* the contents of the Required Time Lapse element to indicate when the product is required by.

Selections do not just apply to I/O Structure Elements; by adding them to structure boxes they can be used to identify whole sequences of inputs and outputs, or sections of the interface, which are mutually exclusive (see Figure 4.24).

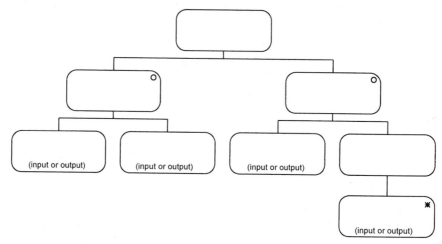

Figure 4.24 - Selection of Structures

Clearly it is possible to have several distinct groups subject to different selections within the same interface. So to identify which components belong to each selection we group them together and attach them below a single structure box. For example, in Figure 4.25(a) by grouping all of a-d under the same structure box we show that only one of a-d would be selected, whereas in Figure 4.25(b) we have a sequence of two selections where one of a or b is selected followed by one of c or d.

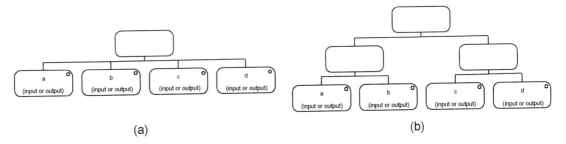

(a)   (b)

Figure 4.25 - Selection Groupings

Some elements in an interface will be entirely optional, i.e. they do not have to be input or output, and there is no alternative. We show optionality using a null box. In Figure 4.26 either 'a' happens or nothing happens.

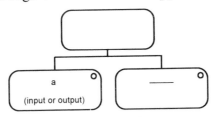

Figure 4.26 - Null Selection (Optional Element)

Iterations

Parts of the structure which repeat within a single execution of the function are indicated by an asterisk in the top right-hand corner. These are known as iterations.

We have to take a little care using an asterisk, as all parts of an I/O Structure Diagram below it will be subject to the iteration.

In Figure 4.21 the asterisk in the 'Product Details' box means that the entire sequence of inputs and outputs attached below it can be iterated (including the selections). That is we can repeat the sequence:

1. Product Number (input)
2. Product Name (output)
3. Product Qty (input)
4. Either - Required Date (input)
   Or   - Required Time Lapse (input)

A common mistake when using iterations is illustrated in Figure 4.27.

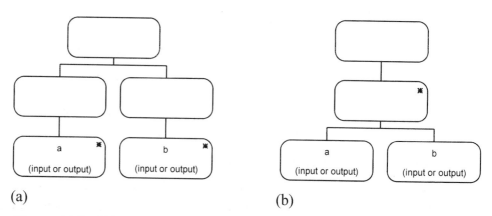

(a)   (b)

Figure 4.27 - I/O Structure Iterations

The structure in Figure 4.27 (a) gives us the sequence a,a,a,a .... *followed by* b,b,b,b .... . This is because a and b are subject to separate iterations denoted by different parent structure boxes. The structure in Figure 4.27 (b) gives us the sequence a,b;a,b;a,b; .... , as they both lie below the same iterated structure box. It is quite easy to confuse these two structures, so we should handle them with care.

Structure Rules

There are a number of basic rules for drawing Jackson-like structures:

- All boxes hanging from a single 'parent' box must be of the same type, i.e. all selections, or all sequence boxes. So (a) and (b) in Figure 4.28 would not be allowed as they have mixed types hanging from a common parent.

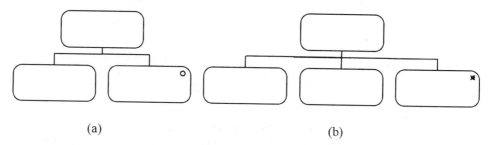

(a)   (b)

Figure 4.28 - Invalid Structures

- All iteration boxes must have a sequence box or selection box immediately above them.
- All selection boxes must have a structure box above them.

Drawing I/O Structures

There are two basic types of I/O Structure:

(i) On-Line

An I/O Structure for an on-line function or part of a function is drawn to reflect the kind of dialogue users will expect, i.e. with inputs paired with appropriate system responses, as in the case of Purchase Order Product Details in Figure 4.21.

(ii) Off-Line

For off-line functions or parts of functions, we will produce one I/O Structure illustrating its input data and one I/O Structure illustrating its output data. This mirrors the way in which dialogues for off-line functions are conducted.

As we have seen, some functions will include both on-line and off-line components (such as Propose Purchase Order), in which case we will have separate I/O Structures representing each component.

The off-line component of Propose Purchase Order (see I/O Description 1.1-a, in Figure 4.20) is concerned only with *outputs*, as all input to the function is via the on-line component of figures 4.21 and 4.22 (see Figure 4.29).

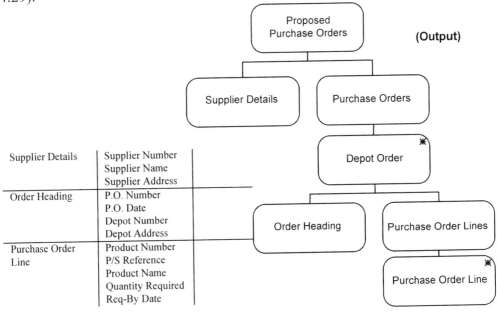

Supplier Details	Supplier Number Supplier Name Supplier Address
Order Heading	P.O. Number P.O. Date Depot Number Depot Address
Purchase Order Line	Product Number P/S Reference Product Name Quantity Required Req-By Date

Figure 4.29 - Off-line I/O Structure Diagram and Description for Propose Purchase Order

Note that we do not need to label the I/O Structure Elements as Input or Output as the entire diagram is output only.

Functions that are largely update in nature are likely to have substantial inputs but only minor confirmation output; whereas enquiry functions will generally have a small amount of triggering input but a large amount of output (after all it is the output which interests us in enquiry functions).

Enquiry functions will be documented mainly in the Requirements Catalogue, so we will not have I/O Descriptions to use as a start point for drawing I/O Structure Diagrams. Instead we will draw them in direct consultation with users.

Some functions will include both enquiry and update components, e.g. Book Delivery. In these cases we can produce a separate I/O Structure for each component. The I/O Structure for the enquiry component Check Available Slots is shown in Figure 4.30, and the remaining update component of Book Delivery is shown in Figure 4.31.

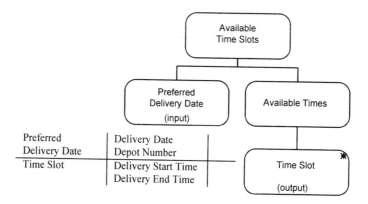

Figure 4.30 - I/O Structure for Check Available Slots Enquiry

The interface of the Book Delivery function is not straightforward since it involves two components and an element of decision making on the part of the stock clerk. For this reason we will single out this function when we introduce some more techniques for dealing with more involved functions a bit later on.

Functions that are system initiated are unlikely to have any input other than user confirmations. For example the enquiry function Produce Stock Listing will contain only outputs as it is triggered by date and time, while the function Remove Old Purchase Orders will only require YES/NO type confirmations of deletions.

(More I/O Structures are included in the Relational Data Modelling section (Step 340) where they are used as input to that technique.)

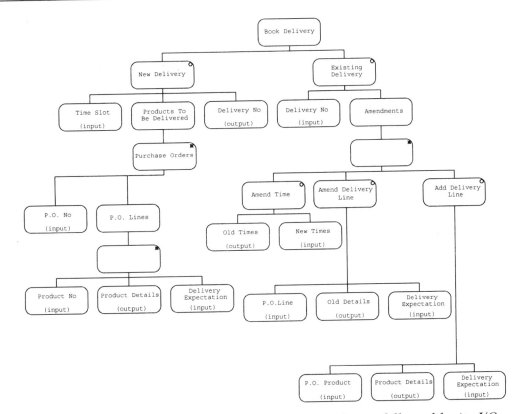

Figure 4.31 - I/O Structure Diagram for Book Delivery followed by its I/O Structure Description

Time Slot	Supplier Number Delivery Date Delivery Start Time Delivery End Time	
P.O. No	P.O. Number	
Product No	Product Number	
Product Details	Product Name P/S Reference Quantity Ordered	The system should also print out the quantity that has already been delivered plus the quantity already arranged for
Delivery Expectation	Quantity Due	
Delivery No	Delivery Number	System assigns a delivery number
Old Times	Delivery Date Delivery Start Time Delivery End Time	
New Times	Delivery Date Delivery Start Time Delivery End Time	System should allow 'old times' to act as defaults to be written over as necessary
P.O. Line	P.O. Number Product Number	
Old Details	Product Name P/S Reference Quantity Ordered Quantity Due	Again, the system should inform if the quantity due exceeds what was ordered plus what has already been delivered or promised.

Events in an I/O Structure Diagram

If a single function handles the processing of more than one different event (for example where a function handles batches of input containing data about a range of events) then I/O Structures should not intermingle the inputs and outputs associated with those different events. This would make it difficult to design distinct event-based processes in later design steps.

We can achieve clear event distinction by creating a separate I/O Structure for each event type, or alternatively we can make sure that the interface elements associated with each event are defined separately within a single structure (see Figure 4.32).

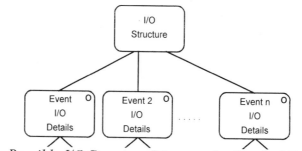

Figure 4.32 - Possible I/O Structure Diagram for Batched Events

The order in which events occur in a single I/O structure must be logically correct. For instance if a structure contained elements dealing with events which create and delete the same entity types then we should sequence the creations first. Allowable or logical sequencing of events will be a lot clearer after Step 360 in which we carry out Entity Behaviour Modelling.

4.5.5 User Interface Design

The I/O Structure does not appear to represent well the richer screen environments which incorporate Windows, Icons, Menus and Pointers (WIMPs). These relatively new environments allow users to perform tasks in which the system itself provides information that helps them take decisions which in turn are input to the system. For example, we have already noticed that the booking of a delivery requires the delivery scheduler to consult the system to find available time slots when a delivery can take place. After agreeing on a provisional time slot, suppliers have to inform SRW of the product quantities they expect to deliver. It is the delivery scheduler's job to make sure that the expected products correspond to undelivered purchase order lines to the point of rejecting a delivery outright if suppliers cannot state the purchase order they are responding to. It is clear therefore that the activity of booking a delivery involves many tasks, each with a different set of expected actions. This means that the design issues to be tackled by system designers are much more complicated now that the richness of computing environments allows for a higher level of sophistication.

SSADM4+ version 4.3 recommends the use of certain techniques from the still evolving arsenal of Human Computer Interaction (HCI). These techniques include Task Modelling, User Object Modelling, Function Navigation Modelling, Window Navigation Modelling as well as mechanisms for prototyping and evaluating Graphical User Interfaces (GUIs).

Task Modelling

To take advantage of a GUI and to not allow the richness of WIMPs to overwhelm the design, we need to tread carefully by first understanding the tasks involved in performing an activity. For example, when arranging a delivery, the delivery scheduler has to first find an available time slot. When a slot is agreed with the supplier, the supplier has to state the contents of the delivery. As each product to be delivered is stated, a check is activated to find the purchase order line which is being dealt with. In the case that this is an extension to a previously agreed delivery, existing delivery lines may be amended while new ones may be added. We can represent all this in a Hierarchical Task Model (HTM) like the one depicted in Figure 4.33.

The HTM is read from left to right and annotated with 'plans' which show the alternative ways in which the activity may be fulfilled. For example, reading the bottom-most plans on every branch of the HTM in Figure 4.33 we see that the most complicated case where a delivery includes the arrangement of a new time, additional delivery lines and the amendment of old delivery lines would need the successful completion of tasks 332, 334, 336, which comprise 33, followed by 3945, 362 and 366.

Task Scenarios

One way of understanding and controlling the tasks involved in the successful completion of an activity is to provide concrete examples of real life situations which describe from beginning to end the actions needed to complete the activity.

Each business activity is influenced by certain happenings and conditions to which users of the system have to react in order to complete the activity. Each set of such conditions represents a task scenario for the activity. For example, each different plan of the HTM represents a Task Scenario.

Task Scenarios are very helpful in validating Task Models. Usually, the task scenarios precede and drive the creation of the Task Model, but, as with all other diagrammatic tools of system analysis, the tables are soon turned and the Task Model generates ideas for Task Scenarios which can be validated with the users.

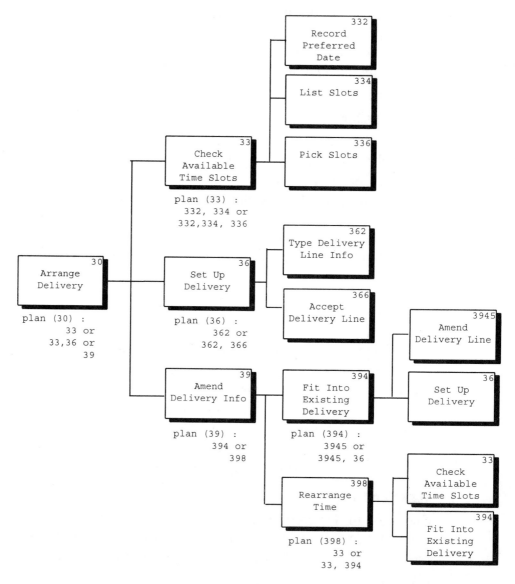

Figure 4.33 The Hierarchical Task Model for the Arrange Delivery Activity

User Object Modelling

Task Models are closely related to User Object Models. A User Object is something the user recognises as being part of performing an action. In information systems, User Objects consist of data items and the actions in which they participate. They are related to each another via associations in a manner similar to entities.

In the case of arranging a delivery for SRW, delivery schedulers perceive that the activity entails the use of a diary which consists of many time slots. During the activity, a delivery note is created. This delivery note is associated with one or more half hour slots and with one or more purchase orders. Figure 4.34 depicts an object model for this activity. The notation used is self-explanatory.

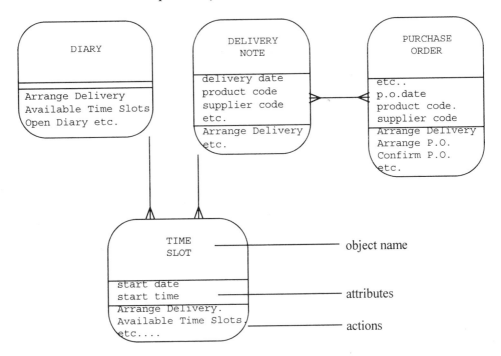

Figure 4.34 The User Object Model for the Arrange Delivery Activity

User Object Models have clear links with Object Oriented Design models. Indeed, the User Object Model notation can be extended to incorporate any Object Oriented (OO) notational convention depending on the prevailing Policies and Procedures.

Function Navigation Model

The Hierarchical Task Model shows all the tasks involved in completing a business activity. When a User Function is defined to support that business activity, each task on the HTM can be seen as a component of the function. If these components lead to the design of separate 'windows', drop-down menus, cut-outs and the like, then it is useful to create a Function

Navigation Model to show how we will move from one component to another. Figure 4.35 shows a Function Navigation Model that represents the plans of the HTM in Figure 4.33.

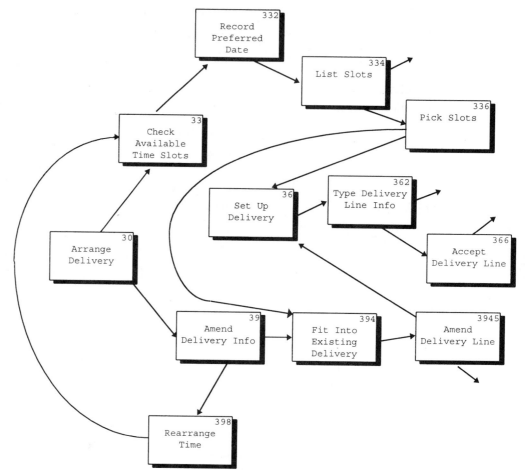

Figure 4.35 A Function Navigation Model

Window Navigation Model

The Function Navigation Model can be transformed into a Window Navigation Model by the addition of the 'window-type' notation of Figure 4.36.

A Windows Navigation Model for the Arrange Delivery function is shown in Figure 4.37.

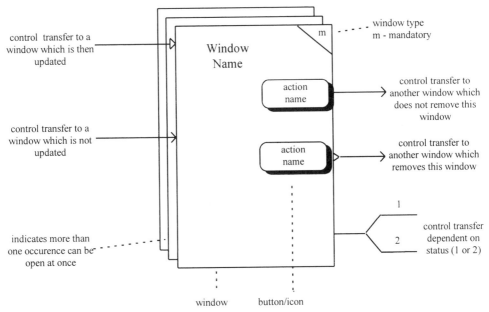

Figure 4.36 The notation for Window Navigation Models

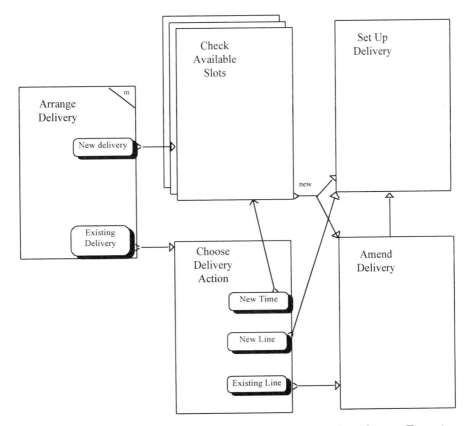

Figure 4.37 A Window Navigation Model for the Book Delivery Function

We now have two representations of the Book Delivery function. The first is shown by the I/O Structure of Figure 4.31 and the second by the Window Navigation Model of Figure 4.36. Neither is totally satisfactory because a) the activity of arranging a delivery is complicated and b) the richness of a WIMP environment needs experience to harness. Nevertheless, both representations have their advantages, each providing a different angle through which to understand the activity. We will single out this function as one that requires clarification and thus submit it for prototyping a bit later on.

4.5.6 Non-Functional Requirements

Our final task in deriving system functions in Step 330 is to add details of related non-functional requirements to our function definitions. These will take the form of approximate volumes of execution, service levels and access controls, and most will be lifted directly from the Requirements Catalogue.

As we have discussed, Function Definition is an on-going activity, but we now have an initial set of building blocks for developing a specification of the processing of the new system. As we create other more detailed models of event processing and dialogue design we will cross-reference them with the relevant function definitions.

4.5.7 Identify Required Dialogues

We now use our Function Definitions and User Role documentation to identify exactly who will require access to each function. The easiest way of documenting this is by using a User Role/Function Matrix (see Figure 4.38).

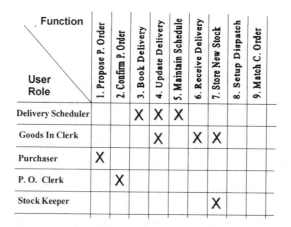

Function \ User Role	1. Propose P. Order	2. Confirm P. Order	3. Book Delivery	4. Update Delivery	5. Maintain Schedule	6. Receive Delivery	7. Store New Stock	8. Setup Dispatch	9. Match C. Order
Delivery Scheduler			X	X	X				
Goods In Clerk				X		X	X		
Purchaser	X								
P. O. Clerk		X							
Stock Keeper							X		

Figure 4.38 - User Role/Function Matrix

Each cross indicates that a dialogue between a user role and a system function is required. We must of course check the matrix with users to verify that we have correctly understood which functions each user role will need access to.

Once the matrix is complete we should identify all dialogues which are critical to the success of the new system (it is possible that they all are). This will help us to make a shortlist of the most important dialogues for prototyping in Step 350, and might be useful in assessing the suitability of various technical system options in Stage 4. It will also help us define the users' work practices in Step 335.

There are a number of questions we can ask when selecting critical dialogues, but any decisions we make must be agreed with users.

- Will the dialogue be used very frequently? Any which are used only once or twice a year are unlikely to be too critical.
- Does the underlying function carry out tasks essential to the success of the business?
- Are large numbers of entities accessed or updated, and are the access paths likely to be complex?
- Is the dialogue associated with new system functionality?
- Does the dialogue represent processing which is likely to be high-profile or politically sensitive?

Once we have identified the critical dialogues we should annotate the User Role/Function Matrix by circling the appropriate crosses (or replacing them with the letter C) as shown in Figure 4.39.

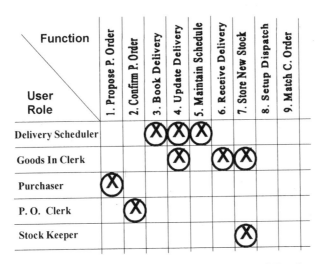

Figure 4.39 - User Role Function Matrix with Critical Dialogues

4.5.7 Summary (Step 330)

The SSADM tasks carried out in Step 330 are:

Task

10   Identify update functions from the DFM with the help and guidance of users. Check that each elementary process is allocated to at least one function. Identify the events and enquiry components of each function.

20   Identify enquiry functions from the Requirements Catalogue and (for major enquiries) the DFM, again with the guidance of users.

30   Create I/O Structures or for each off-line function. Create I/O Structures for on-line functions as appropriate. Study more involved functions using User Interface Design techniques.

40   Create a User Role/Function Matrix. Identify those dialogues that are regarded as critical.

50   Specify service levels for each function.

60   Update the Requirements Catalogue with the resolutions offered by each Function Definition.

4.6 Step 335 - Develop User Job Specifications

The computerised information system we are building will clearly change the way people go about doing their jobs. In Step 330 we concentrate on the activities that involve direct access to the system. In Step 335 we expand our study to include all activities taking place in the environment of the system. This will allow us to understand the whole working practices of our users and so help us integrate the system into their environment.

Until its latest version SSADM took it for granted that the computer system being built will influence the working conditions of the people around it and therefore the project team would deal with any issues as they arose. By not explicitly stating what should be done to study the impact of the system, the impression developed that the SSADM practitioner was meant to look only at the system itself and its direct interaction with its users. Nothing could be further from the truth and Step 335 is designed to redress the balance.

The main product of the step is a complete set of user job specifications. The technique used is Work Practice Modelling.

4.6.1 Work Practice Modelling Concepts

When studying the effects of a system on the working environment, we have to distinguish between the activities that are influenced because of direct use of the system and the activities which get their information via a third party. To clarify the two types of influence some terminology is necessary.

Actors, User Roles, Users and User Classes

Not all job holders will come into contact with the system. For example, the people stacking the SRW shelves will never use the system directly. We will refer to the set of job holders who share a collection of common tasks as 'actors'. By defining all the actors we define each and every person in the system's environment.

Of all the actors, some will require direct access to the system. These actors, i.e. the subsets of all people who share a common user interface, constitute the 'user roles' we have already met.

Users are the people who interact directly with the system. A user uses the system by 'acting' in his or her 'user role'.

When designing an interface it is important to know how frequently each user will be using the system, their computing competence and their experience. If necessary we split users into different 'user classes' and design different interfaces for each class.

Business Events, Activities, Tasks and Basic Tasks

A business event is a happening which triggers one or more business activities. For example, the business event of a truck load arriving at SRW triggers the activities of checking the delivery, placing the goods in the delivery bay, allocating stock locations, removing goods from the delivery bay, storing goods in the depot and updating the stock levels (see left-hand side of figure 2.5). Business events include inputs from outside the business, decisions made within the business boundary and time triggered events.

The complete set of activities triggered by a business event is somewhat clumsily referred to as a 'basic task'. A basic task may involve many people performing their activities in various places (see Figure 4.40).

To complete an activity, humans perform certain tasks which may involve sub-tasks. When an activity is to be supported by the new system, task models may be drawn up as we saw in the previous section.

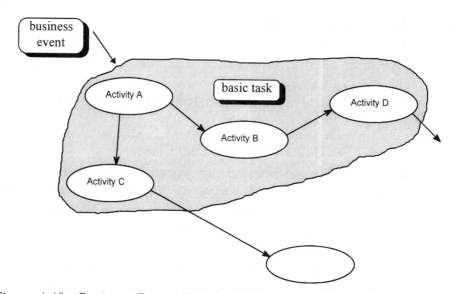

Figure 4.40 - Business Events Trigger the Activities of one Business Task

When a business event occurs, some of the activities it triggers may end up inside the computer system's boundary and some may not. Those that end up inside and also lead to an update of our records give rise to system events.

The BAM shows all activities and their dependencies. Business Process Re-engineering is the discipline which studies the work-flows suggested by a BAM with a view of reducing the number of interactions.

4.6.2   Work Practice Modelling Products

A Work Practice Model (WPM) is a mapping of the Business Activity Model onto the actors whose jobs will be changed by the new system. In many ways we have been doing this from Step 115 when we established the analysis framework by setting up a Business Activity Model (BAM).

While the BAM defines the business activities in terms of what, when, how and why, the WPM specifies who will carry out each activity and where. To achieve this we first define the organisation structure and its actors, we then specify basic tasks, study how these basic tasks interact and then allocate these tasks to actors. The tasks that require direct interaction with the system define the user roles.

The products of Work Practice Modelling include the User Catalogue, Task Models, Task Scenarios, User Roles and User Class Descriptions.

4.6.3 Work Practice Modelling Activities

Work Practice Modelling starts off with Business Activity Modelling. As the BAM is developed, a User Catalogue is set up. This forms the starting point of User Analysis which will, by the end of Step 335 evolve into a complete definition of each user's interface requirements.

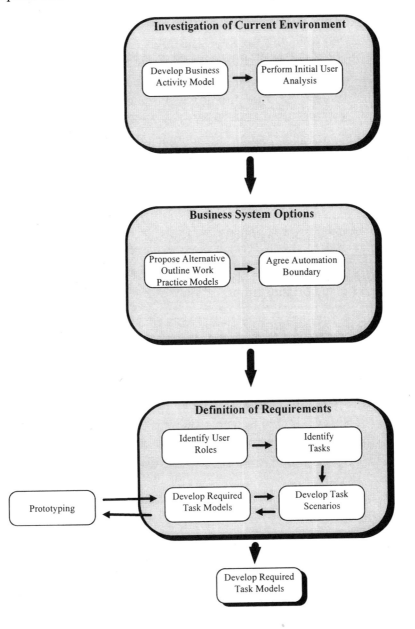

Figure 4.41 - Work Practice Modelling Activities

During Business System Options Work Practice Modelling plays an important part in providing a set of alternative outline Work Practice Models which help illustrate the impact of each BSO.

With an agreed boundary in hand, the technique becomes the forum through which the detail of who does what, down to the level of the user interface, is studied using Hierarchical Task Models and Task Scenarios. This is an iterative process which may resort to prototyping to elucidate complicated tasks. Figure 4.41 illustrates the technique.

Work Practice Modelling straddles the region between IT practitioners and Human Factors specialists. The manner in which it is undertaken will depend largely on the prevailing Policies and Procedures. These will usually define exactly how Business Activity Modelling and Work Practice Modelling will take place. The approach described here is quite general. As the SSADM manual rightly states "the overriding consideration in the approach adopted for Work Practice Modelling is that projects should take account of the complete picture of the business and not just concentrate on the automated system. The automated system must be designed to fit the business needs, not the other way round."

Work Practice Modelling entails the allocation of responsibilities to humans. To do so successfully, experience is needed plus the full backing of the affected organisation.

4.6.4 Summary (Step 335)

The SSADM tasks carried out in Step 335 are:

Task

10	Specify basic tasks.
20	Specify interactions between tasks.
30	Allocate tasks to user roles.
40	Specify interaction between user roles and the computerised system.
50	Define job specifications and assign to user roles.

4.7   Step 340 - Enhance Required Data Model

In Step 320 we completed the top-down analysis of data, and produced the Required System LDM. Logical data modelling is a very useful and powerful technique for analysing data as it concentrates on the concepts which are of significance to the business and allows for subsequent refinement of the model as our knowledge increases. It also allows us to create a system-wide view of information needs right from the very start of analysis.

We now turn our attention to bottom-up data analysis using the technique of Relational Data Analysis (RDA). Our aim is to create LDS extracts from collections of individual data items, which we can then use to enhance or confirm the Required System LDM.

To carry out RDA on all known system data in order to build a complete LDS would be very time consuming and complicated, especially for large systems. So in Step 340 we select some of the most important or most complex I/O Structures (using the kind of criteria mentioned earlier for identifying critical dialogues) and carry out RDA on the data items listed in their I/O Structure Descriptions.

4.7.1   Relational Data Analysis Concepts

RDA is based on material published in the 1970s by Edgar Codd of IBM, proposing the application of mathematical set theory and algebra to the organisation of data. Up to that time data tended to be stored in a relatively ad-hoc fashion, in line with the way in which computer systems had been developed. Computer files frequently mirrored paper documents or the way in which data was entered into the system. Data duplication (and hence data redundancy) was rife, leading to problems with maintenance and flexibility. Codd's aim was to solve many of these problems by applying mathematical principles to the storage and manipulation of data, thereby reducing redundancy and increasing flexibility.

A detailed discussion of the work of Edgar Codd in setting out his theory of the 'Relational Model' of data is well beyond the scope of this book (for a definitive view see Date, 1995, or for a more informal and accessible view see Harris, 1992). Instead we will look briefly at some basic concepts, then move on to the main technique of RDA, that of 'normalisation'.

Relations or Tables

In the relational model, data is viewed as consisting of two-dimensional tables (or more formally, relations), consisting of rows and columns of attributes.

Primary Key

Rows   Columns   Attribute
                                            Names

Supplier Number	Supplier Name	Supplier Address	Supplier Tel. No.	Sup Con
1463	Salami Express	3 Blah St	0171-5630254	John
3621	Johnsons plc	29 Acacia Rd	0181-5814207	...
2321	The Fruit People	115 Cavendish St	...	...
6762	GlobWines Ltd	...	...	...
...	...	...	...	...

Figure 4.42 - Table Elements

In essence a table is the relational equivalent of an entity type in a Logical Data Model.

For a table to be properly relational it must obey a number of rules:

- There must be no duplicate rows. This means that each row will be uniquely identifiable. We use the concept of the primary key as discussed in Chapter 2 to describe the group of attributes which together identify each row.
- The order of the rows is not significant. If a sequence is required to add meaning to the data (for example in a table which holds data on positions in a race) then a new column should be added which stores values for the position attribute.
- The order of the columns is not significant. It makes tables easier to read if the primary key is given as the first column or columns; this is for presentational purposes only.
- Attribute names are unique.
- For a given value of the primary key there must be no more than one value for each attribute in the row, i.e. attributes must be 'atomic'. If we wished to store more than one telephone number for each supplier in Figure 4.42, then the attribute Supplier Tel. No. could have more than one value per row, and this rule would be violated. Collections of attributes which can have more than one value for a given primary key are known as 'repeating groups', and a table which contains them is termed 'unnormalised'. We will look at how we can resolve repeating groups by creating new tables to hold their information a little later in this section.

In SSADM tables are represented by listing their attributes under the table name, with the primary key underlined:

SUPPLIER
<u>Supplier Number</u>
Supplier Name
Supplier Address
Supplier Tel. Number
Supplier Contact Name

Tables which include repeating groups of attributes for a single value of the primary key (i.e. unnormalised tables) are documented with the repeating group indented. For example, consider a list showing all the suppliers of a particular product, like the one in Figure 4.43.

Product Number: xxxxxxxxx
Product Name: xxxxxxxxx
Product Type Code: xxxxxx
Product Type Name: xxxxxxxxxxxx

Supplier Number	Supplier Name	Supplier's Product Ref No	Price	Main Supplier Y/N
xxxxxxx	xxxxxxx	xxxxx	£xxxx.xx	Y
...	...	...	...	N

Figure 4.43 - Sample List of a Product's Suppliers

If we place the contents of the whole list in just one table for the moment, we will represent it as

PRODUCT'S SUPPLIERS
<u>Product Number</u>
Product Name
Product Type Code
Product Type Name
    Supplier Number
    Supplier Name
    Ref. Number
    Product Price
    Main Indicator

The indentation of the attributes below *product type name* indicate that this group of attributes will repeat (with different values) for each value of *product number (the table's primary key)*. The problem with indenting repeating groups is that it is possible to have numerous levels of repeating group within repeating group etc., which leads to presentational problems. An alternative to indenting them is to give repeating groups a level number:

PRODUCT'S SUPPLIERS	level
Product Number	1
Product Name	1
Product Type Code	1
Product Type Name	1
Supplier Number	2
Supplier Name	2
Ref. Number	2
Product Price	2
Main Indicator	2

Foreign keys are indicated by an asterisk to the left of the attribute name:

Functional Dependencies

An attribute X is said to be *functionally dependent* on an attribute Y if each value of Y is associated with only one value of X.

For example, each product is of one product type. This means that each *product number* is associated with only one *product type code*. *Product type code* is therefore functionally dependent on *product number*. The opposite is not true as each *product type code* may be associated with many *product numbers*.

Another way of phrasing functional dependency is to say that the value of X can be *determined* from the value of Y, or that Y *functionally determines* X.

So *product number* functionally determines the value of *product type code*, or the value of *product type code* can be determined from the value of the *product number,* i.e. given the value of a *product number* we can always establish the value of the associated *product type code.*

The concept of functional dependencies is an important one in RDA as we shall see in the next section.

4.7.2   Normalisation

The process of normalisation involves applying a series of refinements to groups of data items in order to produce tables which conform to specified standards, known as normal forms.

Unnormalised tables are converted to First Normal Form by removing repeating groups into separate tables. Second and Third Normal Forms are achieved by reducing and splitting tables so that the only functional dependencies which exist are between the primary keys and the remaining non-key attributes.

There are further normal forms which are beyond the scope of this book and which are not part of SSADM. They address problems with data organisation which are relatively infrequent (for a full discussion see C.J. Date, 1995).

Advantages of Normalisation

Before describing normalisation in detail it is worth mentioning some of its advantages briefly. Data in Third Normal Form (3NF) consists of tables of closely associated attributes which are entirely dependent on 'the key, the whole key, and nothing but the key'

This has the effect of minimising data duplication across different tables, thereby resolving many of the problems associated with data redundancy. In particular it should reduce the incidence of 'update anomalies'.

Update anomalies is the collective term for problems with modifying, inserting and deleting data in an unnormalised environment. These can be illustrated by considering the unnormalised contents of the list of a product's suppliers again.

If we were to implement this data structure as it stands, and to use it as the only place in which product details were stored we would encounter the following problems:

(i) **Insertion Anomalies** No new suppliers could be added to the system without adding a product.

(ii) **Deletion Anomalies** If the last remaining product for a given supplier was deleted, then all information on that supplier would be lost.

(iii) **Amendment Anomalies** Any change to a supplier's details (e.g. to the telephone number) would mean that every product for that supplier would need amending to keep it in line.

(The same anomalies also apply to the supplier information if we were to keep the one data structure alone.)

Many of the problems with poorly organised data arise from failures to deal with these anomalies, especially amendment anomalies which would occur even if some details were also duplicated in a separate table.

The other major advantage of well normalised data is its flexibility or ease of expansion. If new groups of attributes are added to the system they can usually be accommodated with minimal knock-on effects.

There are also disadvantages of course. The principal one is that maintaining and manipulating a large number of tables is often physically slow.

However, these are problems of physical design and implementation and should be ignored at this point, and dealt with in Stage 6 (Physical Design).

Unnormalised Form (UNF)

The first step in normalisation is to identify the group of data items to be normalised and to pick a key which will uniquely identify each occurrence of the group (it may be composite or compound); this gives us a UNF table.

In Step 340 our source of data items will be the I/O Structure Descriptions and/or screen dumps from Step 330. The UNF tables will include all data items, whether input or output. Repeating groups can be identified quite easily by iterations on the I/O Structure Diagram, and need to be indicated in the UNF table by indenting or level numbers. Once again we will use the Product's Suppliers List whose layout is driven by the I/O Structure in Figure 4.44.

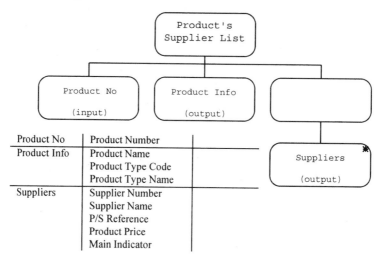

Figure 4.44 - I/O Structure of the Product's Supplier List of Figure 4.43

UNF	level	1NF	2NF	3NF	Table Name
Product Number	1				
Product Name	1				
Product Type Code	1				
Product Type Name	1				
Supplier Number	2				
Supplier Name	2				
P/S Reference	2				
Product Price	2				
Main Indicator	2				

Figure 4.45 - UNF and Levels formally documented using an RDA Working Paper

The contents of the Product's Suppliers List I/O Structure Description provide us with the following UNF table (Figure 4.45).

RDA can be used informally in earlier steps to validate or enhance the LDM as we go along. In these cases our sources of data items might be actual forms or reports when analysing current data, or entity descriptions themselves when creating the Required System LDM.

First Normal Form (1NF)

A table is in *First Normal Form* if it contains no repeating groups.

If our UNF table does include a repeating group then we remove it to form a table of its own, and give it a primary key consisting of the primary key of the parent UNF table plus an additional attribute or attributes to enable unique identification of its rows (Figure 4.46).

UNF	lev	1NF	2NF	3NF	Table Name
Product Number	1	Product Number			
Product Name	1	Product Name			
Product Type Code	1	Product Type Code			
Product Type Name	1	Product Type Name			
Supplier Number	2				
Supplier Name	2				
P/S Reference	2	Product Number			
Product Price	2	Supplier Number			
Main Indicator	2	Supplier Name			
		P/S Reference			
		Product Price			
		Main Indicator			

Figure 4.46 - Moving from UNF to 1NF

The additional attributes required to make the primary key of the new table unique are those which uniquely identify occurrences of the repeating group within the UNF table as a whole.

By including the primary key of the parent table in the new table we maintain the links between them.

Second Normal Form (2NF)

A table is in *Second Normal Form* if, in addition to being in 1NF, it contains no non-key attributes which are dependent on only *part* of the primary key.

Any such attributes in the 1NF tables are removed to form a new table with the relevant partial key as its primary key.

In our example *supplier name* is dependent solely on *supplier number*, which is only part of the key of the second table in Figure 4.46. In other words, given the *supplier number* we can always determine the relevant *supplier name*, regardless of the *product number*. To achieve 2NF we will need to remove these partially dependent attributes to form a new table, Figure 4.47.

UNF	lev	1NF	2NF	3NF	Table Name
Product Number	1	Product Number	Product Number		
Product Name	1	Product Name	Product Name		
Product Type Code	1	Product Type Code	Product Type Code		
Product Type Name	1	Product Type Name	Product Type Name		
Supplier Number	2				
Supplier Name	2				
P/S Reference	2	Product Number	Product Number		
Product Price	2	Supplier Number	Supplier Number		
Main Indicator	2	Supplier Name	P/S Reference		
		P/S Reference	Product Price		
		Product Price	Main Indicator		
		Main Indicator			
			Supplier Number		
			Supplier Name		

Figure 4.47 - Moving from 1NF to 2NF

Note that we could be left with a table without any non-key attributes. This is quite allowable and fairly common. The table concerned may represent the equivalent of a link entity, or an entity for which we will discover additional attributes when we tackle other I/O Structures.

The essential question to ask at this point for each non-key attribute is:

'Does this attribute depend on the *whole* of the primary key?'

If it does not then it should be removed. One thing to take care over is that the primary key of the parent table is left intact - there are usually other attributes which *do* depend wholly on it.

In other words *there is no way* that the keys of 1NF will disappear. When moving from 1NF to 2NF to 3NF, new keys may be identified while existing keys will remain even if they have no other attributes associated with them.

The other 1NF table in our example is automatically carried forward as 2NF, since it has a simple key which cannot be subject to partial dependencies.

Third Normal Form (3NF)

A table is in *Third Normal Form* if, in addition to being in 2NF, there are no non-key attributes which depend on *other* non-candidate key attributes.

Any such dependent attributes are removed from the 2NF table to form a new table having the attribute that determines them (their determinant) as its primary key. The determinant is left in the parent table as a foreign key in order to maintain links between the data.

If we look at our example, the table with a primary key of *product number* contains the *product type name* which is dependent directly on *product type code* rather than the primary key of *product number*. So we need to remove this attribute to form a table with *product type code* as its primary key, while at the same time leaving *product type code* behind as a foreign key in the 'parent' table (Figure 4.48).

UNF	lev	1NF	2NF	3NF	Table Name
Product Number	1	Product Number	Product Number	Product Number	PRODUCT
Product Name	1	Product Name	Product Name	Product Name	
Product Type Code	1	Product Type Code	Product Type Code	*Product Type Code	
Product Type Name	1	Product Type Name	Product Type Name		
Supplier Number	2				
Supplier Name	2			Product Type Code	PRODUCT
P/S Reference	2			Product Type Name	TYPE
Product Price	2				
Main Indicator	2				
		Product Number	Product Number	Product Number	SUPPLIER
		Supplier Number	Supplier Number	Supplier Number	PRODUCT
		Supplier Name	P/S Reference	P/S Reference	
		P/S Reference	Product Price	Product Price	
		Product Price	Main Indicator	Main Indicator	
		Main Indicator			
			Supplier Number	Supplier Number	SUPPLIER
			Supplier Name	Supplier Name	

Figure 4.48 - A complete RDA Normalisation

Dependencies of this sort are slightly more difficult to spot than partial key dependencies, as they involve asking for each non-key attribute:

'Is this attribute dependent on *any other* non-key attribute?'

The other 2NF tables in our example are already in 3NF, so the process of normalisation is complete for the purposes of RDA.

As each normalisation is completed, each 3NF table is given a meaningful name so that we can refer to it easily later on.

Partial Inter-Key Dependencies

The following example exposes a possible RDA pitfall: suppose we wish to list all the purchase orders sent to a particular supplier. (This function does not exist as such in our case, but it would be part of the function that provides a monitor of suppliers' performance. Suppliers' monitoring was required by requirement 8 which did not make it through BSO.)

The I/O Structure for this 'List all Purchase Orders of a Supplier' function would be

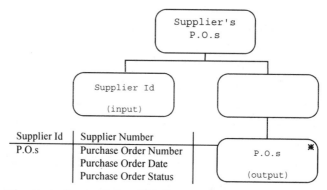

Supplier Id	Supplier Number
P.O.s	Purchase Order Number
	Purchase Order Date
	Purchase Order Status

Figure 4.49 - The Supplier's P.O.s I/O Structure

Moving into 1NF, two data groups appear. The first has *supplier number* as its key. The second appears to have the pair

supplier number

purchase order number

as its key. Before we unquestionably accept this key we have to scrutinise it by enquiring whether any part of it depends on any other part of it. Careful consideration reveals that *supplier number* **depends** on *purchase order number* since a purchase order always has the one supplier. In other words, given a purchase order number we can, without a shadow of a doubt, pinpoint the supplier for which the purchase order was raised or, to use the proper terminology, *purchase order number* **determines** *supplier number.* This means that the key of the second 1NF group is simple. Figure 4.50 shows the full RDA working for this function where we also see that the first normal form groups are in third normal form too.

UNF	lev	1NF	2NF	3NF	Table Name
Supplier Number	1	Supplier Number	→	→	SUPPLIER
Purchase Order Number	2				
Purchase Order Date	2				
Purchase Order Status	2	*Supplier Number			
		Purchase Order Number	→	→	PURCHASE
		Purchase Order Date			ORDER
		Purchase Order Status			

Figure 4.50 - RDA of the I/O Structure of Figure 4.49 which contains an Inter-Key Dependency

So, before moving to 2NF we should look at all composite or compound keys to see if any of the attributes in the primary key are redundant, i.e. are not needed to uniquely identify the rows in the table. This is equivalent to asking whether *all* attributes (including potentially redundant attributes in the primary key) are dependent on the *same part* of the key.

We will now look at a few more examples of normalisation, partly to illustrate one or two additional aspects of the process and partly to provide us with a reasonable set of tables with which to build an LDS extract, for comparison with the Required System LDM.

Reprint Invoice

When an invoice is received, the stock clerk reconciles it against goods already delivered. This is a complicated activity which requires careful study and the application of User Interface design techniques (see exercises). After an invoice has been recorded in the system, we may need to reprint it. The I/O Structure for reprinting an invoice is shown in Figure 4.51.

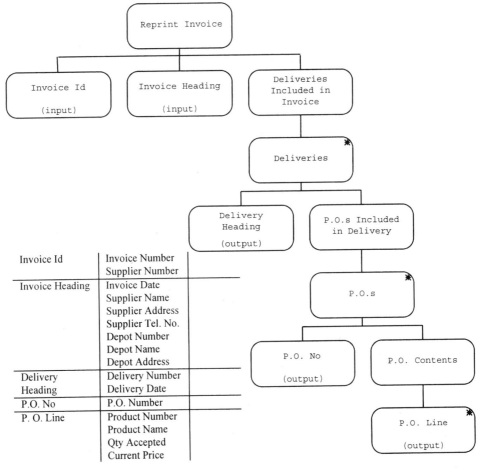

Invoice Id	Invoice Number
	Supplier Number
Invoice Heading	Invoice Date
	Supplier Name
	Supplier Address
	Supplier Tel. No.
	Depot Number
	Depot Name
	Depot Address
Delivery Heading	Delivery Number
	Delivery Date
P.O. No	P.O. Number
P. O. Line	Product Number
	Product Name
	Qty Accepted
	Current Price

Figure 4.51 - The I/O Structure for Reprinting an Invoice

The iterations and level numbers identify a hierarchy of repeating groups: each Invoice can include payment requests for several deliveries; each Delivery may have included goods resulting from several Purchase Orders; each Purchase Order consists of several Purchase Order Lines, some of which were included *at least in part* in the delivery (Purchase Order Lines can be split over several deliveries).

Note that when invoices are printed the output data will include values for the total cost of the invoice. We do not list these in the UNF table as attributes which can be derived from other attributes not normally included in relational tables.

1. 1NF: The removal of repeating groups requires a little more care in this example, as there are several levels of repeat.

For inexperienced analysts the best approach is probably to remove the groups one level at a time, remembering to carry the primary key of the parent table forward at each stage. We will do this step by step since this example is full of pitfalls which go to show just how closely we are forced to examine the details of system data in RDA.

The first point to note is that the primary key of the first group consists of the *invoice number, supplier number* pair, as explained in Step 320.

When we carry this down to the second group, the key of that group appears to be

> *invoice number*
> *supplier number*

and *delivery number*

but careful examination reveals that the *invoice number, supplier number* pair **depend** on the *delivery number* because each Delivery will only ever be included in one invoice. So the *invoice number, supplier number* pair is not needed as part of the primary key and is redundant, leaving

> **invoice number*
> **supplier number*
> *delivery number*

This explains why the *invoice number, supplier number* pair does not appear as part of the key of the second 1NF group in Figure 4.52.

Since now the key of the second group is *delivery number* alone, and since the third group inherits the key of the second group we see that the *invoice number, supplier number* pair should not be present in the third group even though it is the key of the first group. Similarly it should not be present in the fourth group whose key is that of the third group plus *product number* (see Figure 4.52).

UNF	lev	1NF	2NF	3NF	Table Name
Invoice Number	1	Invoice Number	Invoice Number	Invoice Number	INVOICE
Supplier Number	1	Supplier Number	Supplier Number	Supplier Number	
Invoice Date	1	Invoice Date	Invoice Date	Invoice Date	
Supplier Name	1	Supplier Name	Depot Number	*Depot Number	
Suppler Address	1	Suppler Address	Depot Name		
Supplier Tel. No.	1	Supplier Tel. No.	Depot Address	Supplier Number	SUPPLIER
Depot Number	1	Depot Number		Supplier Name	
Depot Name	1	Depot Name	Supplier Number	Suppler Address	
Depot Address	1	Depot Address	Supplier Name	Supplier Tel. No.	
Delivery Number	2		Suppler Address		
Delivery Date	2		Supplier Tel. No.	Depot Number	DEPOT
P. O. Number	3			Depot Name	
Product Number	4			Depot Address	
Product Name	4				
Qty Accepted	4	*Invoice Number	*Invoice Number	*Invoice Number	DELIVERY
Current Price	4	*Supplier Number	*Supplier Number	*Supplier Number	
		Delivery Number	Delivery Number	Delivery Number	
		Delivery Date	Delivery Date	Delivery Date	
		Delivery Number	Delivery Number	Delivery Number	DELIVERY/ P. O. ALLO-CATION
		P. O. Number	P. O. Number	P. O. Number	
		Delivery Number	Delivery Number	Delivery Number	DELIVERY LINE
		P. O. Number	P. O. Number	P. O. Number	
		Product Number	Product Number	Product Number	
		Product Name	Qty Accepted	Qty Accepted	
		Qty Accepted			
		Current Price	P. O. Number	P. O. Number	PURCHASE ORDER LINE
			Product Number	Product Number	
			Current Price	Current Price	
			Product Number	Product Number	PRODUCT
			Product Name	Product Name	

Figure 4.52 - Tne RDA Normalisation of the I/O Structure in Figure 4.51

2. 2NF: We now look for partial key dependencies. Two groups contain compound keys with other associated items. In the first group it is easy to see that *supplier name, supplier address* and *supplier tel. no.* depend on *supplier number* alone while the other four attributes are particular to each supplier's invoice. In the fourth 1NF group only *qty accepted* depends on all three components of the key; *current price* is the price agreed upon while confirming the purchase order so it only depends on the *purchase*

order number, product code pair; and finally *product name* depends on *product number* alone (see Figure 4.52).

3. 3NF: *depot name* and *depot address* clearly depend on *depot number* so we remove them from the Invoice table (see Figure 4.52).

Transfer Request

This is another straightforward example, but one which will prove useful in enhancing the Required System LDM (Figure 4.53).

UNF	lev	1NF	2NF	3NF	Table Name
Transfer Number	1	Transfer Number	→	→	TRANSFER
Transfer Date	1	Transfer Date			
Depot Number [from]	1	Depot Number [from]			
Depot Number [to]	1	Depot Number [to]			
Stock Id.	2				
Qty Transferred	2	Transfer Number	Transfer Number	→	TRANSFER LINE
Product Number	2	Stock Id.	Stock Id.		
Product Name	2	Qty Transferred	Qty Transferred		
Zone Type Code	2	Product Number			
Depot Zone Letter	2	Product Name			
Bin Number	2	Zone Type Code	Stock Id.	Stock Id.	STOCK
		Depot Zone Letter	Product Number	*Product Number	
		Bin Number	Product Name	Zone Type Code	
			Zone Type Code	Depot Zone Letter	
			Depot Zone Letter	Bin Number	
			Bin Number		
				Product Number	PRODUCT
				Product Name	

Figure 4.53 - The RDA Normalisation of the Data concerning Transfer Request

Book New Delivery

As we have seen, the Book Delivery function is quite complicated. Nonetheless, the I/O Structure in Figure 4.31 suggests two clear structure branches; one for booking new deliveries and one for amending existing ones. The two branches have a lot in common. It therefore pays to study each separately. We will show here the normalisation of the left-hand side branch.

The trick here is to spot that the level 1 data item that becomes the key of the first group is found in the rightmost, i.e. last, element of the structure. Figure 4.55 contains the RDA working for this function.

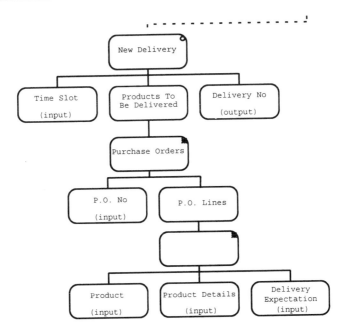

Figure 4.54 - I/O Structure branch first seen in Figure 4.31

UNF	lev	1NF	2NF	3NF	Table Name
		Delivery Number			DELIVERY
Supplier Number	1	Supplier Number	→	→	
Delivery Date	1	Delivery Date			
Delivery Start Time	1	Delivery Start Time			
Delivery End Time	1	Delivery End Time			
P. O. Number	2				DELIVERED
Product Number	3	Delivery Number			PURCHASE
Product Name	3	P. O. Number	→	→	ORDER
P/S Reference	3				
Quantity Confirmed	3				DELIVERY
Quantity Due	3	Delivery Number	Delivery Number		LINE
Delivery Number	1	P. O. Number	P. O. Number		
		Product Number	Product Number		
		Product Name	Quantity Due		
		P/S Reference			
		Quantity Confirmed	P. O. Number		PURCHASE
		Quantity Due	Product Number		ORDER LINE
			P/S Reference		
			Quantity Confirmed		
			Product Number		
			Product Name		PRODUCT

Figure 4.55 - The RDA Normalisation of the I/O Structure in Figure 4.54

Locate Stock

Each zone in a depot is of a specific type. Requirement 19 requests a more precise location for stock. This has led to splitting each zone into aisles and each aisle into sections. Each zone is split into three aisles, 1 being at ground level, 2 intermediate and 3 the highest. Sections, which are designed to take a pallet-full of goods, are numbered from 1 to whatever, depending on the length of the zone. A combination of aisle and section constitutes a 'bin'. Thus bin 3-24 is the 24th section of the highermost aisle (of a particular zone).

When new stock arrives, available space has to be found in the appropriate depot's zone. The stock clerk inputs the *zone type code, depot number* and *depot zone letter* which pinpoint a particular zone type in a depot, and the system responds with the bin numbers that are free. For example, on typing FRO 101 A, the following may be output

$$1-1$$
$$1-3$$
$$1-9$$
$$2-2$$
$$2-3$$

indicating that five bins are free, three ground level and two intermediate. The normalisation of the above implied I/O Structure is shown in Figure 4.56.

UNF	lev	1NF	2NF	3NF	Table Name
Zone Type Code Depot Number Depot Zone Letter Bin Number	1 1 1 2	Zone Type Code Depot Number Depot Zone Letter	→	→	DEPOT'S ZONE
		Zone Type Code Depot Number Depot Zone Letter Bin Number	→	→	BIN

Figure 4.56 - The RDA Normalisation of the Data concerning Stock Location

4.7.3 Rationalising 3NF Tables

Once we have carried out normalisation on a number of I/O Structures we will have several sets of tables in 3NF, which we now rationalise into a single, larger set. Any tables that share a primary key should be merged, as should tables with matching candidate keys. We will also look for attributes which now act as foreign keys when compared with primary keys in other

3NF sets. A little care is needed to ensure that any synonyms or homonyms are identified, as failure to do so could lead to missing or spurious merges.

The list of tables resulting from our six examples is:

PRODUCT'S SUPPLIERS LIST:

1. PRODUCT

Product Number
Product Name
*Product Type Code

2. PRODUCT TYPE

Product Type Code
Product Type Name

3. SUPPLIER PRODUCT

Product Number
Supplier Number
Ref. Number
Product Price
Main Indicator

4. SUPPLIER

Supplier Number
Supplier Name

LIST SUPPLIER'S PURCHASE ORDERS:

5. SUPPLIER

Supplier Number

6 PURCHASE ORDER

Purchase Order Number
*Supplier Number
Purchase Order Date
Purchase Order Status

REPRINT INVOICE:

7 INVOICE

Invoice Number
Supplier Number
Invoice Date
*Depot Number

8. SUPPLIER

Supplier Number
Supplier Name
Supler Address
Supplier Tel. No.

9. DEPOT

Depot Number
Depot Name
Depot Address

10. DELIVERY

Delivery Number
*Invoice Number
*Supplier Number
Delivery Date

11. DELIVERY/ P.O. ALLOC

Delivery Number
P. O. Number

12. DELIVERY LINE

Delivery Number
P. O. Number
Product Number
Qty Accepted

13. P. ORDER LINE

P. O. Number
Product Number
Current Price

14. PRODUCT

Product Number
Product Name

TRANSFER REQUEST:

15. TRANSFER

Transfer Number
Transfer Date
Depot Number [from]
Depot Number [to]

16. TRANSFER LINE

Transfer Number
Stock Id.
Qty Transferred

17. STOCK

Stock Id.
*Product Number
Zone Type Code
Depot Zone Letter
Bin Number

18. PRODUCT

Product Number
Product Name

BOOK NEW DELIVERY:

19. DELIVERY
Delivery Number
Supplier Number
Delivery Date
Delivery Start Time
Delivery End Time

20. DELIVERED PURCHASE ORDER
Delivery Number
P. O. Number

21. DELIVERY LINE
Delivery Number
P. O. Number
Product Number
Quantity Due

22. P. ORDER LINE
P. O. Number
Product Number
P/S Reference
Quantity Confirmed

23. PRODUCT
Product Number
Product Name

LOCATE STOCK:

24. DEPOT'S ZONE
Zone Type Code
Depot Number
Depot Zone Letter

25. BIN
Zone Type Code
Depot Number
Depot Zone Letter
Bin Number

There are several tables which can be merged or dropped:

- **PRODUCT**: Tables 14, 18 and 23 are identical subsets of 1 so we drop them.

- **SUPPLIER**: Tables 4 and 5 are subsets of 8 so we drop them.

- **PURCHASE ORDER LINE**: Tables 13 and 22 have the same key, so we merge their contents:

  22. P. ORDER LINE
  P. Order Number
  Product Number
  Current Price
  P/S Reference
  Quantity Confirmed

- **DELIVERY LINE**: Tables 12 and 21 have the same key, so we merge their contents.

- **DELIVERY**: Tables 10 and 19 have the same key, so we merge their contents. We take care to preserve *supplier number* twice since in table 10 it appears as part of a foreign key that links the entity to a supplier's invoice and in table 19 it appears on its own accord. Since the action through which we identified table 19 takes place before an invoice is even contemplated, we have to ensure that a link between Delivery and Supplier always exists.

- **DELIVERY/PURCHASE ORDER ALLOCATION** and **DELIVERED PURCHASE ORDER**: Tables 11 and 20 have the same key, so we merge their contents. For no particular reason we choose to drop table 11.

When we merge tables formed in this way there is a danger that we may introduce new functional dependencies that take us out of 3NF (this is especially true for merges involving large numbers of non-overlapping attributes). To check that the resulting tables are still in 3NF we can apply a couple of tests, known as the TNF tests:

(i) For a given value of the primary key, is there one and only one possible value for each attribute in its row?

(ii) Are all attributes in the table dependent on the key, the whole key and nothing but the key?

All merged tables that result from rationalising the SRW tables pass the TNF tests. One point to note is that the Transfer table contains *depot number* (twice in fact). This table arose as a result of normalising the 'Request Transfer' function. During that normalisation there was nothing to suggest that *depot number* is a key of another table. After completing the normalisation we find out that *depot number* is indeed a key of another table. As such it is a foreign key for the Transfer table and we will mark is so

15. TRANSFER

<u>Transfer Number</u>
Transfer Date
*Depot Number [from]
*Depot Number [to]

In practice the tables and attributes created as a result of normalisation are likely to have a wide variety of names. So the exercise of recognising redundant or 'mergeable' tables can be far from trivial, involving the application of a detailed understanding of the semantic meaning of the data.

4.7.4 Converting 3NF Tables to LDSs

The prime objective of RDA is to enhance the Required System LDM using the results of the close examination of data items enforced by normalisation. In order to compare our 3NF tables with the Required

System LDM we will convert them into an LDS extract, which will hopefully represent a subset of the entire Required System LDM.

The conversion process is a fairly mechanistic one, following four basic steps:

1. Represent each table as an entity type box. List primary and foreign key attributes inside the box. Clearly annotate the foreign key elements of hierarchic keys with an asterisk (Figure 4.57).

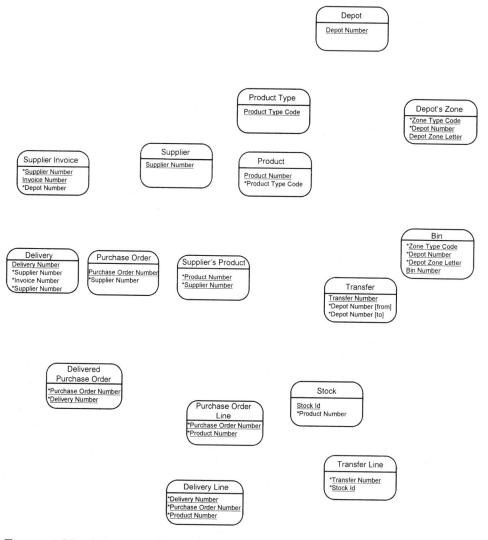

Figure 4.57 - 3NF 'Entities'

2. For each element of every compound key, check that an entity exists which has that element as its primary key. If any such entities are missing they should be created with their sole attribute being the required primary key.

   For example, the key of Depot's Zone contains *zone type code*. We have not formally identified a table with this as its primary key but from Logical Data Modelling we know that such an entity exists. We therefore include it in our diagram as in Figure 4.58.

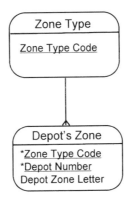

Figure 4.58 - The Entity Zone Type is identified because one Element of the Compound Key of Depot's Zone is a Foreign Key which does not belong to any of the Entities of Figure 4.57

   Note that we would also need to look for non-key attributes in other relations to check if they contain the new key, as they would now become foreign keys.

3. Add a master-detail relationship between every pair of entities where the *entire* primary key of one (the master) is an attribute or collection of attributes in the *compound* key of the other (the detail) (see Figure 4.59).

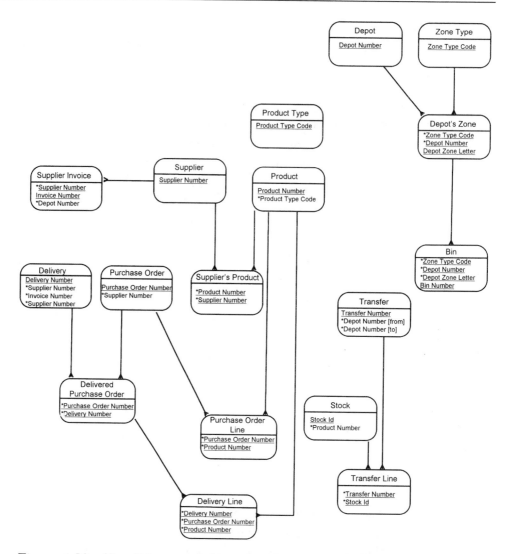

Figure 4.59 - 'Small keys grab large keys'

4. Add a master-detail relationship between every pair of entities, where the primary key of one (the master) is a foreign key of the other (the detail), see Figure 4.60.

The resulting LDS will not have relationship names, or include details of optionality or exclusivity. Don't worry about this as these features are not required for the purposes of comparison with the Required System LDM, and the LDS extract will not be carried forward beyond this comparison.

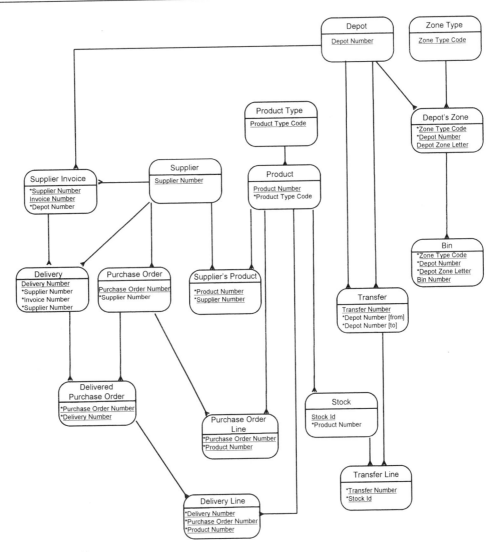

Figure 4.60 - 'Crows feet grab asterisks' to complete RDA

4.7.5 Comparing LDSs

We now compare our two LDSs (the extract with the Required System LDM) and decide whether any discrepancies are due to errors in Logical Data Modelling or whether they represent redundant information resulting from RDA.

In practice there may be large numbers of entities involved in the comparison, so a fair amount of time is likely to be spent in identifying corresponding entities in the two models. Probably the best starting point is to look for common attributes, in particular common primary keys or candidate keys.

When comparing the two models we should look for:

- **Differences in Attributes**. RDA will frequently uncover additional attributes as it concentrates much more on data item detail than Logical Data Modelling. It may also allocate some attributes to different entities than in the Required System LDM. These differences should be discussed with users in order to decide on the correct interpretation.

- **Additional Entity Types**. Logical Data Modelling may result in entities which are not in 3NF. This may lead to additional entities in the LDM extract produced using RDA which should be incorporated in the Required System LDM. On the other hand RDA may result in extra entities which are redundant. For example, if we compare the RDA and Required System LDMs for the SRW system we find two additional entities in the RDA model: Delivered Purchase Order and Bin. If we look at Delivered Purchase Order closely we find that it is in fact a link entity which resolves a m:n relationship between Delivery Line and Purchase Order Line. This can already be resolved using Purchase Order Line and Delivery Line so Delivered Purchase Order and its associated relationships are redundant. Bin on the other hand is an entity we wish to retain. Doing so means that we have to reconsider the relationship between Stock and Depot's Zone since now Bin comes between them. This leads to detaching Stock from Depot's Zone and attaching it to Bin so that the attributes of Stock become

  STOCK
  Stock Id
  *Delivery Number
  *Purchase Order Number
  *Product Number
  *Depot Number
  *Zone Type Code
  *Depot Zone Letter
  *Bin Number
  *Transfer Number
  *Stock Id [Transferred]
  Quantity Stocked
  Quantity Reserved

- **Additional Relationships.** Any additional relationships in the RDA model should be looked at carefully to check that they have not been missed out in the Required System LDM intentionally, to reduce redundancy.

In the RDA model we have a relationship between Supplier Invoice and Depot which is not present in the Required System LDS; this is an omission, as there is a clear requirement to tie each Supplier Invoice to a single depot (leading to the addition of a 1:m relationship between Depot and Supplier Invoice).

The RDA model also shows relationships between Product and Purchase Order Line and between Product and Delivery Line. These two relationships are maintained in the LDM by the link from Delivery Line to Purchase Order Line to Supplier's Product to Product. This link is much stronger because it enforces the fact that we order only what is on a supplier's catalogue and we only accept deliveries of what we have ordered. We therefore drop these two relationships from our enhanced model.

For the same reasons, namely that we can transverse our LDM to arrive at Product from Stock via Delivery Line, Purchase Order Line and Supplier's Product, we will ignore the RDA relationship between Stock and Product. (Since this relationship will be resurrected for reasons of efficiency later on it is important to understand why it actually is redundant in *logical* terms.)

4.7.6 Summary (Step 340)

The SSADM tasks carried out in Step 340 are:

Task

10	Identify which I/O Structures are to be normalised.
20	Carry out normalisation to produce tables in 3NF.
30	Use the 3NF tables to build a mini LDM.
40	Compare the mini LDM with the Required System LDM, and resolve any differences.

4.8   Step 350 - Develop Specification Prototypes

Step 350 provides us with an opportunity to demonstrate and verify our understanding of system requirements by presenting users with physical prototypes of critical dialogues.

It is important to realise that within core SSADM prototyping is used to correct and enhance our specification of user requirements. It is *not* used to incrementally develop the final system. If any of the prototypes developed in Step 350 can be used in physical design and implementation then this should be regarded as a bonus and not our specific objective.

Specification prototyping is an optional technique within SSADM, requiring careful handling and management. As we shall see it is not appropriate to all projects, but when used properly it can lead to enhancement of a wide range of products, and to increased user commitment.

In many ways specification prototyping can be considered as a mini-project in its own right, set slightly aside from the mainstream of SSADM, and as such it requires its own project management procedures. SSADM offers some guidance in this area which will be discussed briefly in the next section.

4.8.1   Specification Prototyping Issues

Once a decision to undertake prototyping has been made and management procedures set up, the activities involved are quite easy to understand and satisfying to carry out. However before we can proceed there are a number of issues which need addressing.

Project Suitability

Specification prototyping can involve a great deal of time and effort, so for each project we should assess its suitability before committing the necessary resources.

Suitable Projects

Projects which are likely to benefit from specification prototyping will generally fall into one or more of the following categories:

- High risk projects.
- High cost projects.
- Projects which are likely to result in large-scale changes to working practices.
- Politically sensitive projects.
- Projects involving users with little or no experience of computer systems, or analysts with little experience of the business area.
- Projects which involve large elements of new functionality, or for which there is no existing system.

Unsuitable Projects

Projects which are unlikely to benefit substantially from specification prototyping will generally fall into one or more of the following categories:

- Projects which merely aim to replace existing systems, with little or no extra functionality.

- Low cost projects, where specification prototyping would have significant impact on cost/benefit.
- Projects where user requirements are very precisely and rigidly defined.

Benefits of Specification Prototyping

For suitable projects there are a number of potential benefits which may justify the use of specification prototyping:

- **Improved Communication:** Users can immediately understand and relate to actual screens or reports, in a way which is just not possible with a paper-based specification. Although some training may be necessary in the prototyping tool, this is likely to be far less than in the interpretation of diagrams, etc.
- **Verification of User Requirements:** Users will be able to provide feedback quickly and effectively on which aspects of the system requirements have been correctly interpreted.
- **Assessment of System Capabilities:** Users may not be familiar with the capabilities of computer systems. Using an appropriate prototyping tool to present a mock-up or simulation of a system may help users to more fully understand these capabilities. This in turn may lead to additional or modified user requirements.
- **Increased User Commitment:** In large projects users can feel alienated or even forgotten as time progresses without anything concrete for them to get involved with. The central and highly practical role of users in specification prototyping often leads to a greater sense of commitment and project ownership in users.
- **Improved Project Morale:** Analysts and users usually find prototyping a satisfying and enjoyable activity, leading to improved morale and a greater feeling of teamwork.

Risks of Specification Prototyping

Virtually all of the risks involved with Specification Prototyping are associated with its management and presentation:

- **False User Expectation:** When users are shown a superficially working system they may believe that final implementation is imminent. Users must be made aware that prototypes are just highly visual and sophisticated simulations or models of systems.
- **Limits of Prototyping Tool:** Users may receive a misleading impression of the final solution's likely appearance. In many cases the prototyping tool will not use the same technical

platforms as the final system and may be less sophisticated, or alternatively offer more facilities than the implementation environment (for example where a PC based 4GL is used for prototyping, giving a colourful and a highly graphical user interface, while a mainframe based 3GL will be used to build the final system, with monochrome screens etc.).

- **Uncontrolled System Design:** Prototyping can be difficult to control. An atmosphere can develop where a prototype is demonstrated to users, changes made and then re-demonstrated to users and so on, almost indefinitely. The rather informal physical design of prototypes can also lead to non-standard designs and constant uncontrolled changes to the project's scope.
- **Lack of Documentation:** It is extremely important that the results of Specification Prototyping are fully documented and that appropriate updates to function definitions, the LDM, the Requirements Catalogue, etc. are applied. If this is not done then the purpose of prototyping will have been missed.

Management of Specification Prototyping

The management of specification prototyping requires careful handling. Prototyping activities and control are less rigorously defined than most other SSADM techniques, but there are some basic guidelines for us to follow.

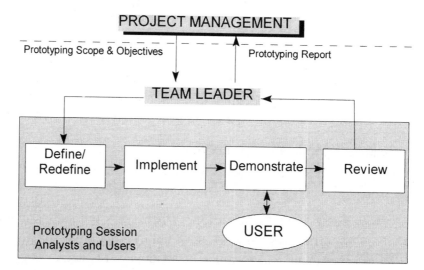

Figure 4.61 - Prototyping Cycle

SSADM uses the concept of the Prototyping Cycle (see Figure 4.61), in which each prototyping session consists of four steps:

(i)   Define or redefine the prototype.

(ii) Implement the prototype.

(iii) Demonstrate the prototype to users.

(iv) Review the results of the demonstration.

These steps are carried out by analysts and users, with the results being reported to the prototyping 'Team Leader'. The team leader will then examine the results of the session and decide whether to carry out a further session based on a refined prototype, or to stop the prototyping cycle at this point. This decision will be based on an assessment of the likely benefits of further prototyping sessions against the costs and time involved.

The Team Leader will also be responsible for the following:

- Agreeing the initial scope of prototyping with management. This scope should define the areas of the requirements specification to be prototyped, the objectives of the prototyping, time scales and project resources (such as personnel).
- Agreeing which dialogues are to be prototyped.
- Monitoring changes to SSADM products.
- Reporting the results of the prototyping exercise to management.

Selection of Prototyping Tool

If the final implementation environment is known at this stage, then the prototyping tool should match the characteristics of that environment as closely as possible.

If this is unknown we should select a tool which supports rapid development of screens, reports and menus, etc. It is also helpful to have a good data dictionary and version control.

If we are using a CASE tool to support the project it may provide an integrated prototyping tool. If not, the chosen prototyping tool should ideally interface with at least the LDM elements of the CASE tool.

4.8.2   Development of Specification Prototypes

Define Prototype Scope

The overall scope of the prototyping exercise will have been agreed with management already. We now extend this by examining the outputs from Steps 330 and 335 to assess which specific on-line dialogues and reports should be prototyped.

The User Role/Function Matrix will be annotated with detail of critical dialogues, and these will be the obvious first candidates for prototyping.

We should also consider any other dialogues that users wish to view, to confirm that their requirements are properly understood.

For each on-line dialogue we will have one or more potential screen prototypes. To help us decide which of the candidate dialogues are suitable for prototyping we can look for:

- High levels of user interaction.
- Complex data manipulation.
- Dialogues supporting functions which have been difficult to define, or where requirements were vague.

For each potential report prototype we should pay particular attention to the following:

- Legal constraints, e.g. disclaimers or registration numbers.
- The requirements of external organisations, e.g. Inland Revenue standard forms.

Prototype Initial Menu Structures

We begin the prototyping process by looking at menu structures for each user role within the prototyping scope. This involves the application of dialogue design techniques, which are discussed more fully in Chapter 6.

A menu structure is essentially a hierarchical diagram of menus and dialogues for a given user role. It details how the user role will access all of the functions assigned to it in the User Role/Function Matrix. In Stage 5 the entire system will be covered by a full set of menu structures. In specification prototyping we are interested in building a set of menu structures for the subset of the system to be prototyped.

For example, let us suppose that in the SRW system for the User Role Delivery Scheduler we have agreed to prototype dialogues associated with the following functions:

- Book Delivery
- Book Transfer
- Check Available Slots

This does not represent a full list of functions for Delivery Scheduler; just those required for prototyping.

Notation

We represent menus by 'square-cornered' boxes as in Figure 4.62, whereas individual dialogues are represented by round cornered boxes as in Figure 4.63.

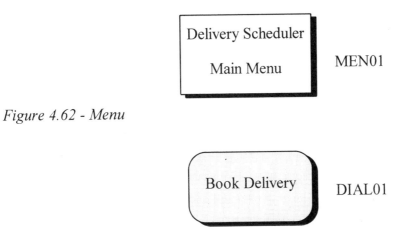

Figure 4.62 - Menu

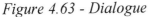

Figure 4.63 - Dialogue

We then combine these basic elements to represent a hierarchy of menus and dialogues for the user role (see Figure 4.64).

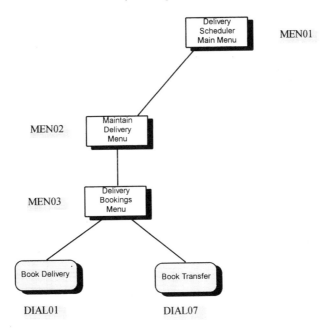

Figure 4.64 - Menu Structure (section of Figure 6.12)

As we can see, dialogues and menus can exist together on the same level, indicating that we may need to access both from a single menu. Once a dialogue is reached in the hierarchy we have a 'dead-end' and no further levels of dialogues or menus can be accessed below it. Guidelines for grouping menu structure elements together will be discussed in Chapter 6.

Once the structures are completed, we should build the actual menu elements of the structures using the prototyping tool and demonstrate them to users. Any comments or changes requested by users should be fed back to the Team Leader who will decide on the action to be taken.

Cosmetic or aesthetic changes (e.g. user preferences for vertical or pop-up menus) can be made and re-demonstrated quite easily. More significant changes may indicate that we have misunderstood a user role or requirement, and we may need to update the User Role documentation, Requirements Catalogue and User Role/Function Matrix, in addition to appropriate menu structures.

Prototype Initial Dialogues

Once the menu structure has been agreed we have a framework for putting together dialogue or report prototypes. The basic idea is to create a proto-typing session which takes the user from the main menu, via any necessary sub-menus, through all of the screens and reports that together constitute a dialogue. The route to and through each dialogue or report is referred to as a Prototype Pathway. Figure 4.65 shows the pathway required to prototype the dialogue 'Book Delivery' (DIAL01). The formal notation for documenting the pathway will be discussed a little later.

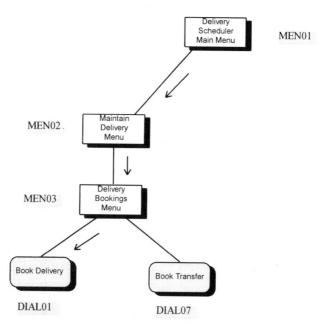

Figure 4.65 - Pathway

Before physical screens and reports are created we must identify the logical components of each dialogue, i.e. we must design logical screens and reports. This involves employing either the techniques covered in more detail in Chapter 6 or the Windows Navigation Models we may have created.

Identify Logical Screen Components

The I/O Structure for the dialogue we wish to prototype gives us our basic Dialogue Structure. We now look at this, with users, to establish which on-line Dialogue Elements (previously called I/O Structure Elements) should be logically grouped together when navigating through the dialogue. SSADM provides a few guidelines on allowable groupings, but our main consideration is to identify which elements the *users* regard as forming logical groups. This usually means that there is a strong correlation between Hierarchical Task Model sub-tasks and logical screens.

Identify Report Output Components

The logical report components are identified by looking at the I/O Structure of the function and establishing which elements refer to the report's output data items.

Create Prototype Pathways

Once we have established all screen and report components we are in a position to decide on the Prototype Pathways to be demonstrated in the prototyping session. The notation for a Prototype Pathway is quite simple:

- Each component (menu, screen or report) is shown as a box.
- The boxes are linked by arrows showing the sequence of the boxes required for the prototyping session (see Figure 4.66).

Each session may involve a number of pathway demonstrations. Figure 4.66 illustrates the pathway used to demonstrate the Book Delivery dialogue for the case when new lines are to be added onto an existing delivery.

Pathways will always end in a series of screen components or a report (and not a menu), with the dialogue to which they refer named in a box immediately before it.

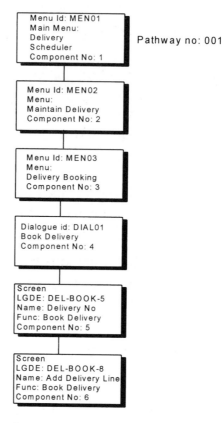

Figure 4.66 - Prototype Pathway

Implement Prototype Pathway

We can now implement the Prototype Pathways on the prototyping tool. Menus will probably be in place already. If not they can usually be generated quickly using most tools.

Screen and report design is beyond the scope of SSADM and in any case will be determined largely by organisational standards. Installation style guides will often be available and the kind of material which they might be expected to include should be clear before the onset of prototyping.

In Specification Prototyping our main consideration is verification of user requirements, so the content of screens and reports, rather than their layout, are of primary concern. We should make no attempt at this stage to provide a sophisticated all-singing all-dancing interface; not least because it may divert attention from our main objectives and will in any case necessarily result in greater development effort and time.

The guiding principle in designing prototypes is to keep the layout clear, well structured, and above all accurate. The content of each screen and report should be validated against the data items in the relevant I/O Structure Descriptions, against the Attribute Descriptions in the Required System LDM or Data Catalogue, and against the task descriptions in the Hierarchical Task Models.

Preparing for the Prototype Demonstration

Before we demonstrate prototypes to users, we should draw up specific objectives and agendas for the session as it is all too easy in the rather informal atmosphere of prototyping to get side-tracked and to waste valuable time on trivial issues.

To help in this task we can draw up a Prototype Demonstration Objective Document for each pathway. As well as listing specific discussion points for each dialogue, we can use this document to note down general tasks, such as an explanation of procedure, in the form of an agenda for the entire prototyping session.

The Prototype Demonstration Objective Document for Update Stock Levels is shown in Figure 4.67.

As part of preparing for the demonstration we should also design some test data. This will often include both input and output data, as the prototype may not possess any true processing capabilities, but merely simulate the correct responses to pre-specified inputs. We should make test data comprehensive enough to illustrate all the relevant user requirements, and to simulate a full range of system responses (including major error processing or validation).

Prototype Demonstration Objective Document		
Pathway No: *001*	Function Name: *Book Delivery*	User Role: *Delivery Scheduler*
Agenda: *1. Discuss Prototyping aims and procedures.* *2. Explain operation of prototyping tool.* *3. Carry out demonstration.* *4. Discuss feedback and possible re-demonstration.*		
Component No.	**Discussion Point**	
5	*Check input data items if Id unknown.*	
6	*Check field sizes.*	
6	*Check output details are sufficient.*	
6	*What if stated quantity exceeds expected?*	

Figure 4.67 - A sample Prototype Demonstration Objective Document

Demonstrating and Reviewing Prototypes

We will demonstrate each pathway to one or more users belonging to the appropriate user role. Ideally, demonstrations should be conducted by two analysts from the project team.

The 'lead' analyst will be the designer of the prototype and will be the one who actually demonstrates the prototype. The second analyst will act as note-taker and help to keep the demonstration to the pre-set agenda. The designer of a prototype will often feel defensive about any criticisms of it, so the second analyst should also act as an objective observer, ensuring that the wishes of the *user* are fully recorded.

We document the results of the demonstration in a Prototype Result Log (Figure 4.68). This will detail each request made by the user during the demonstration, which we will later annotate with a change grade. There are seven grades suggested by SSADM:

N. No change needed.

C. Cosmetic. This refers to change requests associated with layout and format, not content. If the only change requests logged are in this category, we would not carry out any further iterations of the Prototyping cycle.

D. Dialogue level, i.e. changes which affect the content of the dialogue only.

P. Pathway changes. These will generally refer to requests regarding the sequence of the pathway. They may lead to changes in the I/O Structure for the function.

S. This indicates a possible need to change installation standards.

A. Analysis errors. Any changes in this category will indicate that errors have been made in systems analysis. If the errors are very great they may lead to repeats of earlier steps.

G. Global change requests. Some requests may have implications outside the business area under investigation.

We pass the completed Pathway Result Logs, along with our recommendations, to the Team Leader, who will decide on what will happen next. This may involve carrying out further demonstrations using refined prototypes, or halting the cycle if there is likely to be little benefit gained from continuing. If any major problems have arisen from the demonstration then these may need reporting to management.

Prototype Result Log				
Pathway No:	Function Name:		User Role:	
Component No	Result No	Result Description		Change Grade

Figure 4.68 - A sample Prototype Result Log

The Team Leader will also ensure that any relevant SSADM products are updated. Any entirely new requirements should be added to the Requirements Catalogue. We should review changes of all types other than N or C to make sure that all of their implications are understood, and that they are practical when the requirements of the system as a whole are taken into account.

Produce Final Prototyping Report

Once all of the prototype demonstrations have finished the Team Leader should prepare an overall report of their results. This should include comments on the prototyping exercise as a whole, e.g.:

- Were the objectives of the step met?
- Was the original scope adhered to?
- Was the exercise a success?

It will also summarise any changes to the requirements specification, and refer to SSADM products which have been updated or amended as a result.

We will retain and document our menu and dialogue structures for input to Stage 5 (Logical Design) where they may prove useful during formal Dialogue Design.

4.8.3   Summary (Step 350)

The SSADM tasks carried out in Step 350 are.

Task

10	Identify which dialogues are to be prototyped.
20	Prototype the menu structures.

30	Create Prototype Pathways detailing which screen and report components of each dialogue are to be prototyped, and in which order.

Repeat tasks 40 - 70 for each Pathway:

40	Build the prototype.
50	Prepare for the prototyping session.
60	Demonstrate the prototype to representatives of the relevant user role.
70	Review the prototyping session and consider whether another demonstration would be worthwhile.
80	Update the requirements specification with the results of the prototyping exercise. Report on the exercise as a whole.

4.9   Step 360 - Develop Processing Specification

In a large number of projects this will be the critical step in the analysis and design of the new system. It marks the end of analysis and the beginning of rigorous detailed specification.

Through Data Flow Modelling and Function Definition we have built up high level views of processing, and have defined our basic units of specification (i.e. Functions). Through Logical Data Modelling and Relational Data Analysis we have developed a detailed model of the required data structure and content of the new system.

We now apply Entity Behaviour Modelling and Conceptual Process Modelling to bring together processing and data requirements to form the third view of the required system, illustrating the effects of time (and therefore of events) on data.

Entity Behaviour Modelling involves two related techniques: Event Identification and Entity Life History Analysis. Conceptual Process Modelling is an umbrella term for the development of Enquiry Access Paths, Effect Correspondence Diagrams, Update Process Models and Enquiry Process Models.

Entity Life Histories are diagrammatic representations of how entity types are or can be affected by events. They detail the allowable sequence, iterations and optionality of events for each entity, and thus further document business rules. Entity Life History Analysis often requires a great deal of effort and discipline in order to reduce ambiguity and ensure completeness. The rigour of the technique should repay this effort by producing a greater understanding of system needs and revealing flaws or omissions in our specification to date. It will also provide the basis for detailed design of system processing in the steps which follow.

The involvement of users at this point is essential to the success of the exercise, as only they are likely to have a full and detailed enough understanding of events and their effects. In particular we will rely heavily on users to provide details of exceptions to the normal lives of entities, the specification of which will frequently take far longer than that of standard processing.

Effect Correspondence Diagrams place the project firmly in the design phase. Having modelled the effects of events from the perspective of the entity, we then take the opposite view and model the effects on entities from the perspective of the event. In other words we will specify all of the effects on the Logical Data Model of each event type in turn. The resulting Effect Correspondence Diagrams will then be carried forward into Stage 5 to be used as the basis for more detailed specification of update processing.

Entity Behaviour Modelling is only concerned with the processing of events, i.e. with updates. In Step 360 we will also begin the detailed specification of enquiries, by formally documenting the required database navigation of each enquiry using Enquiry Access Paths.

The level of detail and rigour involved in this step is likely to lead to fairly extensive modifications and additions to the Required System Logical Data Model, Required System Data Flow Model and Function Definitions, as we uncover new or revised user requirements. For this reason Step 330 - Derive System Functions - is not considered to be complete until Step 360 is finished.

4.9.1 An introduction to Entity Life Histories

As we have discussed, Entity Life Histories document all of the events which can affect - i.e. cause a change to or constrain the life of - an entity type. They model the business rules applicable to the processing of a particular entity type, and thus specify allowable sequences and combinations of events. It is important to realise that an Entity Life History applies to all occurrences of an entity type and so must cope with all possible lives of that entity type.

Concepts

Before looking at the technique in detail, it is worth reconsidering the concepts of events and effects.

Events

An event is real world action which causes an update to the data held within the system. Therefore it acts as a trigger for a defined set of processing, and does not represent the processing itself.

If the reader thinks of the information system as storing facts about some aspect of the real world, then it follows that when that part of the real world changes, the stored data must change too.

The information system does not get to know about the changes in the real world by magic. The users of the system have to constantly feed it with new data which describe the changes that have taken place.

This is the purpose of an update function: to provide an interface by which the users of a system can inform the system of a real world event.

In this chapter, when we talk about an event, we mean a conceptual model event. This is a real world happening whose effects can be described in terms of changes to the data represented by the Logical Data Model.

There are many other events, *business events*, that the systems analyst will encounter. These are relevant to the running of the organisation, but will not be reflected in the conceptual model. Thus the event 'purchaser goes sick' is of no relevance to the system we are developing, although it could of course be an important event in some other system.

Once again the skill of the systems analyst is to work with the users to clarify which events are to be considered relevant in the context of the current project.

Effects

Each event will cause updates to at least one entity type; these updates are called *effects*.

It is quite possible for a single event to have two or more mutually exclusive effects on an entity occurrence, dependent upon the state of that entity occurrence. For example the effects of the event Archive Stock on the entity Delivery Line depend on whether we are deleting the last occurrence of Stock of the Delivery Line or not. If it is the last one, we delete the Delivery Line as well as the Stock occurrence; if there are other Stock occurrences belonging to the Delivery Line, then the Delivery Line is not deleted. It is not possible to know which effect is going to take place without reading the database to see what the situation is.

It is also possible for a single event to simultaneously affect more than one occurrence of an entity, but in differing ways. For example, the event Merge Stocks will cause one stock of a product to be added to another. The quantity of the first stock will thus be reduced to zero, while the quantity of the second stock will be increased by the original quantity of the first. In cases such as this, the entity is said to be taking on different roles.

Mutually exclusive effects and entity roles form an important part of the specification of effects and so will need highlighting in Entity Behaviour Modelling.

Notation

With one or two minor differences, Entity Life Histories use the same Jackson-like structure notation as I/O Structure Diagrams. This causes us to issue a word of warning to the novice reader: the *notation* is the same, but the *context* of the diagrams is completely different.

On the Entity Life History the root node (the top box) contains the name of the entity being described. The leaves of the diagram (boxes which have no children) represent effects and each effect box carries the name of the event which causes that effect.

On the I/O Structure Diagram the root node contains the name of a function and each leaf represents a data item, or a group of data items, which is input to, or output from, that function.

Sequence

Entity Life Histories comprise of a sequence of events read from left to right i.e from birth to death. In the most trivial of cases an Entity Life History may include only an insertion (creation, or birth) event, but the majority will include some form of mid-life and a deletion (or death) event as well.

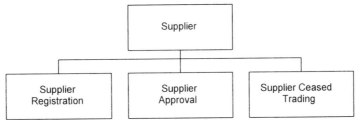

Figure 4.69 - Sequence

In Figure 4.69, the Entity Life History for Supplier, we see that the Supplier entity has three events in its life, and that each occurrence of Supplier can experience each event just once.

The system is notified of a new Supplier when the Purchasing Department identifies a new company from whom they want to buy products. This is the Supplier Registration event.

Suppliers have to undergo a number of checks to make sure that they can meet SRW's standards (relating to timeliness of deliveries, quality of goods, ability to deliver in sufficient quantities etc.). When these checks have been completed the Supplier record will be updated. This is the Supplier Approval event.

It is possible that the Supplier will go out of business. If this is the case, then the Supplier record has reached the end of its life and may be deleted, or marked for deletion. Hence the event Supplier Ceased Trading.

The Supplier Entity Life History of Figure 4.69 is not complete. It is a first-cut diagram which shows only the main events in the life of the Supplier entity. It is usual to develop Entity Life Histories in a number of passes, with each pass adding greater detail to the life.

Note that there will be many events in the life of the real world Supplier which will not be reflected in the Supplier Entity Life History. For example: Supplier Celebrates 50 Years in the Trade may be an important event in the history of the Supplier in question, but it is not of any great interest to our purchasers.

Selection

Some effects are options of a selection, meaning that each time that the selection is reached, one and only one of the effects can occur.

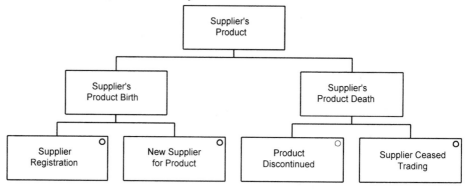

Figure 4.70 - Selection

Thus in Figure 4.70, we see two selections: Supplier's Product Birth and Supplier's Product Death (these are structure boxes, and it is not necessary to name them, but is often convenient to do so).

The diagram tells us that an occurrence of Supplier's Product gets created either by the Supplier Registration event (when the details of the Supplier are first recorded) or by the New Supplier for Product event (when a decision is taken to source a product from an existing supplier). Similarly, each occurrence of Supplier Product is killed off by either the Product Discontinued event, or the Supplier Ceased Trading event. In other words, an occurrence of Supplier's Product will die when one of its masters dies: whichever dies first.

Iteration

Iterations are used to illustrate cases where an event can affect an entity occurrence more than once:

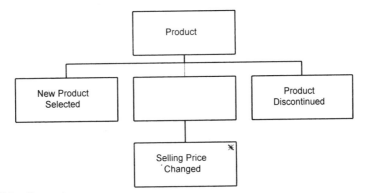

Figure 4.71 - Iteration

Figure 4.71 uses the first-cut Entity Life History for the Product entity to illustrate iteration. The Selling Price Changed event can affect an occurrence of Product more than once because a given Product can have its Selling Price increased or reduced many times: one week we reduce the price of Haggis as part of a special promotion; the next week we put it back to its original price; a year later a Haggis shortage means that the selling price of Haggis has to be increased by 50 %.

This leads us to a further point. The business events Sales Promotion and Price Revision both have the same effect on our system: an update to the Selling Price attribute of Product. Because their effects are the same, we only need to define one conceptual model event for these two business events.

Again, the precise requirements of the users have to be considered. We could imagine that the Sales Promotion event requires us to record two dates between which a lower price is to be charged for a product, whilst the Price Revision event requires us to record only the date from which the price increase is to take place. Then the two events would be different and we would need to name two different events in our Entity Behaviour Model. The Required System Logical Data Model for SRW does not support these requirements and we will consider them no further, but the reader might like to consider the ways in which the Logical Data Model and Entity Life Histories might be changed in order to support them.

It is important to remember that by definition an iteration occurs *zero*, one or many times, which means in this case that an occurrence of Product might experience its death event without ever having been affected by the Selling Price Changed event. Some Products will be discontinued before they have their prices changed.

Remember also that although an iteration can have only one child (a box marked with an *) that child can be the parent of an entire substructure (see Figure 4.74 for example).

Rules for Jackson structures

The rules for drawing Jackson structures have already been discussed in the section on Function Definition. The same rules apply to the drawing of Entity Life Histories as to the drawing of I/O Structure Diagrams:

- An iteration has just one child.
- All the children of a parent must be of the same type.

These rules are described in section 4.5.4.

4.9.2   Developing Entity Life Histories

The development of Entity Life Histories is best carried out in a number of stages:

1. Identify events and document them on the Entity Access Matrix.
2. Analyse the basic behaviour of the entities.
3. Perform an up-pass analysis of entity behaviour. Starting from the bottom of the Required System Logical Data Model (i.e. with those entities which are details only) and working upwards through the structure, document the life of each entity. Try to identify mutually exclusive behaviour patterns. For iterated patterns of events identify the way in which the iteration stops.
4. Perform a down-pass analysis of entity behaviour. Starting from the top of the Required System Logical Data Model (i.e. with those entities having no masters), work down through the data model reviewing each Entity Life History, looking in particular for death events, and examining the way that the death events of masters and details interact. Identify super-events.
5. Consider deletion strategy.
6. Add operations and state indicators.

Identifying events and documenting their effects

Event Identification

There are a number of ways in which events can be identified.

During Function Definition the Required System Data Flow Model is examined for updates, which are indicated by the presence of an arrow pointing towards a main data store. These updates are responses to events (remember that an event is a trigger to a set of update processing), and these events are named and documented as part of the Function Description.

In the section on Function Definition (Step 330) we discussed the identification of the events Purchase Order Proposal and Purchase Order Confirmation from the Required System Data Flow Model. The reader might like to review the Required System Data Flow Model and try to identify further events.

Another good way of identifying events is to examine the Required System Logical Data Model. For each entity we ask the following questions:

- Which events cause occurrences of this entity to be created?
- Which events cause occurrences of this entity to be deleted?
- Which events set the values of non-key attributes?
- Which events create and delete occurrences of relationships?
- Which events cause changes to the state of an entity?

When we ask of Delivery 'which event creates occurrences of Delivery' we find that these are created when the supplier 'phones to confirm the delivery date and time: the Delivery Confirmation event.

Having identified an entity's birth event, a further question that we should always ask is whether the entity shares the birth event with any of its masters or details.

A clue here is the presence of a fully mandatory relationship between master and detail. This suggests that the master and one or more detail occurrences will be created at the same time i.e. in response to the same event. It also suggests that they will be deleted together.

A further question that can be asked when identifying a detail which shares a birth event with its master is 'does the detail have its own independent birth as well?' Again, a similar question can be asked of entities which share a death event.

An example is Supplier's Product, which shares a birth event with Supplier: when suppliers are first registered the purchaser can also record any products that they are thinking of using that supplier for, hence the sharing of the Supplier Registration event. However, purchasers often decide to extend the range of products that they buy from an existing supplier. When this happens the system must be updated by creating new Supplier's Product records. Hence the alternative birth event for Supplier's Product: New Supplier for Product.

Mandatory attributes (those that are defined as 'not null' in the attribute/data item descriptions) will have their values set by the birth event, but we should still ask if there are any other events which cause those values to change.

We have seen one example of this already: the Selling Price Changed event (see Figure 4.71). The price of a product is recorded when the details of a product are first recorded, but prices change, and there is an event to reflect this.

This does not mean that we have to have a separate event for each non-key attribute that can change its value. Often there are a number of attributes, e.g. name, address, telephone number, which the user might want to edit from time to time. We can define a single change of details event for this situation.

Some attributes are optional: they may be set to null when an entity is created. Again we should look for the event which leads to a value being given to that attribute. In SRW, Purchase Order has the attributes Quantity Requested: a mandatory attribute input with the Purchase Order Proposal event; and Quantity Confirmed: set to null at first and then updated as part of the Purchased Order Confirmation event.

In SSADM the relationship between two entities is represented by a foreign key attribute in the entity which is at the detail end of the relationship. When an occurrence of a relationship is created this foreign key attribute is given a value. The value ties the detail occurrence to the master entity which has that value as its primary key.

In Entity Behaviour Modelling we talk about masters gaining details and details being tied to masters. This is another way of saying that a relationship occurrence is being created, that a foreign key is being given a value.

We should look for events which cause gains and ties. When an end of a relationship is mandatory, there will be a gain (for a master) or a tie (for a detail) as part of the birth effect of the entity at the mandatory end of the relationship. Thus Supplier's Product is tied to Supplier and tied to Product at the time of its creation.

When an end of a relationship is optional, we can expect the event which causes a gain or tie to occur in the mid-life of the entity at the optional end of the relationship. Thus the Invoice Arrival event will be a mid-life event in the Entity Life History for Delivery (when a delivery is set up, it has no related invoice because the invoice is not sent by the Supplier until after the delivery has been made).

Another point to consider with relationships is whether they are fixed or transferable. In our system most of the relationships are fixed: once we create a relationship between a Purchase Order Line and a Purchase Order, those two occurrences remain linked together i.e, the Purchase Order Line will never be linked to a different occurrence of Purchase Order.

An exception is the relationship between Stock and Bin. Stock can be moved, or merged with other stocks (of the same delivery). When this happens, the stock location changes, e.g. stock which was in bin number 3456 is now in bin number 7689. We have to cut the Stock occurrence from one Bin occurrence, and tie it to a different one. The relationship between Stock and Bin is said to be transferable, because the detail can be attached to more than one master during its lifetime (but only one master at any one time of course).

Event Identification can start early on in a project, perhaps as early as Business Activity Modelling in Step 115. However, we can't fully identify and analyse events until we have a stable Logical Data Model and a well defined set of requirements and it isn't until Function Definition and subsequently Entity Behaviour Modelling that events are identified and documented in earnest.

Events are informed to the system by users, via functions. It follows that every event must have at least one related Function Definition, and every update function should be related to at least one event. Events and Function Definitions should be cross-checked to ensure that this is the case.

In Step 360 previously unidentified events will be discovered, so we will have to define new functions for these events because there are unlikely to be any existing Function Definitions which cover them.

Event and Enquiry Catalogue

By now it should be obvious that there are many ways in which events can be identified and that events can be identified at many points in a project. Whenever and however events are discovered we should document the following information:

- Event name and id (if necessary)
- Event description
- Related business activities or business events
- Average and maximum occurrences
- Event data
- Entry point entity
- Entity accesses

The cross-referencing of events to the Business Activity Model is good practice because it reminds us that the purpose of our work is always to support business activities. It lends our project further traceability from the early stages of investigation through to the later stages of design.

The volumetric information is important because in Physical Design and Technical Systems Options we will need to have an idea of the volumes of transactions that the Technical Systems Architecture must support.

The event data is the data that must be provided by the user (input via a function), or by another process, in order for the processing of the event to take place (see the sections on Conceptual Process Modelling).

The entry point entity is the first entity accessed by the event (again, see the sections on Conceptual Process Modelling).

The entity accesses are the effects of the events and the type of those effects (see the section on the Entity Access Matrix).

Similar information should be recorded for each enquiry.

Entity Access Matrix

As events are identified we should document their effects on the Entity Access Matrix. This is a grid which lists all the entities of the Required System Logical Data Model along the top and all the known events and enquiries down the side.

Each column-row intersection of the matrix can be used to record the effect of an event on an entity. Each effect can be described with one or more letters each of which gives an indication of the type of effect taking place (see table in Figure 4.72).

The matrix can also be used to show which entities are read by each enquiry.

I	Insert	Indicates that one or more occurrences of the entity are created by an occurrence of the event.
M	Modify	Indicates that one or more occurrences of the entity have their attribute values modified by an occurrence of the event.
D	Death	Indicates that one or more occurrences of the entity are killed by an occurrence of the event (the occurrences remain, but only for enquiry purposes).
B	Bury	Indicates that one or more occurrences of the entity are deleted by an occurrence of the event (the occurrences are physically deleted, archived or marked for deletion; the user can no longer see them).
T	Tie	Indicates that one or more occurrences of the entity are linked to a master entity, via a relationship. (The corresponding effect on the master is shown on the matrix using a G.)
C	Cut	Indicates that one or more occurrences of the entity have the relationship with their master deleted. (The corresponding effect on the master is shown on the matrix using an L.)

G	Gain	Indicates that one or more occurrences of the entity have their relationships with one or more detail entities created. (The corresponding effect on the detail is shown on the matrix using a T.)
L	Lose	Indicates that one or more occurrences of the entity have their relationships with one or more detail entities deleted. (The corresponding effect on the detail is shown on the matrix using a C.)
S	Swap masters	Indicates that one or more occurrences will be cut from one master and tied to another. (The corresponding effect on the master is shown on the matrix using an X.)
X	Swap details	Indicates that one or more occurrences of an entity lose their details and that one or more occurrences of the entity gain them. (The corresponding effect on the detail is shown on the matrix using an S.)
R	Read	Indicates that one or more occurrences of the entity are read to access attribute values, or to navigate the Logical Data Model.

Figure 4.72 - Allowable Effects of an Entity Access Matrix

The above letters can only be used for events, except for R which can be used for enquiries as well as events.

The matrix can help in identifying events. We look down each column of the matrix and ask:

- *Does the entity have at least one creation and one deletion event?* If not, then the reasons should be investigated and if the omission is valid they should be documented in the Required System Logical Data Model. If the omission is not valid we should try to identify the missing event and we will have to alter Function Definition and possibly the Required System Data Flow Model (if we think it is important to keep it up to date).

Similarly we can look across each row of the matrix and ask:

- *Does every event affect at least one entity?* If it does not then we have definitely made an error, as events only exist to trigger update processing.

Entity Life Histories for SRW

In the following sections we will develop Entity Life Histories for some of the entities in the case study. As we do so we will introduce the further concepts and notation of Entity Life History Analysis: effect qualifiers, entity roles, parallel lives, super-events and quits and resumes.

We do not have the space to develop the full set of Entity Life Histories, so we will concentrate on the section of the data model containing the Purchase Order, Purchase Order Line, Supplier, Supplier's Product and Product entities.

Entity Access Matrix

The Entity Access Matrix for the part of the case study we are concerned with is shown in Figure 4.73. In practice it is not possible to entirely complete the Entity Access Matrix before starting to draw the Entity Life Histories. Rather, an initial Entity Access Matrix is drawn up, the drawing of Entity Life Histories commences, and the Entity Access Matrix is kept up to date as the behavioural analysis progresses.

Some will prefer to use the Entity Access Matrix as a working document - a rough starting point for Entity Behaviour Modelling and nothing more. Others will want to keep the Entity Access Matrix entirely consistent with the Entity Life Histories as they develop. A good CASE tool should do this automatically, but CASE tools tend to be poor in their support for the Entity Access Matrix. Maintaining consistency by hand can be a tiresome task.

Entity Event	Product	Supplier	Supplier's Product	Purchase Order	Purchase Order Line
Product Substitute Defined	G				
Ad Hoc Purchase Order Raised		G	G	I T G	I T T
Purchase Order Proposal		G	G	I T G	I T T
Purchase Order Confirmation			M	M	M
Delivery Confirmation		G			G/D
Purchase Order Cancellation				D	D
Supplier Ceased Trading		D	D	D	D
Out of Time					D
☺ End of Purchase Order Line				M/D	
Invoice Arrival		G			
Supplier Details Change		M			
Supplier Suspension		M			
Supplier Reinstatement		M			
New Supplier for Product	G	G	I T T		
Supplier Registration	G	I	T		
Product Withdrawal			D		
Product Discontinued	D		D		
New Product Selected	G	G	I T T		
Priority Supplier Changed			M		
Selling Price Changed	M				

Figure 4.73 - Partial Entity Access Matrix for SRW

Basic behaviour

We will start by reviewing the Entity Life Histories of Figures 4.69, 4.70 and 4.71. These were somewhat simplified. For instance, the mid-life of Product contained no *gain* effects. Product is a master of two entities: Supplier's Product, and Product Substitute. The birth events of these entities should be placed in the mid-life of Product, because relationships with Product are created each time one of these events takes place. This pattern (birth event of detail, iterated in mid-life of master) is a very common one. In fact, where we have a mid-life iteration of effects, and no detail entity, we should ask if a detail entity needs to be created.

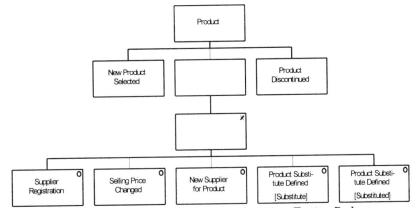

Figure 4.74 - Product Entity Life History showing Entity Roles

The keen-eyed reader will have spotted something unfamiliar in the mid-life of Product: the event Product Substitute Defined appears twice. In each case the event name is followed by a role name in square brackets.

Entity Roles

An event can appear more than once on an Entity Life History, but only in two well-defined circumstances:

- *Entity roles*: one occurrence of the event affects two or more occurrences of the same entity type, each in different ways.
- *Effect qualifiers*: one occurrence of the event can have different effects on an entity occurrence, depending on that entity's current state.

In the Product Entity Life History, we are dealing with the first of these situations.

When a Product Substitute entity is defined, it is tied to *two* Product occurrences, each via a *different* relationship. One Product is the substitute, the other Product is the one which can be substituted. Therefore two different gains take place, one via the Substitute relationship, and one via the Substituted relationship.

In Supplier's Product we meet another example of entity roles:

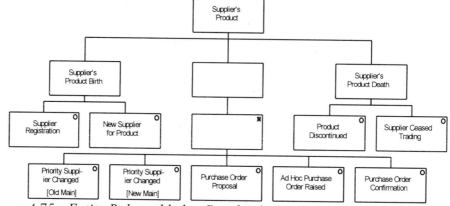

Figure 4.75 - Entity Roles added to Supplier's Product ELH

Supplier's Product contains an attribute 'Main Y/N?'. When a product is ordered it will be ordered from the main supplier, and the other suppliers are only used if the main supplier cannot meet the order. Each product has only one main supplier at any one time.

The preferred supplier of a product can change. When this happens, the purchaser goes to the system and updates the relevant Supplier's Product record by changing the Main Y/N attribute to Y. The system must find the record of the previously preferred Supplier's Product, and update its Main Y/N attribute to N.

Thus for each occurrence of the Priority Supplier Changed event, there are two Supplier's Product occurrences affected.

Note that square brackets are used for entity roles.

Effect Qualifiers

The above example raises a question as to what happens when a new Supplier's Product occurrence is created. If there is already a main supplier for the product, and if the new Supplier's Product is to become the main source for the product, then we again have two entity roles. However, if there is no existing main supplier for the product, or if the new Supplier's Product is to be a secondary source, then only one occurrence of Supplier's Product is involved: the new one. It isn't possible to tell which of the two alternative sets of effects is going to take place without enquiring to see if an existing main supplier for the product exists and there is no particular reason why the user of the system should be aware of the need to do this.

Thus the processing of the event will have to take account of the two possibilities, and our Entity Life Histories will have to show that there are alternative, mutually exclusive, effects of the event.

In Figure 4.76 we show an extract of the Supplier's Product Entity Life History. The Supplier Registration event appears twice as a birth effect, each time being qualified with the possible case. If the new Supplier's Product is replacing another as the main source of a product, then two occurrences of Supplier's Product will be affected: one taking the role of 'new main', another taking the role of 'old main'. Thus the event appears a third time in the mid-life of Supplier's Product.

If the new Supplier's Product occurrence is not replacing any other occurrence as the main source of the product, then the only effect on Supplier's Product is to create a new occurrence.

Effect qualifiers can be used together with entity roles, as they are in this example, but they can occur independently of entity roles. Effect qualifiers are shown in round brackets.

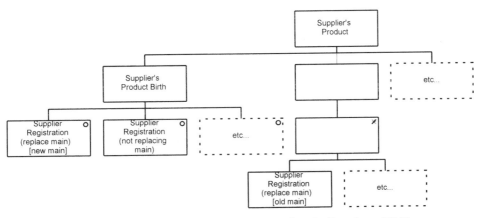

Figure 4.76 - Effect Qualifiers added to Supplier's Product ELH.

It goes without saying that the same need for effect qualifiers applies to the other birth event of Supplier's Product. For reasons of space, our subsequent models of Supplier's Product will not show any of the qualified birth effects, but as an exercise the reader might like to redraw the Entity Life History to include them.

Mid-life sequence of events

In the two Entity Life Histories reviewed so far, the mid-life was an iterated selection of effects. But we should always examine the mid-life of an entity to see if there is any sequence to the mid-life effects.

A little care is required here, because the events which occur in a sequence for one entity, may occur in a selection for a different entity.

For instance, the Purchase Order Proposal and Purchase Order Confirmation events both affect Supplier's Product and Purchase Order Line. In Purchase Order Line these events are in sequence (see Figure 4.79). A real world purchase order line cannot be confirmed before it has been placed. However, the same two events appear in a selection in the Entity Life History for Supplier's Product. For Supplier's Product the occurrence of these events is not ordered. Many purchase orders can be placed before one is confirmed.

When a mid-life sequence of events is discovered, we should consider other mid-life effects for that entity: do they fit into the sequence, are they independent of it, or are they constrained by it?

SRW monitors the performance of its suppliers, and if it falls below acceptable standards the supplier may be suspended. This means that purchasers are restricted from placing any further business with the supplier, until such time as the supplier is reinstated.

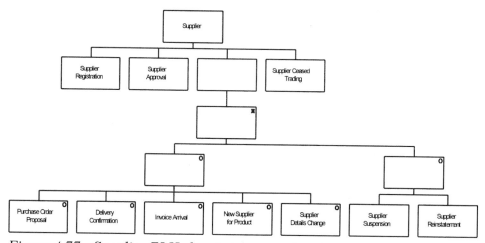

Figure 4.77 - Supplier ELH showing 'suspensions'

Our first attempt at showing this is given in Figure 4.77.

Figure 4.77 now says that once the Supplier Suspension event has happened to an occurrence of Supplier, no other events will be allowed to affect that occurrence until the Supplier Reinstatement event has happened.

For the last two entities in our discussion, initial Entity Life Histories are shown in Figures 4.78 and 4.79.

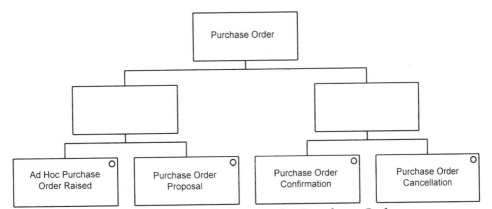

Figure 4.78 - First-cut Entity Life History for Purchase Order

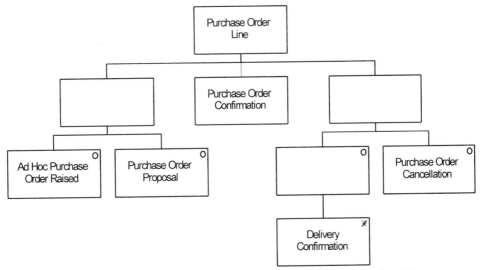

Figure 4.79 - First-cut Entity Life History for Purchase Order Line

A structure of the type shown in Figure 4.78 (a sequence of two selections) will always raise a question as to its correctness: is it really the case that either of the first two events can be followed by either of the second two events?

Often the answer is no. We will deal with this shortly.

Up-pass analysis of behaviour

We will now work our way back up our section of the Logical Data Model, from detail to master, looking for mutually exclusive behaviour patterns, and asking the question 'how does an iteration end?'.

When a purchase order is first raised, SRW waits for confirmation from the supplier that they can supply the quantities requested. If the supplier cannot supply the requested amount, then an alternative supplier will be contacted to make up the shortfall. These ad-hoc purchase orders are confirmed, over the 'phone, before they are actually raised. There is no separate Purchase Order confirmation event for an ad-hoc purchase order. This is why the Entity Life Histories of Figures 4.78 and 4.79 did not show a true picture of events.

A better representation of the life history of Purchase Order Line is shown in Figure 4.80, where the Purchase Order Confirmation event has been placed in a sequence with the Purchase Order Proposed event. A similar technique is used on the Purchase Order structure as well.

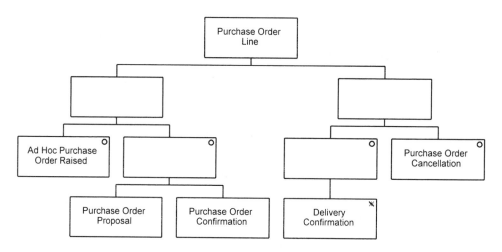

Figure 4.80 - Restructured Entity Life History for Purchase Order Line

Note that in solving one problem, we have introduced another. The structure now suggests that a Purchase Order which has been proposed, but not confirmed, cannot be cancelled. But of course it can.

Quit and Resume notation

The quit and resume is a useful device for separating out exceptional events, or events that can occur in more than one place in an entity's life. Readers who are familiar with previous versions of SSADM should be aware that the method now uses disciplined Quits and Resumes.

In Figure 4.81 the life of Purchase Order Line is modelled as a high level selection. The left-hand option of the selection shows the normal sequence of events: the assumed case.

We assume that events are going to occur in the way that the assumed case describes unless an event occurs that proves otherwise: we expect that a purchase order proposal will be followed by a confirmation. We know that sometimes it will be followed by a purchase order cancellation instead, but at the time of proposal, we do not know which of these two events will take place, so we assume that confirmation will take place.

If the cancellation event occurs, then it becomes clear that the confirmation event will not happen, that the alternative life has happened instead.

The 'Q' on the Purchase Order Confirmation effect indicates that it is possible that this effect can be replaced by the Purchase Order Cancellation event marked 'R' in the alternative life.

The iteration of 'events' which starts the alternative life is a convention: it represents the events in the assumed case life which might happen before the events in the alternative life occur.

When using Quits and Resumes, SSADM follows the convention that the resume event *replaces* the quit event. Furthermore, Quits and Resumes are only used to jump from one side of a selection to another, or to jump out of an iterated sequence of events; always from an assumed case to an alternative case.

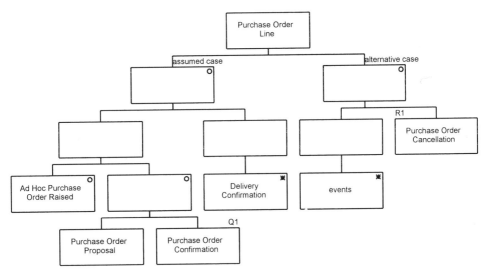

Figure 4.81 - Quit and Resume notation

Sharp eyed readers will notice that there is no sequence of events in the ELH of Figure 4.81 that allows for the cancellation of an ad-hoc purchase order. Yet in SRW, purchasers can cancel any order, provided that no delivery has been arranged for that order. If we put a quit on the iterated effect Delivery Confirmation, then the structure will permit a sequence of events that includes the cancellation of a purchase order after one or more deliveries has already been arranged.

A purchase order line can be met by more than one delivery (which is why the Delivery Confirmation event appears as an iteration in the life of Purchase Order Line). In order to describe *exactly* the sequence of permissible events for Purchase Order Line we have to distinguish between the first delivery, and any subsequent delivery, for an order line. To do this, we use effect qualifiers (see Figure 4.82). Having done this, we can put a Quit on 'Delivery Confirmation (first)', to allow for the fact that a cancellation can take place any time up to the point at which a delivery has been arranged for a purchase order (or part of a purchase order).

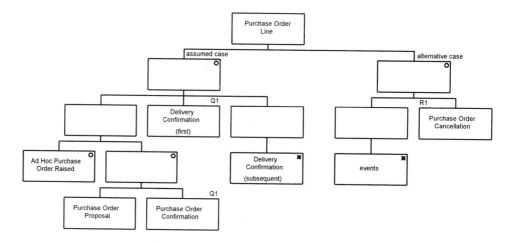

Figure 4.82 - Effect Qualifiers used in combination with Quit and Resumes

The Entity Life History for Purchase Order Line has now become rather elaborate. Readers who find this approach to Entity Life History Analysis unnecessarily complicated might like to consider ways of 'cheating'. In the example just discussed we could attach an operation to the Purchase Order Cancellation event which says 'fail if Delivery Lines exist'. Then we would not need to distinguish between first and subsequent delivery confirmation events on the Purchase Order Line Entity Life History.

Before we finish looking at the Purchase Order Line Entity Life History, we should ask a further question of it: how does the iteration of delivery confirmations end? Put another way, how do Purchase Order Lines die, assuming that they do not get cancelled?

There are two possibilities:

The last delivery of goods required by a Purchase Order Line is confirmed (most Purchase Order Lines will be met by a single delivery, but some will have two or more deliveries; the last delivery is the one which brings the quantity of goods delivered equal to the quantity of goods promised when the order was confirmed).

Alternatively, it is possible that the time limit for delivery expires before delivery is arranged.

These two events are reflected in the Entity Life History of Figure 4.83.

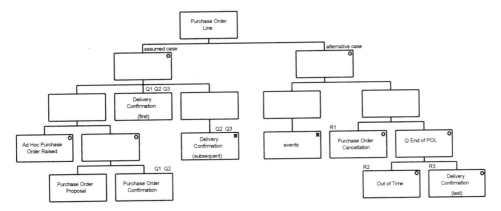

Figure 4.83 - Further Death Events for Purchase Order Line

A new function will have to be defined for the Out of Time event. This will be an off-line function, which will run overnight, when the system is not busy. It will identify all Purchase Order Lines for which the required by date has expired, a report of the products and quantities on these Purchase Order Lines will be printed for the purchasers' information.

As with the cancellation event, we do not know at the outset how the life of any given Purchase Order Line will end, so the two extra death events have also been placed in the alternative life, with appropriate quits and resumes.

Note that it is possible to quit from more than one place in the assumed case to the same resume point, and that the quits and resumes are numbered to distinguish between the different possible resume events.

The reader is invited to return to Figure 4.78 and consider how, in the light of the treatment of Purchase Order Line, the Purchase Order Entity Life History should be developed.

Our suggested solution to this exercise is shown in Figure 4.84.

Super-events

When two or more effects appear at the same point in an Entity Life History, and have the same effects, we can identify a super-event.

Super-events simplify Entity Life Histories by reducing the number of boxes appearing on them. They also identify common processing, thereby promoting re-use and reducing the amount of effort involved in specifying the update processing.

In the Entity Life History for Purchase Order Line (Figure 4.84) the super event ☺End of POL is identified. We use a ☺ to denote a super-event, but any special symbol will do.

In the Entity Life History for Purchase Order (Figure 4.84) the normal death of Purchase Order is the death of its last Purchase Order Line. Instead of showing both possible ways in which a Purchase Order can be killed by the death of its last detail, the super-event is used instead.

Note that the Purchase Order Cancellation event kills a Purchase Order and all its Purchase Order Lines in one go, whereas the normal death of Purchase Order is a lingering one, with its Purchase Order Lines being killed off one by one, till none remain.

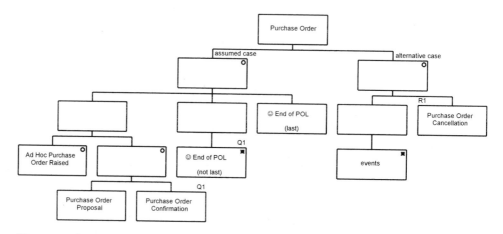

Figure 4.84 - Purchase Order Entity Life History

Continuing our up-pass analysis of behaviour, we have only one change to make to Supplier's Product - the addition of a third death event. The Product Discontinued event takes care of the situation where SRW stops stocking a product, but we need an event to cover the case where a supplier withdraws a product from its range (see the final Entity Life History for Supplier's Product in Figure 4.85).

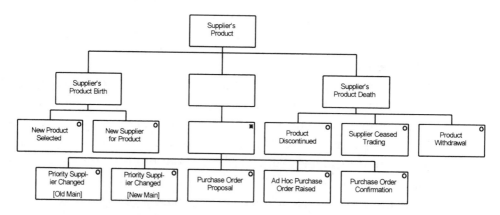

Figure 4.85 - Supplier's Product Entity Life History

Moving on to consider the Supplier Entity Life History, we find that we have a problem. In the structure of Figure 4.85 we have a mid-life sequence which says that for a given occurrence no events can intervene between Supplier Suspension and Supplier Reinstatement.

Unfortunately, this is not quite in tune with SRW's business rules. Firstly, if a supplier is suspended, SRW will still have to honour payment on any deliveries which have already been accepted. This means that Invoice Arrival event should be able to affect a suspended Supplier. Secondly, if the supplier's details (address, telephone number, contact name) change, then SRW will want these changes updated on the system, even if the supplier is currently suspended.

So we have some events which can happen regardless of the Supplier Suspension event, and some events which cannot happen once the Supplier Suspension event has happened (until the Supplier Reinstated event occurs).

Parallel Lives

In Entity Life History Analysis we use a parallel life to separate groups of unrelated effects in an entity's life history. In Figure 4.86 the parallel life is denoted using a double line which straddles two sub-structures. On the left-hand side of the parallel life we have the suspension-reinstatement sequence. The other events on that side of the parallel life can not occur if the Supplier Suspension event has just occurred.

The events on the right-hand side of the parallel life continue without regard for the supplier suspension-reinstatement sequence.

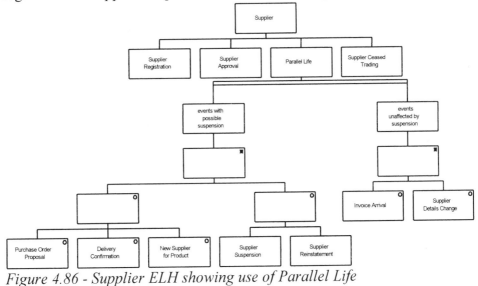

Figure 4.86 - Supplier ELH showing use of Parallel Life

Note that the Supplier Ceased Trading event is one which is outside of SRW's control. It is quite possible that this event could happen whilst a supplier is suspended. Unfortunately the Entity Life History for Supplier does not allow for this. Following the rules of the notation, the only event which is allowed to follow Supplier Suspension is Supplier Reinstatement (ignoring events in the parallel life). This is a problem which we can again deal with using the Quit and Resume notation (see Figure 4.87).

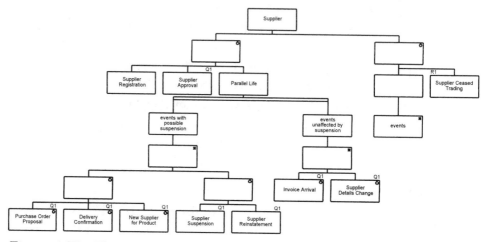

Figure 4.87 - The Supplier ELH

One final observation; we have forgotten to include the second of Purchase Order's birth events as a gain effect in the Supplier Entity Life History.

Down-pass analysis of behaviour

We should complete our Entity Life History Analysis by working from master to detail, looking in particular for extra death events, and at how death events cascade to detail entities. Finally we might consider the strategy for deleting entities.

In considering the Product and Supplier Entity Life Histories we have nothing else to add.

When it comes to the Supplier's Product Entity Life History, we have already shown the effects of the cascading death events of its masters. There are no further death events to add. We must, however, consider how the death of a Supplier's Product might affect its details.

In the case of Product Withdrawal we assume that any existing orders for this product will either be honoured by the supplier, or lapse when the required-by date expires.

In the case of Product Discontinued we find that this only constrains the placing of future purchase orders: existing orders for the discontinued product will not be automatically cancelled.

In the case of Supplier Ceased Trading, there will be a cascading of this event: it will result in the death of all Purchase Order, Purchase Order Lines and Deliveries of the Supplier in question. The effect on Purchase Order and Purchase Order Line can be seen in Figures 4.88 and 4.89.

The box named Death of Purchase Order in Figure 4.88 looks like a candidate for a super-event. We might hope to replace the two events Purchase Order Cancellation and Supplier Ceased Trading on the Purchase Order Line Entity Life History of Figure 4.89 with this super-event.

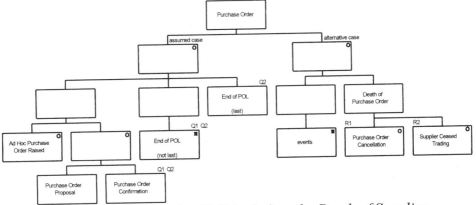

Figure 4.88 - Purchase Order ELH including the Death of Supplier

Unfortunately, the quit points for these two events in the life of Purchase Order Line are not the same, so we cannot replace them with a single super-event.

The astute reader will notice that there are several common patterns in the deaths of entities. The one we have just been considering is the cascading death (death of master is also the death of its details). Another common one is the death of last detail causing the death of the master (considered earlier).

Sub-types and aspects

In dealing with mutually exclusive behaviour patterns we have used the quit and resume notation. This enabled us to model as an assumed case the behaviour which was common to several lives, with the alternative cases dealing with the differences in those lives. Where there are several complex and mutually exclusive behaviour patterns to be dealt with the analyst may find it helpful to model these as separate structures by defining sub-types or aspects.

When dealing with sub-types there will be two structures: a super-type structure consists of super-events which represent the processing common to all the sub-types; and a sub-type structure which has a high level selection and an option for each sub-type life history.

For entity aspects, each aspect is modelled as a separate Entity Life History.

Deletion strategy

A death event does not remove an entity occurrence from the system; the entity remains available for enquiry purposes. Often users will require historical information based on dead entities. If this is not the case then we might consider deleting an entity upon its death.

If historical information is to be kept on the system, then we need to identify the event which will eventually cause its deletion (although some entities, may remain on the system for the life of that system).

We are likely to get the same patterns in deletion events as in death events e.g. deletion of master causes deletion of details.

In SRW, we have to keep an audit trail, meaning that each stock must be traceable to the delivery that gave rise to it. This means that the delivery and purchase order entities and their details cannot be deleted until all related stock records have been deleted. Stock records die when the quantity in stock reaches zero. They are deleted six months later (we have to introduce a new attribute to record the date of death in order to allow for this).

As an exercise the reader might like to complete the Entity Life Histories by adding deletion events.

4.9.3 ELH Operations and State Indicators

Operations

Each end-leaf on an ELH represents an effect on an entity. We have to describe each effect in detail, and to do this we add operations to the effects.

SSADM provides a standard set of logical operations to be used with Entity Life Histories:

- **Create *<Entity>***: creates a new occurrence of the entity. In this book we will omit the create operation from our Entity Life Histories and add it when we develop our Effect Correspondence Diagrams. The need for a create operation on an Entity Life History is implicit: it applies to every birth effect.
- **Set *<Attribute>***: changes the value of the named attribute to the new value input with the event.
- **Set *<Attribute>* using *<Expression>***: Sets *attribute* to the value resulting from the application of *expression* (e.g. a numeric calculation of the type "Today's date plus seven days").
- **Tie to *<Entity>***: Establishes a relationship with the master *entity*.

- **Cut from *<Entity>*:** Removes the relationship with the master *entity*.
- **Gain *<Entity>*:** Establishes a relationship with the detail *entity*. Where an occurrence of the event may cause more than one detail to be gained, we can use '*gain set of <entity>* '.
- **Lose *<Entity>*:** Removes the relationship with the detail *entity*. Again, we can use '*lose set of <entity>*' where more than one detail is being lost.
- **Invoke *<Process>*:** Invokes a named process. The process could be a super-event, common process or enquiry.

Operations have been added to the Entity Life Histories of Figure 4.89. Not every effect carries an operation. The death events of Purchase Order Line affect only its state (see next section). Operations that reflect changes in state will be built into the Effect Correspondence Diagrams, as will operations to read, write and delete entity occurrences. These are not usually added to the Entity Life History.

For every Gain in a master entity's Entity Life History there should be a Tie in the detail entity's Entity Life History and for every Lose in a master there should be a Cut in the detail.

In most environments gain and lose have no implementation, acting only to validate the Entity Life Histories by forcing the analyst to consider the interaction between events in a detail's life and those in its master. Gains and Losses can be omitted if they are found to be unhelpful.

Organisations may wish to define their own local standards for operations rather than using the default set suggested by SSADM.

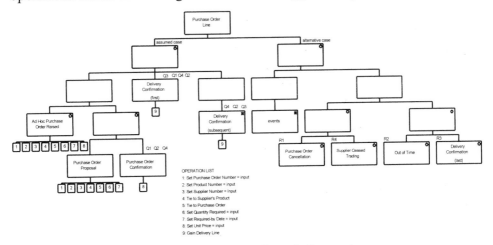

Figure 4.89 - Purchase Order Line ELH with Operations

State indicators

During Stage 3 we have used Entity Life Histories to model the required or allowed sequence of events for each entity. For example the Entity Life History fragment in Figure 4.90 tells us that the effects of event B cannot be applied to the entity until event A has finished.

In other words event B can only take place if it affects entity occurrences which are in the state resulting from event A.

The validation of event occurrences forms an important part of Conceptual Process Modelling, but specifying the checking of a *diagram* in a way that is implementable in program code is rather tricky.

So we will now make the state of an entity explicit by adding an extra attribute called a state indicator.

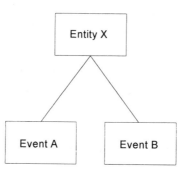

Figure 4.90 - Event B cannot precede Event A

By inspecting the state indicator of an entity occurrence we can answer two questions:

- Which event occurred last? Upon completion of an event the state indicator is set to a unique value within the entity.
- What events can occur next? For each event we will specify which state indicator values the entity must have for the event to be allowable.

This information is added to the ELH of each entity using the following notation:

*<Valid Previous Values>/<Value Set by Event> *

Valid Previous Values represents a list of the values that the state indicator can have for the event to be allowed.

Value Set by Event specifies the value the state indicator will be set to on completion of the event.

The values can be numbers, with a unique number for each state within an entity, or they can be words, reflecting the names of states.

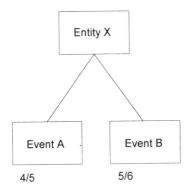

Figure 4.91 - ELH section showing State Indicators

For example, looking at Figure 4.91 we can see that event A can only take place if the state indicator has a previous value of 3 or 4. Once event A is complete the state indicator will be set to 5. Event B is then allowed to take place, and will result in a state indicator value of 6.

The values set by each event are only meaningful within the context of a single Entity Life History. The convention is for the first birth event in an Entity Life History to set the value to 1. As an entity occurrence will have no state indicator prior to its birth, the valid previous value for a birth event is -. Similarly, the value set by a deletion event would also be -.

State Indicator Rules

State Indicators are usually added to Entity Life Histories in two passes:

- The values set by each event are added.
- By examining the allowed sequences of events the valid previous values are added for each event.

Sequence

If the Entity Life History contains a sequence of events the value set by one event is the only valid previous value of the next event (as no other events can occur in-between) as in Figure 4.92.

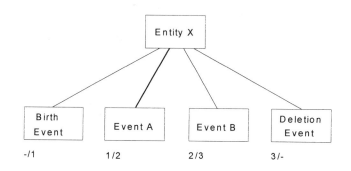

Figure 4.92 - State Indicators for Birth and Death Events

Selection

The valid previous values for all events in a selection will be the same. The values set by each event in the selection will be unique, unless one is a null selection, in which case it will leave the state indicator unchanged (denoted by /*).

The event that immediately follows the selection must include the 'set to' values of all selection events in its list of valid previous values (as any of them can occur) as shown in Figure 4.93.

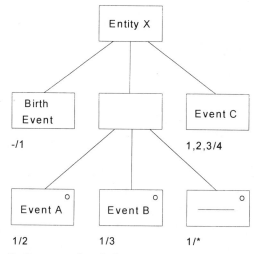

Figure 4.93 - State Indicators for Selections

Iteration

As an iterated event must include the possibility of being preceded by itself, the list of valid previous values must include its own 'set to' value.

The event that follows an iteration will include the valid previous values of the iteration in its own list of valid previous values, as an iteration can occur '*zero* or many' times, i.e. not occur at all (Figure 4.94).

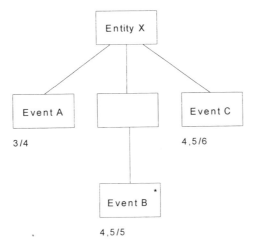

Figure 4.94 - State Indicators for Iterations

Quits and Resumes

The valid previous values of a resume effect are the same as the valid previous values of the corresponding quit effects.

Parallel Structures

The 'main leg' of a parallel structure will update the state indicator as normal. However, any parallel legs will leave it unchanged. This is because events in a parallel life have no effect on the position of the entity occurrence within its main life.

As a parallel life can occur at any point in the main life, the valid previous values for all parallel life effects will be made up of all valid previous values *plus* all set to values from the main life. The set to value for all events in the parallel life will be * as the indicator is unchanged.

If a parallel life itself contains a sequence of events then we will need to specify this in the same way as the main life sequence. This means introducing secondary state indicators that apply only to the parallel life structures. The notation for a parallel life state indicator is the same as for the main life indicator, but is differentiated from it by the use of brackets.

Adding State Indicators to an Entity Life History requires a little practice at first, but rapidly becomes a straightforward mechanistic process. No knowledge of the underlying effects or meaning of events is required, just an understanding of how to navigate through Entity Life History structures.

For this reason CASE tools will often generate state indicators automatically.

Optimised State Indicators

The optimisation of state indicators helps to make the update processes that check them easier to maintain, this will become clearer when we have developed Effect Correspondence Diagrams in the next section. Optimisation also facilitates the use of super-events. Furthermore, it helps us to identify named states which are probably more meaningful to the user.

State indicators are optimised in the following way:

- the set to values for each option of a selection are made the same
- the set to values of an iterated component can be made the same as the state which precedes the iteration

Figure 4.95 shows the same Entity Life History with normal, optimised and named state indicators.

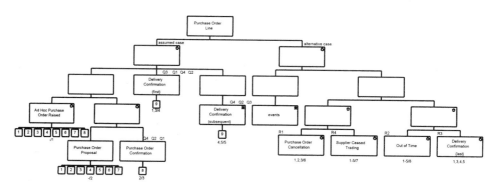

Figure 4.95a - Purchase Order Line ELH with Normal State Indicators

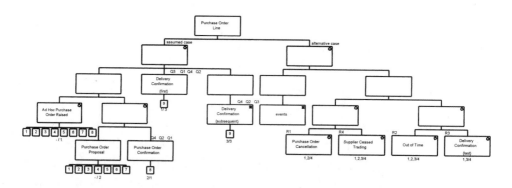

Figure 4.95b - Purchase Order Line ELH with Optimised State Indicators

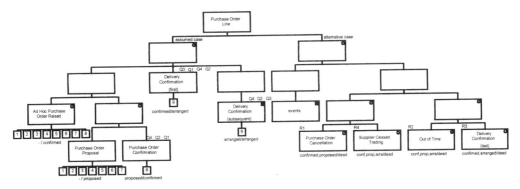

Figure 4.95c - Purchase Order Line ELH with Named State Indicators

4.9.4   Effect Correspondence Diagrams

Once we have completed Entity Life Histories for all entities in the Required System Logical Data Model we turn our attention to analysing effects from the perspective of the event, using Effect Correspondence Diagrams.

We develop Effect Correspondence Diagrams in order to illustrate which entities are affected by a given event. We also use them to define how the effects on these different entities correspond with each other, and ultimately to provide us with a specification of *update* processing. The development of Effect Correspondence Diagrams helps to clarify the work done during Entity Life History Analysis, and often the two techniques are used in tandem in order to validate each other.

Drawing Effect Correspondence Diagrams

The simplest and most effective way of drawing Effect Correspondence Diagrams is to follow the eight steps given below. A separate Effect Correspondence Diagram is developed for each event.

Draw a box for each entity

The Entity Access Matrix will show which entities have been affected by the event. Alternatively these could be identified from the Entity Life Histories directly. A good CASE tool will perform this step automatically.

If Entity Life History Analysis has not been performed then the analyst will have to develop Effect Correspondence Diagrams by reference to the Event and Enquiry Catalogue, Function Definitions and Logical Data Model, trying to gain as full an understanding of the effects of the event as possible.

In any case, the analyst should refer to the Event and Enquiry Catalogue to gain an overview of the processing which is triggered by the event.

Each entity affected is represented as a soft box containing the entity name. A separate box is drawn for each aspect, super-type and sub-types, where these have been used.

For the Purchase Order Proposal event, the following boxes will be drawn:

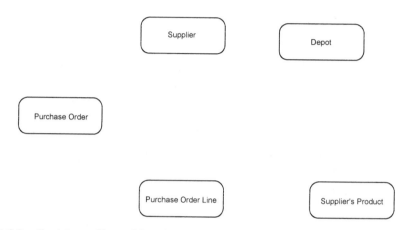

Figure 4.96 - Entities affected by the Purchase Order Proposal Event

Add all effects of events

Where entity roles (simultaneous effects) and effect qualifiers (alternative effects) have been shown on Entity Life Histories, these have to be added to the Effect Correspondence Diagram:

- alternative effects are represented by making the entity a selection, with each option showing one of the possible effects (each box will contain the entity name with an effect qualifier in round brackets)
- simultaneous effects are represented by drawing a separate box for each effect (each box will contain the entity name, with the role name in square brackets).

Again, a good CASE tool will assist in this step.

Readers will remember that the Product Substitute Defined event affects two occurrences of product:

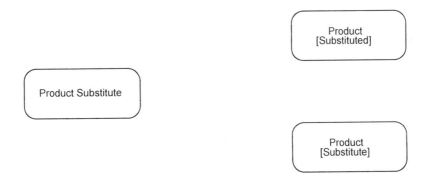

Figure 4.97 - Representation of Entity Roles on an ECD

And if we refer back to the Entity Life History for Purchase Order Line, we will see that the Delivery Confirmation event can have one of three different effects on Purchase Order Line:

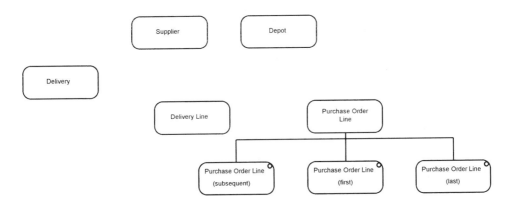

Figure 4.98 - Representation of Effect Qualifiers on an ECD

Identify entry point

This is the first entity to be processed. The input data must contain enough information to identify the required occurrence(s) of the entry point entity.

There may be more than one potential entry point entity. In this case, several entry points can be defined, and the order of processing can be deferred as an implementation decision.

For the Purchase Order Proposal event we will choose Purchase Order as the entry point; for Product Substitute Defined we will choose Product Substitute; and for Delivery Confirmation the entry point will be Delivery.

The entry point is shown on the Effect Correspondence Diagram using an arrow, against which is listed the data which is required as input to the event (see Figure 4.99).

Define correspondences

A correspondence shows an access to a non-entry point entity. A correspondence is shown with an arrow. We have to be sure that for each entity there is a way of identifying which occurrences are to be affected. Usually a correspondence arrow will trace a relationship between two entities, but there are two exceptions:

- a detail is not directly related to a master, but contains its key as part of a compound key
- there is enough data in the event data to identify the correct occurrence(s).

Sometimes it will be necessary to navigate via another entity to identify an affected entity. This access should be shown as a read on the Entity Access Matrix.

Returning to the Purchase Order Proposal event, for each Purchase Order which is affected there will be one Supplier affected, and for each Purchase Order Line affected there will be one Supplier's Product affected:

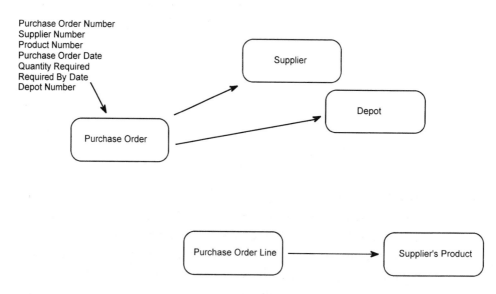

Figure 4.99 - Correspondence of Effects

Deal with iterations

Where there is navigation from a master to a detail, it is necessary to decide how many occurrences of the detail are affected per occurrence of the event. Where more than one detail occurrence can be affected, we use a 'Set of' box, and connect it to the iterated effect, which is marked with an asterisk.

The creation of a Purchase Order will result in the creation of one or more Purchase Order Lines. Thus the effect on Purchase Order Line is iterated. Note that many occurrences of Supplier's Product will be affected too - one for each Purchase Order Line. This correspondence was identified in the previous step.

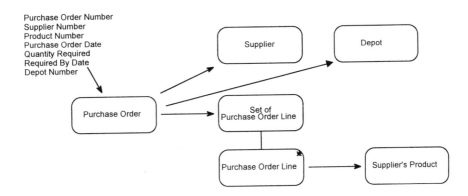

Figure 4.100 - Iterated Effects

The Effect Correspondence Diagrams for Delivery Confirmation and Product Substitute Defined are similarly developed by defining entry points, identifying correspondences and considering iterations:

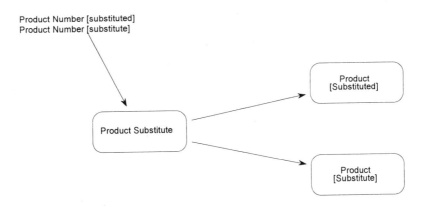

Figure 4.101 - Effect Correspondence Diagram for Product Substitute Defined

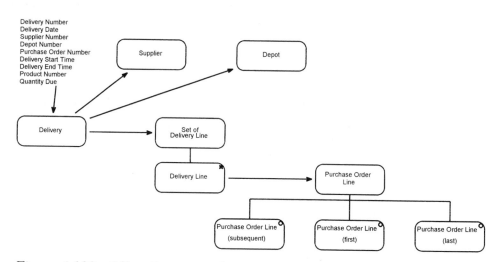

Figure 4.102 - Effect Correspondence Diagram for Delivery Confirmation

Add conditions

A condition can be added to each option and each iteration. The condition must state the circumstances under which an option is to occur, or an iteration is to continue.

Typically a condition which is attached to an option will evaluate an attribute value (this might include state indicator values).

Add operations

The effects that appear on Effect Correspondence Diagrams are the same effects that appear on Entity Life Histories. On the Effect Correspondence Diagram the effect carries the name of the entity affected, whilst on the Entity Life History the effect carries the name of the event which causes the effect.

Thus each effect on an Effect Correspondence Diagram has already been described with operations on an Entity Life History. These operations can be carried forward to the Effect Correspondence Diagram.

There are further operations to add. These are database operations to create/read and write/delete entity occurrences; and integrity operations to check and set state indicator values. A checklist of the necessary operations is given in Figure 4.103.

The fail operations are used whenever an entity is read. The format of a fail operation is *Fail if SI value of entity outside 'range'* where *'range'* is the valid previous value(s) for the effect, as shown on the Entity Life History. Similarly, the Set SI operation is of the form *Set SI of entity =*

'*value*' where '*value*' is the set to value for the effect, as shown on the Entity Life History.

For a birth effect:	For a deletion effect:	For other effects:
Create <entity>	Read <entity>	Read <entity>
ELH operations	Fail if SI of <entity> <>	Fail if SI of <entity> <>
Set SI =	ELH operations	ELH operations
Write <entity>	Delete <entity>	Set SI =
		Write <entity>

Figure 4.103 - Operations for Effect Correspondence Diagrams

The Effect Correspondence Diagram for Purchase Order Proposal, complete with operations and conditions, is shown in Figure 4.104.

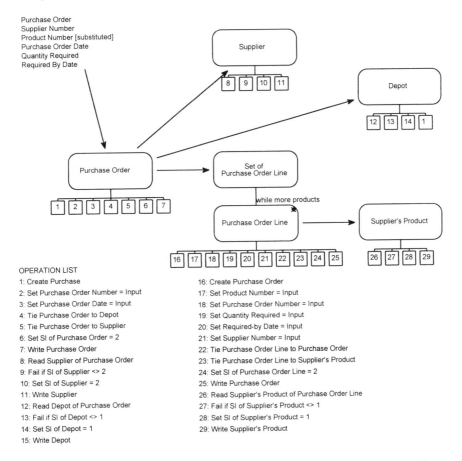

Purchase Order
Supplier Number
Product Number [substituted]
Purchase Order Date
Quantity Required
Required By Date

OPERATION LIST

1: Create Purchase
2: Set Purchase Order Number = Input
3: Set Purchase Order Date = Input
4: Tie Purchase Order to Depot
5: Tie Purchase Order to Supplier
6: Set SI of Purchase Order = 2
7: Write Purchase Order
8: Read Supplier of Purchase Order
9: Fail if SI of Supplier <> 2
10: Set SI of Supplier = 2
11: Write Supplier
12: Read Depot of Purchase Order
13: Fail if SI of Depot <> 1
14: Set SI of Depot = 1
15: Write Depot

16: Create Purchase Order
17: Set Product Number = Input
18: Set Purchase Order Number = Input
19: Set Quantity Required = Input
20: Set Required-by Date = Input
21: Set Supplier Number = Input
22: Tie Purchase Order Line to Purchase Order
23: Tie Purchase Order Line to Supplier's Product
24: Set SI of Purchase Order Line = 2
25: Write Purchase Order
26: Read Supplier's Product of Purchase Order Line
27: Fail if SI of Supplier's Product <> 1
28: Set SI of Supplier's Product = 1
29: Write Supplier's Product

Figure 4.104 - Final Effect Correspondence Diagram for Purchase Order Proposal

4.9.5 Enquiry Access Paths

We considered informal validation of access paths earlier in the text, but in Step 360 we build formal access models for all enquiries (other than ad-hoc enquiries). Each Enquiry Access Path will document the required data model accesses resulting from an enquiry trigger (the non-update equivalent of an event), using the same notation as that used for Effect Correspondence Diagrams.

Enquiry Access Paths serve two very important purposes. Firstly they validate the Logical Data Model against the users' information requirements. In other words, they demonstrate that the database design is capable of providing the reports and answering the queries that users have identified. Secondly they provide an unambiguous specification of each enquiry process. Therefore they can be used by the database programmer as the basis for writing code.

Understanding Enquiry Access Paths

Before we look at the technique for drawing them we will try to get an understanding of Enquiry Access Paths by walking through a typical diagram. In Figure 4.105 we have an Enquiry Access Path for the Purchase Order Query. The Function Definition for this enquiry reads:

> For a given supplier return details of all confirmed purchase orders, giving the numbers and names of the depots that placed them, and giving a full description of each purchase order line, including the name and quantity of the product ordered.

We will start at the top left-hand point of the diagram where there is an arrow labelled Supplier Number.

Supplier Number is part of the enquiry trigger; it is the data item entered by the user in order for this enquiry to take place. You can think of the arrow as saying 'find the Supplier with the Supplier Number that matches the one input by the user'. This arrow is known as the entry point arrow.

The soft box marked Supplier represents an access to the Supplier entity: the reading of one instance of Supplier. On an Enquiry Access Path the entity access which is annotated with the enquiry trigger is known as the entry point of the enquiry. So for this enquiry Supplier is the entry point entity.

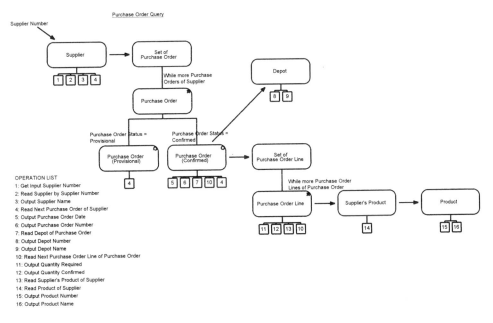

Figure 4.105 - EAP for Purchase Order Query

The access to Supplier is described in detail by the operations which are attached to it:

- Get Input Supplier Number accepts the enquiry trigger which is input by the user via the function which invokes the enquiry.

- Read Supplier by Supplier Number is an instruction to find the one entity occurrence which matches the input Supplier Number.

- Having read an occurrence of Supplier it is possible to output to the user (via the function which invoked the enquiry) the required attribute instances of Supplier. Hence the operation: output Supplier Name.

The arrow from the box named Supplier, to the one named Set of Purchase Orders says 'find all the Purchase Orders where the Supplier Number foreign key in Purchase Order matches the Supplier Number of the Supplier just found' i.e. find the Purchase Orders of the Supplier chosen by the user.

Because there is a one-to-many relationship between Supplier and Purchase Order there is a good chance that the enquiry will find more than one matching Purchase Order, hence the iteration 'Set of Purchase Orders'. The box labelled Purchase Order (with an asterisk in the top right-hand corner) represents each matching Purchase Order found. Of course there is the possibility that no Purchase Order will be found for the selected Supplier.

Each arrow on the diagram is described by a read operation. The arrow from Supplier to Set of Purchase Orders is described by the operation Read Next Purchase Order of Supplier. This operation appears twice. An iterated access on an Enquiry Access Path represents the one-by-one processing of a set of entity occurrences. To perform this processing the first occurrence has to be read, the processing of that occurrence can then be carried out, and then the next occurrence can be read and processed. This loop continues until there are no more occurrences to be processed.

This enquiry only requires details of confirmed Purchase Orders. For this reason the Purchase Order access is a selection, with two options below it labelled Purchase Order (Confirmed) and Purchase Order (Provisional). The Purchase Order (Provisional) access has no further arrows emanating from it, and only one operation: Read Next Purchase Order of Supplier. This means that if the enquiry finds a provisional Purchase Order it will do nothing except go on to read the next Purchase Order of the selected Supplier and see whether that one is provisional or confirmed (this cycle will continue until all the selected supplier's purchase orders have been processed).

When the enquiry finds a confirmed Purchase Order there is further processing to be done. The arrow to Depot says 'for each confirmed Purchase Order find the Depot whose primary key value matches the foreign key value of Depot Id in Purchase Order'. The box labelled Depot represents an access to the Depot entity, and the output operations identify the Depot attributes which are required as output.

In following the arrow from confirmed Purchase Order to set of Purchase Order Lines, we see a similar pattern repeating itself. The arrow says 'for each confirmed Purchase Order find all the Purchase Order Lines which belong to it'; the iterated Purchase Order Line represents a one-by-one access to each Purchase Order Line; the arrow to Supplier's Product says 'for each Purchase Order Line read the one Supplier's Product which matches it'; and the arrow to Product says 'for each Supplier's Product read the one Product which matches it'.

Drawing Enquiry Access Paths

SSADM suggests a number of steps for drawing Enquiry Access Paths:

Define enquiries

Enquiries should already be documented in the Requirements Catalogue and each one should be named in at least one Function Definition. An enquiry should have a unique name and because we develop one Enquiry Access Path for each enquiry, we use the enquiry name as the title of the Enquiry Access Path.

Each enquiry should be entered on to the Entity Access Matrix and documented in the Event and Enquiry Catalogue, as discussed earlier.

We will take the Purchase Order Query as our initial example.

Note that the enquiry requests details 'for a given supplier'. In order that this enquiry can take place, the user will have to supply the system with the Supplier Number. If we looked at the I/O Structure for the Purchase Order Query we would see that the Supplier Number appears as an input on the I/O Structure Diagram.

Data items which are input to an enquiry process so that the required information can be produced are known as the enquiry trigger. We should cross-check every Enquiry Access Path with the Function Definitions to ensure that any data which is required by an enquiry as a trigger is supplied by its related function.

Identify the entities we require access to

We do this by looking at the required output of the enquiry and identifying the entities which have as their attributes the output data items.

For the Purchase Order Query we will need access to Supplier, Purchase Order, Purchase Order Line, Product and Depot.

If the only information we required on Depot was Depot Id, it would be available as a foreign key in the Purchase Order entity (as Depot is a master of Purchase Order), and so we would not need to access the Depot entity itself. However we will assume that we require Depot Name as well, and so will need to read Depot.

Draw the required view of the Logical Data Structure

Having identified the required entities we can draw an extract of the Logical Data Model containing only those entities. A good CASE tool will remove the need for this step by allowing the user to select the required entities from the Logical Data Structure and then automatically generating a first cut Enquiry Access Path.

The required view of the Logical Data Structure includes the Supplier's Product entity. None of the attributes of Supplier's Product are required by the enquiry, but it provides an access path to product.

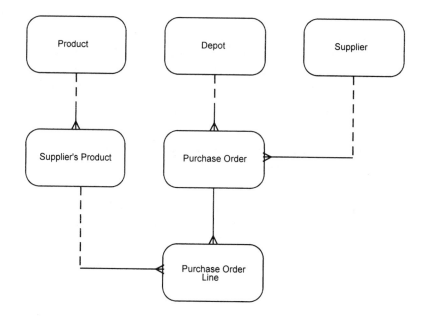

Figure 4.106 - Required View of Logical Data Structure

Develop an initial Enquiry Access Path

Enquiry Access Path diagrams use the same notation as Effect Correspondence Diagrams.

Accesses to detail entities from a master entity are shown as iterations. The entity name is placed in the iterated box and a parent box is placed above with the words 'Set of' followed by the entity name (Figure 4.107).

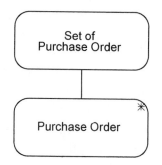

Figure 4.107 - Accesses to Detail Entities are shown as Iterations

Selections are added where necessary. Selections are used where the processing will follow a different path, depending on the state of the entity occurrence accessed. Each option of a selection will contain the relevant entity name, qualified in some way (see Figure 4.108). Note that a condition will be attached to each selection, and that the condition must have a way of being evaluated. In the example below, there must be an attribute of Purchase Order which tells us whether a purchase order is confirmed or provisional.

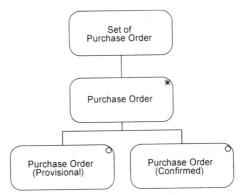

Figure 4.108 - Adding Selections to EAPs

Where access is required from one entity to another we connect the relevant boxes with a single-headed arrow, indicating the direction of the access (Figure 4.109). When the access is from master to detail there will always be a 'set of detail entity' box at the head of the arrow. We try to have the arrows pointing horizontally, which has the effect of showing master to detail accesses cascading down the page.

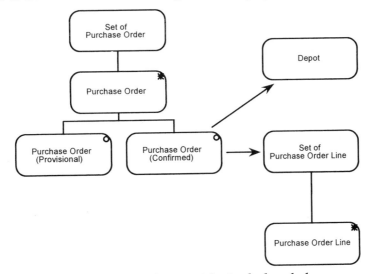

Figure 4.109 - Accesses are shown with single-headed arrows

Applying these rules to Purchase Order Query results in the Enquiry Access Path shown in Figure 4.110.

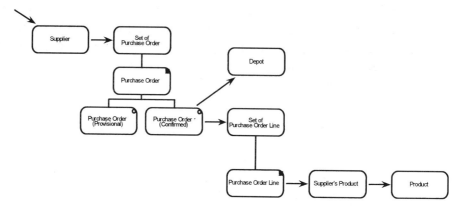

Figure 4.110 - Purchase Order Query

Add entry points

There are two main types of entry allowed on Enquiry Access Paths: single occurrence and multiple occurrence.

- When the enquiry trigger contains the primary key of the entry point entity then only one occurrence of the entry point entity will be read.
- When the enquiry trigger contains non-key attributes of the entry point entity, or parameters for selecting occurrences of the entity within some range of attribute values, then many occurrences of the entry point entity will be read.
- A special case is where the enquiry trigger contains no selection criteria and all occurrences of the entry point entity are to be read.

In the Purchase Order Query example we are dealing with a single occurrence of Supplier, so Supplier Number is added to the Enquiry Access Path alongside the entry point arrow.

If we wanted the enquiry to return details of confirmed purchase orders for all suppliers then the Enquiry Access Path would start like the one shown in Figure 4.111.

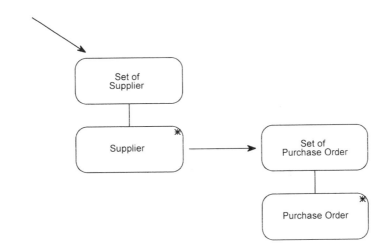

Figure 4.111 - Selecting all Occurrences of Supplier

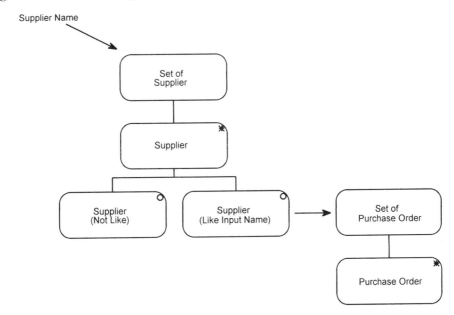

Figure 4.112 - Selecting Suppliers with name matching input string

Entry via a foreign key is *not* allowed. If we identify a need to access an entity via a foreign key, we do so via the relevant master entity's primary key.

Add operations

The operations which can be added to an Enquiry Access Path are a subset of those used on Effect Correspondence Diagrams. There will be one read operation for each arrow on the Enquiry Access Path. The allowable read operations are:

- Read using the primary key (for a single occurrence entry point).
- Read next detail entity of a master (for an access to a 'set of')
- Read the master entity of a detail.

If the Enquiry Access Path does not give us access to all required data using only these kinds of read, then we may need to introduce new relationships or attributes to the Required System Logical Data Model. In this way we may uncover business rules which have been missed from the Logical Data Model.

If we look again at the Enquiry Access Path in Figure 4.104 we find the following read operations taking place:

- Direct read of Supplier using Supplier Number (the primary key).
- Read next Purchase Order (a detail) of Supplier (the master).
- For each confirmed Purchase Order read the master entity Depot, and the next Purchase Order Line (a detail).
- For each Purchase Order Line read the master entity Supplier's Product.
- For each Supplier's Product read the master entity Product.

All of these operations are of allowable types, and so the Enquiry Access Path reveals no obvious problems with the Logical Data Model.

One point to note is that the access to Supplier's Product was made purely for navigation i.e. as a way of reading the Product of the Purchase Order Line. The enquiry did not require any output from Supplier's Product.

As it happens, there is a direct access path from Purchase Order Line to Product. Product Number appears in Purchase Order Line as part of the foreign key which has cascaded down from Supplier's Product. This access path has not been shown as a relationship on the Logical Data Structure because it is redundant, but it would be more efficient to use it. This case is the one exception to the rule that a non entry-point arrow on an Enquiry Access Path must be supported by a relationship on the Logical Data Structure.

As well as read operations we can also add operations to output the data items required by the enquiry. These data items will be attributes of the entities concerned, or derived from those attributes.

A note on the placement of operations

Operations should be added to each entity access, from left to right, in the order in which they are going to be executed.

To simplify the placing of operations on Enquiry Access Paths, we have adopted a convention which says that when a read operation is reached, the operations of the entity which is the subject of that read operation will be carried out. When these are complete, processing will return to the next operation after the read operation, where there is one.

Referring to Figure 4.104, this means that upon reaching the Read Depot of Purchase Order operation, the Depot access will be made, the Output Depot Name and Output Depot operations will take place, followed by the Read Next Purchase Order Line of Purchase Order operation, followed by the operations under Purchase Order Line etc., before returning to read the next Purchase Order and start the process all over again.

If preferred, extra structure boxes can be added to the Enquiry Access Path, and operations can be added to it just as they would on an Enquiry Process Model.

In Step 530 we have the option of converting each Enquiry Access Path into an Enquiry Process Model. An Enquiry Process Model is a proper Jackson structure and is totally unambiguous in describing the order in which operations are to be executed. The placement of operations on Enquiry Access Paths is optional, although it is a good idea if the Enquiry Access Path is to be the final process specification i.e. if Enquiry Process Models are not going to be developed. Since read operations are implied by arrows, the addition of read operations to an Enquiry Access Path could be considered unnecessary: a compromise might be to record only get, set and output operations on the Enquiry Access Path.

Document entry point on the Required System Logical Data Model

This simply involves annotating the Logical Data Structure with a small arrow pointing to the entry entity, with the entry attributes listed below. This information will be useful in Physical Design, as we shall see.

More than one access type per entity

In the above example each entity or set of entities was accessed just once. However this is not always the case. For example, let us consider the following enquiry:

> For a given Depot output the Depot Number and Depot Name and list all Transfers (Transfer Number, Transfer Date) made from that Depot since a given date. For each

Transfer output the Depot Number and Depot Name of the Depot which received the Transfer.

In this case we require more than one visit to the Depot entity. The first access is a direct one using the primary key value provided. We will then need to access all Transfers of the selected Depot, via the 'From' Relationship.

For each Transfer we then read the Depot occurrence which is related via the 'To' relationship.

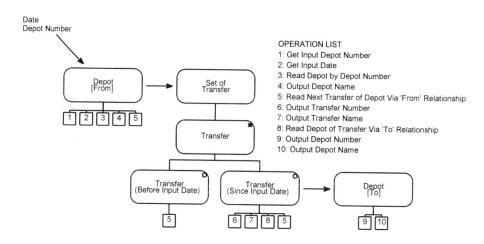

Figure 4.113 - Enquiry Access Path for Transfer Enquiry

Note that the operations for this Enquiry Access Path identify which of the two relationships between Transfer and Depot is being used at any one time. If the read from the original Depot was made along the 'To' relationship, we would find all the transfers *in* to that Depot. This is not what the user wants.

Derived output data items

Our final example of an Enquiry Access Path involves the calculation of a derived data item. A derived data item is one which is not stored as an attribute of an entity type, but is calculated from stored attributes.

In our example we suppose that a purchaser requires a report which lists the total value of all orders placed with a given supplier.

There are three operations to take note of:

Operation number four declares a variable named Total Value and sets its value to zero. This has to happen once, at the beginning of the enquiry, which is why the operation has been placed on the Supplier access.

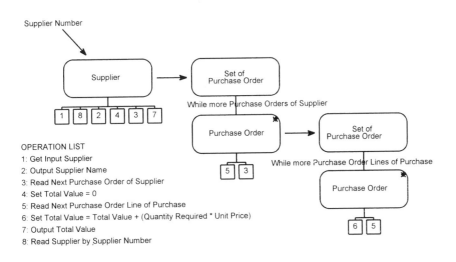

Supplier Number

OPERATION LIST
1: Get Input Supplier
2: Output Supplier Name
3: Read Next Purchase Order of Supplier
4: Set Total Value = 0
5: Read Next Purchase Order Line of Purchase
6: Set Total Value = Total Value + (Quantity Required * Unit Price)
7: Output Total Value
8: Read Supplier by Supplier Number

Figure 4.114 -Enquiry Access Path showing calculated totals

The next operation of note is operation number six. This calculates the value of the Purchase Order Line and adds it to the Total Value. This operation has to happen once per Purchase Order Line, which is why it is placed on the Purchase Order Line access.

Finally, when all the Purchase Order Lines of the selected Supplier have been processed, we have to output the Total Value. This will happen once per running of the enquiry, which is why operation number seven appears on the Supplier access.

4.9.6   Logical Data Structure Volumes

Before leaving Step 360, we have one final task to perform, that of annotating the Logical Data Structure with estimated entity and relationship volumes.

A knowledge of the expected volumes is important in the Technical System Options stage, and in Physical Design. Although this information will probably be used by experts in database tuning and Capacity Planning, rather than by SSADM analysts, it is the systems analyst who is best placed to collect the information in the first place.

Figure 4.115 shows an extract of the SRW Logical Data Structure with volumes and entry points added.

The number in the top right-hand corner of each entity is an estimate of the average number of occurrences of that entity. The number on each relationship is an estimate of how many detail entity occurrences will be related to each master entity occurrence.

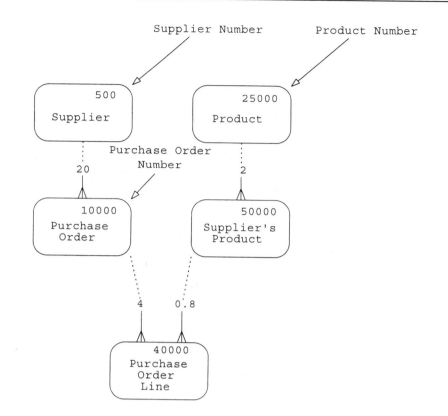

Figure 4.115 - Logical Data Structure Volumes

4.9.7   Summary (Step 360)

The SSADM tasks carried out in Step 360 are:

Task

10   Develop the Entity Access Matrix, and document each event and enquiry in the Event and Enquiry Catalogue.

20   Develop Entity Life Histories incrementally.

Add operations and state indicators to the Entity Life Histories.

30   Create an Effect Correspondence Diagram for each event and an Enquiry Access Path for each enquiry.

Cross-check the event data and enquiry triggers with input data on each related function.

40   Update the Requirements Catalogue and Logical Data Model to reflect any new requirements identified during Entity Life History Analysis.
Define or redefine functions (by repeating Step 330) for any new events.

50   Annotate the Logical Data Model with entry points and volumetric information.

4.10   Step 370 - Confirm System Objectives

During Stage 3 we will continually uncover additional or revised user requirements. The purpose of Step 370 is to carry out a formal review of functional and non-functional requirements to ensure that they are fully described and associated with relevant requirements specification products. We will then be in a position to move on to the Logical System Specification module and detailed process design, with a verified and complete Requirements Specification under our belts.

The following review tasks should be carried out:

Task

10   Ensure that all functional and non-functional requirements are fully defined. Check that each Requirements Catalogue entry is cross-referenced with the Function Definition which satisfies it, and that this is cross-referenced with the other products that specify it.

20   Define any new or outstanding non-functional requirements in the Requirements Catalogue, Function Definitions or Required System Logical Data Model.

30   Ensure that each Function Definition is fully defined, including service level requirements.

40   Ensure that the Required System Logical Data Model is fully defined.

4.11   The products of Requirements Specification

The products below should be checked for completeness, cross-checked for consistency and published along with any covering summary or project management reports required by the organisations standards.

- Data Catalogue
- Requirements Catalogue
- Entity Life Histories

- Event and Enquiry Catalogue and Entity Access Matrix
- Function Definitions
- User Role/Function Matrix
- Effect Correspondence Diagrams and Enquiry Access Paths
- Required System Logical Data Model

These are the products which SSADM regards as comprising the Requirements Specification and which will be carried forward into the Logical Design.

The Required System Data Flow Model is not included in the list as it has in effect served its purpose as an analysis tool. Further detailed specification of the new systems processing will revolve around the concept of the function and associated events and enquiries. However, in practice, the Required System Data Flow Model will remain a useful reference document, so we might choose to include it in our completeness and consistency checks.

4.12 Requirements Definition Exercises

4.1 *(I/O Structures)* Produce an I/O Structure (diagram and description) for the following Treebanks enquiry function description:

'When a playing court number is entered into the system it should return a list of all the sessions for which the court has been booked, giving details of the member or team that placed each booking.'

Assume that the following attribute names are all that are needed:

> Court No.
> Session No.
> Session Start Time
> Session End Time
> Member No.
> Member Name
> Team No.
> Team Name

4.2 *(I/O Structures)* Produce an I/O Structure (diagram and description) for the following Natlib off-line function description:

'Every Friday at 11.00 a.m. the system should produce a report of all overdue loans. The report should be broken down by due return date (longest overdue first), and provide details of the reader, book title and copy for each loan.'

Assume that the following attribute names are all that are needed:

Due Return Date
Loan No.
Book ISBN
Book Title.
Reader No.
Reader Name
Reader Address
Reader Tel. No.
Book Copy No.

4.3 *(I/O Structures)* Produce an I/O Structure (diagram and description) for the Bodgett & Son function 'Record Estimate Decision':

'The estimate number should be entered and the customer's details displayed for confirmation. The user should then have a choice of entering an acceptance or rejection for each individual job within the estimate. When decisions are entered there will often be a mix of acceptances or rejections, and job details should be displayed for each job number for confirmation. Details of any jobs for which no decision has been recorded should then be displayed.'

The following attribute names are derived from the I/O Description associated with this function along with appropriate system responses:

Estimate No.
Customer No.
Customer Name
Customer Address
Job Decision
Job No.
Job Description

4.4 *(Relational Data Analysis)* Normalise (to 3NF) the I/O Structure produced in exercise 4.1.

4.5 *(Relational Data Analysis)* Normalise (to 3NF) the I/O Structure produced in exercise 4.2.

4.6 *(Relational Data Analysis)* Normalise (to 3NF) the I/O Structure produced in exercise 4.3.

4.7 *(I/O Structures)* Translate the 'Customer Invoice' and 'Customer Request Form' physical layouts overleaf into I/O Structures. These two reports are required by the current system of the Fresco ticket agency of exersises 2.1 & 2.2. You may assume that all Fresco's customers are allocated a customer number, each performance has a number, e.g. 2341, and a performance may be requested at more than one venue.

```
FRESCO TICKET AGENCY
        1 High Street
          London
          W1 1AA
      Tel: 0171 911 5000
Invoice No:  12345
Date: 29/02/00

Customer:        113557
                 F. Bloggs
                 25 Low Rd
                 Hightown NE4 8QT
                 0155 23675

Performance:     Mozart Symphony 40, LCO      (No: 2341)
Venue:           London Concert Centre
                 25 South St
                 London

Date: 14/03/00   Time: 8.00 p.m.

Tickets:         2 at £10
                 2 at £12

Performance:     Macbeth                      (No: 2452)
Venue:           London Theatre
                 1 The Parade
                 London

Date: 19/04/00   Time: 7.00 p.m.

Tickets:         4 at £20

                            Total Cost:  £124
                            Payment by:  Credit Card
                            Number:      6319 0621 9914
```

```
                    CUSTOMER REQUEST FORM

Customer:        113557
                 F. Bloggs
                 25 Low Rd
                 Hightown  NE4 8QT
                 0155 23675

Performance:     Mozart Symphony 36, LCO
Venue:           London Concert Centre
                 25 South St
                 London

Preferred Dates:  07/03/00   14/03/00   21/03/00
Price Range:      £10 - 12
Number of Tickets: 4

Performance:     Haydn Symphony 104, LCO
Venue:           London Concert Centre
                 25 South St
                 London

Preferred Dates:  13/04/00
Price Range:      £20 - 25
Number of Tickets:  6
```

4.8 *(Relational Data Analysis)* Normalise the I/O Structures produced in exercise 4.7. Produce a Logical Data Structure from them.

4.9 *(Entity Life Histories)* Using the information below produce an ELH for the Treebanks entity 'Session':

Every Friday the manager of Treebanks arranges the playing sessions for the week beginning in four weeks time. At the same time the records of playing sessions from four weeks ago are deleted.

Each session is booked either by a team or a member. The booking may subsequently be cancelled, in which case it will become available for re-booking. When the team or member arrives to play on the booked court the session is marked as played.

The Entity Access Matrix for Treebanks records the following events for the entity Session:

Make Team Booking	(M)
Make Member Booking	(M)
Cancel Booking	(M)
Play Session	(M)
Arrange Sessions	(C/D)

4.10 *(Entity Life Histories)* Using the write-up for exercise 2.27 and the information below produce an ELH for the Bodgett & Son entity Estimate:

Estimates are always booked to be carried out either by a surveyor or by an employee right from the start. However, it will sometimes be necessary to change this booking before the estimate is completed.

Customers may respond to a completed estimate in several stages; accepting or rejecting some of the constituent jobs on each occasion.

If no response is received from customers after five weeks a reminder letter is to be sent. If there is still no response after a further four weeks the estimate will be marked as expired.

Records of estimates will be kept for twelve months following their expiry or completion of the last job detailed on them.

Some of the more important attributes of Estimate are:

> Estimate No.
> Estimate Request Date
> Estimate Booking Date
> Estimate Completion Date
> No. of Jobs
> No. of Jobs Responded To
> Reminder Letter Date
> Expiry Date

Hint: Begin the exercise by listing the events that affect Estimate, as in the row of an Entity Access Matrix.

4.11 *(ELH operations)* Add operations to the ELH for Estimate.

4.12 *(Effect Correspondence Diagrams)* Using the write-up for exercises 2.27 and 4.10 produce an ECD for the event Respond to Estimate in the Bodgett & Son system. The ELHs for Bodgett & Son reveal that the following entities are affected by Respond to Estimate:

> Estimate
> Job

Assume that the Current Environment LDS from exercise 2.28 still applies in the Required System.

4.13 *(Effect Correspondence Diagrams)* Using the write-up for exercise 4.9 produce an ECD for the event Arrange Session.

Hint: The LDS from exercise 2.8 will provide the basis for the ECD structure but you will need to consider the effects of this event on any link entity between Session and Equipment.

4.14 *(Enquiry Access Paths)* Produce an EAP for the Treebanks enquiry report in exercise 4.1, using the LDS from exercise 2.8.

4.15 *(Enquiry Access Paths)* Produce EAPs for the reports in question 4.7.

4.16 *(Method)* In the context of the SSADM default structure, explain why Function Point Analysis performed after Function Definition and Relational Data Analysis would be more accurate than Function Point Analysis done during Business Systems Options.

4.17 *(Entity Life Histories)* Using the information given below complete the Entity Access Matrix for the video rental system and develop Entity Life Histories for each entity.

A video rental system is described by the logical data model in Figure 4.116. An (incomplete) Entity Access Matrix for the system is given in Figure 4.117. The system keeps information about the hire and return of videos by customers of a chain of video stores. Customers register at a specific video store. The chain maintains a list of video titles, and copies of each title are available for hire at each store. Customers hire one or more videos at a time, and although each copy of a title can only be on loan to one member at a time, there is a need to keep a historical record of who has borrowed what.

Video titles can be withdrawn at any time, after which no more copies of the title will be purchased by the video stores. A record of a video title will not be deleted from the system until the last copy of that title has been sold or destroyed.

When a video store closes, all its video copies, and all its members are transferred to a replacement store (i.e. they are all transferred to one store, as designated by the company's head office).

Sometimes a member of a video store will lose or damage a video that they have rented. This is treated as "copy sale or destruction".

A member cannot be removed from the system whilst he or she still has videos out on rent.

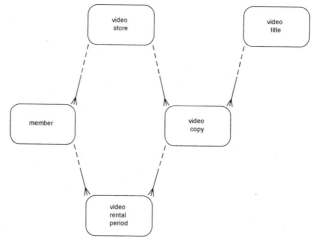

Figure 4.116 - Video Store LDS

Video Copy
(Title Code)
(Copy Number)
*Store Number
Date of Purchase
Daily Rate
On Rental Indicator

Video Rental Period
(Title Code)
(Copy Number)
Member Number
Video Rental Date
Return Date
Amount Charged

Video Title
Title Code
Title Name
Title Description
Number of Copies Held

Video Store
Store Number
Store Name
Store Address
Store Manager
Total Video Stock

Member
Member Number
Member Name
Member Address
*Store Number
Copies Currently On Rental

NB. the 'on rental indicator' attribute of video copy is set to yes when the copy is on loan, and to no when it is available for hire.

ENTITY EVENT/ ENQUIRY	Title	Video Store	Member	Video Copy	Video Rental Period
Copy Purchase					
Copy Sale or Destruction					
Membership Approval					
Membership Removal					
Store Closure					
Store Opening					
Title Release					
Title Withdrawal					
Video Rental					
Video Return					

Figure 4.117: Incomplete Entity Access Matrix

4.18 *(Effect Correspondence Diagrams)* Use the Entity Life Histories of question 4.17 to develop Effect Correspondence Diagrams for the events Copy Sale or Destruction, and Store Closure. For Copy Sale or Destruction the event data is Title Code, Copy Number; for Store Closure the event data is Store Number [closing store] and Store Number [opening store].

4.19 *(Effect Correspondence Diagrams)* Use the Entity Life Histories of question 4.17 to develop Effect Correspondence Diagrams for the rest of the events shown in Figure 4.117.

4.20 *(Enquiry Access Paths)* Draw Enquiry Access Paths for the following enquiries: 1) List all stores. For each store give store number, store name, and manager name. 2) For a given member, find the number of copies currently on rental, their title names, and rental dates.

5   Technical System Options

5.1   Introduction to Logical System Specification Module

The Logical System Specification module consists of two stages carried out in parallel.

In Stage 4 (Technical System Options) we address in detail the question of how the new system is to be implemented in terms of the technical environment it will operate in, the development approach we will use to build it and the need to get the best possible value for money from the new system.

In Stage 5 we continue the task of specifying the new system by creating a detailed logical design for the new system. This design will be in the form of components which, taken together with the implementation plans from Stage 4, can be translated directly into a physical design in Stage 6. An important objective here is to have a design which is as far as possible implementation-independent. This provides us with a product which is portable across different hardware and software environments.

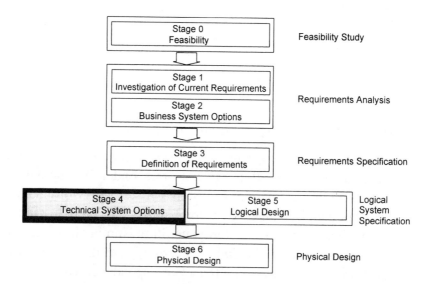

Figure 5.1 - The Stages of SSADM

Stages 4 and 5 can be initiated as soon as Stage 3 is complete, since the specification of user requirements produced by the Requirements Definition module will form a firm basis for both. Stage 4 will require volumetric information and service level requirements from Stage 3, whilst Stage 5 will further develop the Conceptual Model and External Design.

The desire for an implementation-independent design is the main reason for conducting Stages 4 and 5 separately: in this way the logical design is as free from physical constraints as possible. However, we may uncover information while developing TSOs which is of such significance that it requires adjustments to user requirements (and consequently to logical design). An extreme case of this would be abandonment of the entire project on cost grounds, while a more limited case might be the dropping of functions which turn out to be impossible or impractical to implement using any of the available technical options.

5.2   Stage 4 - Technical System Options

The TSOs we develop in Stage 4 will need to provide information and planning in four main areas:

(i)   **Technical environment**. If no feasibility study has been carried out, or if the organisation does not have an overall technical strategy, this may include consideration of the type of technical platform we require (e.g. mainframe or PC). Usually decisions of this type will already have been made, in which case the concern is with the specifics of hardware and software configuration and procurement.

(ii) **Development strategy**. Whether, for example, the system is to be developed in-house, or by some outside agent.

(iii) **Organisational impact**. This may include impact on working practices, other projects and even the IS department itself.

(iv) **System functionality**. Although this is addressed at the BSO stage, the selection of a technical environment may affect the viability of some functions, or the way in which a function is to be carried out.

The skills needed for establishing or assessing TSOs include capacity planning and system sizing; hardware and software procurement; and the knowledge of current and anticipated technologies. These lie outside the scope of SSADM and so it is highly unlikely that all of the skills required to carry out the tasks of Stage 4 will lie within the project team. We may even need to go outside the organisation to talk with suppliers of hardware and software to assess the capabilities of any proposed technical environments.

5.3   Structure

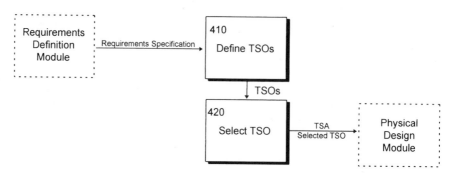

Figure 5.2 - Stage 4

Stage 4 consists of two steps, which bear more than a passing resemblance to the structure of Stage 2 (BSOs):

Step 410 - Define Technical System Options

Constraints on the choice of technical environments are established in order to provide a realistic framework for the definition of TSOs.

A range of up to six TSOs are outlined and discussed with users and technical experts. Three or four of the TSOs will be selected for further expansion.

Step 420 - Select Technical System Options

The expanded TSOs are presented to the project board who, with assistance from the project team, will select a final TSO which may be a hybrid of more than one of those proposed.

The selected TSO will then be developed further to provide a detailed Technical Systems Architecture for use in Physical Design (Stage 6).

5.4   Step 410 - Define Technical System Options

The Requirements Specification that we developed in such detail in Stage 3 was completed with little or no consideration of technical issues. An underlying assumption of SSADM is that an understanding of the user's requirements is best kept separate from a discussion of the hardware and software upon which the system is to be implemented.

Having defined in Stage 3 *what* it is that we want the system to do, we can now turn our attention to *how* the system is going to do it. Thus it is the purpose of Step 410 to identify the possible ways of physically implementing the Requirements Specification. In so doing, we must try to ensure that each proposed technical solution is capable of meeting the service level requirements which are spelt out in the function definitions.

SSADM does not provide a set of specific techniques which can be applied to all possible technical and organisational scenarios. This is not really surprising as the number of possible combinations of hardware, software and implementation strategies is almost limitless. Once again what SSADM does provide are guidelines on issues that should be addressed at this point, whatever the circumstances; and procedures that should be carried out as part of any selection process.

5.4.1 Identify Constraints

Before developing options for expansion and selection we clearly need to establish the constraints on our selection of possible technical environments and on how the system is to be implemented. After all, it would be pointless to waste time in developing plans to implement the system on a mainframe platform using an outside software house if the organisation has a mini-computer technical policy requiring in-house developments using a specific 4GL.

In general constraints fall into two categories:

- External: outside or global constraints applicable to the project as a whole.
- Internal: constraints imposed by the users on specific areas within the project.

External Constraints

These should have been noted in the Business Systems Options stage and should already be documented in the Requirements Catalogue (as indeed should internal constraints). The kinds of constraint commonly encountered in this area are:

- **Hardware and software platform**. On one project we may find that a specific language and operating system must be used, and that hardware must be of a particular type purchased from a pre-specified manufacturer. On another project we may have freedom to suggest hardware types, manufacturers and development software (although this kind of decision should really have been made at the Feasibility stage).
- **Organisational policy**. There may be policy on the use of packages, software houses, facilities management, etc.
- **Time**. The required delivery date for the new system will often have an enormous influence on implementation planning, possibly ruling out entire strategies.
- **Cost**. Most projects will have a maximum cost and/or minimum savings figure imposed on them.

External constraints may have been set up long before Stage 4, perhaps as part of the initial project proposal. For this reason it is worthwhile confirming that they still apply and whether they are negotiable, as they are likely to dictate the nature of all the proposed TSOs.

Internal Constraints

During our analysis of user requirements we will have uncovered a growing number of non-functional project specific requirements which will now act to constrain our choice of technical options. Possible areas of internal constraint include:

- **Service levels** e.g. percentage availability of system, recovery time (in case of system failure), contingency measures.
- **Performance** e.g. response time.
- **Capacity** e.g. maximum number of users/transactions, data storage volumes.
- **Security**.
- **Priority**. All TSOs will inevitably lead to compromises in some areas in order to achieve targets in others. Therefore, we should identify which areas have priority or whose performance is critical.

5.4.2   Produce Outline TSOs

We now investigate possible TSOs using the identified constraints. One of the best ways of identifying potential TSOs is to use brainstorming sessions involving both the project team and outside technical experts. We will also often need to contact suppliers for information on costs, facilities and configurations.

Our aim should be to produce up to six outline TSOs, each satisfying our requirements and constraints. Generating six options at this point might appear extremely difficult, but the main problem may actually be in keeping the number that low. Even if constraints appear very rigid, there is almost always room for adjusting configurations or balancing costs in different areas. For example we might suggest increasing the storage capacity of the system, at the expense of slightly slower or poorer printing. As a general rule, outline TSOs should be as distinct as possible, as they can always be adjusted or fine-tuned later if necessary.

If the new system is intended to replace an existing manual system then one of our options might be a manual one; if there is a current computer system we might propose the use of existing hardware only, or even a *no change* option resulting in termination of the project.

5.4.3   Produce Shortlist of TSOs

A fair amount of effort can go into fully defining a TSO, so we should try to reduce the number of TSOs to around three.

Users must be involved in this shortlisting process as it is they who will eventually have to live with the implementation. To help them we should produce outline impact analyses and attempt to quantify the benefits and drawbacks of each option.

In reality we are unlikely to come out of the shortlisting process with a shortlist consisting of three unchanged TSOs, but rather with a number of combined options.

We must avoid the temptation to select a single option at this stage. It is all too easy to opt for an obvious solution which turns out on closer examination to be more expensive or less reliable than we first thought.

5.4.4   Expand Shortlisted TSOs

We should now develop all of the shortlisted TSOs to a level which will enable them to be fully evaluated, and a final selection of TSO made. This will involve us in applying several non-SSADM techniques such as capacity planning and risk assessment in order to test the viability of the options.

Each TSO specification should contain the following components:

Outline Technical System Architecture (TSA)

As an input to the selection of TSOs the TSA will only be an outline of the proposed environment. After selection the TSA will be fully defined to provide the basis for translating the logical system design into a physical design in Stage 6.

Outline TSAs give us an idea of how the system will operate, of how it will be configured, and of its likely cost. It will help to make the proposed configurations clearer if we draw diagrams illustrating how the different hardware (and software) components will interconnect. We will also need to include information on system sizing, security and back-up arrangements, and maintenance costs.

System Description

As we develop the TSOs we will need to balance the various constraints, with possible trade-offs between costs and performance, or development time and functionality (although any reduction in functionality must be considered as a final option only).

Each System Description must describe the functionality which is to be met by the option it describes. This description can be provided by modifying existing SSADM products such as the Logical Data Model and Function Definitions. The significance of each option can be made clearer by highlighting in the System Description any functionality which is *not* being met.

Impact Analysis

We should explain the impact of the TSOs on the organisation using various non-SSADM techniques and products. Selection of the final TSO will often hinge on a comparison of each TSO's impact, so we are likely to put a lot of work into this area.

Impact analysis should include consideration of the following:
- Organisational and personnel changes.
- Operating changes.
- Training requirements.
- System documentation (e.g. user guides).
- System take-on requirements. Take-on (or cut-over) is often more complicated for TSOs based on the existing technical environment, than for entirely new TSOs.
- Savings.
- Testing requirements.
- Relative merits or drawbacks of each TSO (e.g. in the areas of reliability, performance, implementation time, costs and functionality).

Outline Development Plan

For each TSO we will need to produce an outline development plan for use by project management in estimating and scheduling the rest of the project. It is here that we will also outline the likely development costs of each TSO and propose how the option would be developed and implemented.

Issues to be covered include:
- Overview plan for the remainder of the project.
- Physical Design stage plans, giving details of how standard SSADM tasks will be tailored.
- Resource requirements.
- Construction strategy. For example, will we use contractors, purchase a package or opt for a turnkey solution?
- System testing requirements.
- Cut-over plans.

Cost/Benefit Analysis

Cost/Benefit Analysis (CBA) is one of the most frequently used and most objective of all non-SSADM techniques in assessing the viability and relative merits of different system options. The results of CBA are frequently crucial to the adoption or total elimination of options, so accurate collection and estimation of data is extremely important.

Costs will include:

- Development and implementation costs.
- Operating and maintenance costs.

Benefits or savings will include:

- Displaced costs (costs of operating the current system which will not exist for the new).
- Avoided costs (costs of continuing with the current system, e.g. increased maintenance to deal with business expansion).
- Tangible benefits such as increased sales.
- Intangible benefits. This is the difficult category to place a value on. Benefits such as improved management information or increased customer goodwill are not easy to quantify, but it is often these benefits which make an option attractive to users. Some attempt should be made to cost them if possible.

5.4.5   Summary of Step 410

The SSADM tasks carried out in Step 410 are:

Task

10   Use the Requirements Catalogue, Selected Business System Option, Project Initiation Document and any other strategic planning documents to identify constraints on the Technical System Options.

20   Within the identified constraints produce up to six outline TSOs.

30   Discuss these TSOs with users and reduce to a shortlist of two or three options.

40   Add more detail to the shortlisted options, including an outline Technical System Architecture and System Description.

50   Use capacity planning information to check that service level requirements can be met.

60   Fully define each Technical System Option by adding an Impact Analysis, an Outline Development Plan and Cost/Benefit Analysis.

5.5   Step 420 - Select Technical System Options

The tasks and organisation of TSO selection are very similar to those of BSO selection.

We will present each TSO to the project board (supported by appropriate technical advisors) in a way which emphasises their relative advantages and disadvantages.

The selected TSO may, as with BSOs, be a hybrid, in which case we must be prepared to carry out further capacity planning and impact analysis to ensure that it still lies within the identified constraints.

Once selection is complete we will extend the TSA with further details of hardware, software, sizing and operating procedures. At this point it is not essential to commit a project to a specific supplier. However, procurement procedures can be very drawn out, so it will be in the project's best interest to ensure that delivery of the development environment can be made in time for the end of Physical Design.

At this point we will incorporate the System Description and Impact Analysis within the TSA, to ensure that all of the documentation relating to implementation issues is in one place for input to Physical Design.

If the project board decides that the required system cannot be justified using any of the TSOs it may call a halt to the entire project. Otherwise it might decide to reduce service level requirements or drop some areas of functionality. In this case we would probably need to substantially update some SSADM products, such as the Requirements Catalogue, Function Definitions or the Required System LDM. In extreme instances we may even need to partially repeat Stage 3.

In any event the decisions made by the project board must be recorded for future reference, along with the shortlisted TSO specifications.

As soon as the final implementation environment is known, we can begin work on producing an application-specific style guide based on the organisation's standard style guide.

Capacity Planning

In Step 330 functions are defined; for each function we have to make a statement of the service level requirement. For instance, for an on-line function, we might specify a response time of five seconds or less. At the same time we have some system-wide service level requirements, such as the hours of availability of the system.

With many users accessing the system at the same time, and with many thousands of records in our database, and with the overheads of network communications, we have to be sure that we select hardware and software which can cope with the large number of transactions taking place and that it is possible to meet all the service level requirements.

In order to reduce the risk of the new system not performing to our expectations we employ a technique called capacity planning. This is not a core SSADM technique but SSADM analysts have some responsibility for it. They share this responsibility with specialists in the area of capacity planning.

The systems analyst will have to provide information on the following:

- Target values and acceptable ranges for each functional requirement.
- The frequencies of each event and enquiry, highlighting any peaks or troughs in the frequency of these transactions.
- Number of disk accesses and CPU time for each transaction.
- The size and number of occurrences of each entity. These are used to calculate the data storage requirements.

Capacity planners will use this data to create workload models and to evaluate the hardware configurations of any particular technical system architecture. The resulting predictions of system performance can be used to decide if a proposed TSA can meet the required service levels. If it can not do this then the hardware configuration can be revised, otherwise the service level requirements must be renegotitated.

Application Style Guide

Readers who are familiar with the Microsoft Windows interface will understand the benefits of having a consistent look and feel across different applications. The user of a Windows word processing application should find that they already know how to save a file, copy, paste or format text, or print a document in a Windows application that they have not used before. There are benefits for developers too: design effort is reduced, and component libraries reduce the amount of code that has to be written.

These benefits are achieved through the use of a style guide which defines things like:

- Menus.
- Forms and dialogue boxes.
- User guidance.
- Use of colour.
- Tailoring of the interface (for or by the different users).
- Use of keyboard and mouse.
- Font size, headers and footers on reports.

SSADM anticipates the existence of an Installation Style Guide which sets standards for the organisation as a whole; and an Application Style Guide, developed in Step 420 to provide any extra detail which is necesary for the current project.

5.5.1 Summary of Step 420

The SSADM tasks carried out in Step 420 are:

Task

10	Present the Technical Systems Options.
20	Modify the selected Technical System Option to reflect any decisions taken.
30	Use capacity planning to confirm that the service level requirements can still be met.
40	Develop an Application Style Guide.

6 Logical Design

6.1 Stage 5 - Logical Design

Stage 5 (Logical Design) continues the process of system specification begun in Stage 3. The aim of Stage 5 is to produce a set of implementable components by decomposing the products of Requirements Specification into units of logical processing.

The resulting specification should have the following properties:

- It is non-procedural. In other words it will state what the system is required to deliver and how it will react to events and enquiry triggers; but will not present procedural algorithms or program specifications (these are developed as appropriate to the chosen technical environment in Stage 6 (Physical Design)).
- It is not implementation specific, i.e. is not tied to a particular technical environment.
- It is capable of re-use. This is really an extension of the previous point, with emphasis on the fact that the specification can be re-used either as a whole or in parts, by virtue of its logical and modular nature.

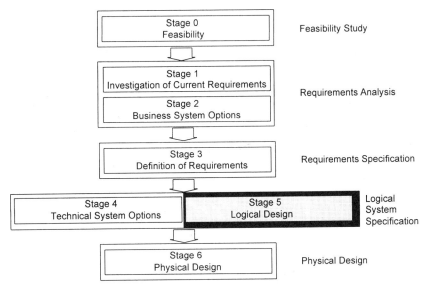

Figure 6.1 - The Stages of SSADM

6.2   Structure

Stage 5 consists of three main steps covering the detailed design of Dialogues, Update Processes and Enquiry Processes, followed by a standard assembly step:

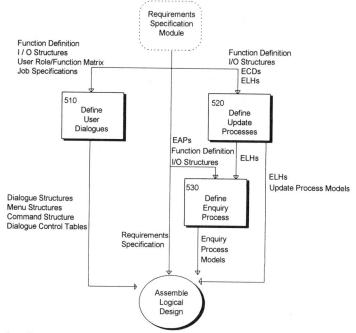

Figure 6.2 - Stage 5

Step 510 - Define User Dialogues

A set of Dialogue Structures is developed to support the interfacing of on-line functions.

Navigation within and between dialogues is documented.

Menu standards are defined, and the issues of how users will move around the system are addressed using command structures.

Step 520 - Define Update Processes

State indicators are assigned to the ELHs developed in Stage 3. These reflect the stage in the life of each entity at which each event is allowed to take place, and what stage the entity will reach as a result of its effects.

ECDs are transformed into update processing structures and operations are allocated governing the effects of each event, along with integrity error checking.

Conditions are allocated to each selection and iteration of processing.

Step 530 - Define Enquiry Processes

Enquiry processing structures are developed by merging EAPs and I/O Structures; operations and conditions are allocated to each processing structure in a similar manner to the update structures.

Assemble Logical Design

The products of Stage 5 are checked (along with relevant Stage 3 products) for consistency and completeness.

The Logical Design is then published for input to Stage 6 (Physical Design).

6.3 Step 510 - Define User Dialogues

Dialogues represent all on-line interactions between users and the system functions. To many users the internal workings of a computer system are entirely unknown and to some extent irrelevant. The important things to them are the inputs and outputs from the system, i.e. their dialogues with the system.

In SSADM terms a Dialogue provides the 'front-end' to a function definition for a given user role. The process of developing dialogues can be seen as having two fairly distinct elements: Dialogue Identification and Dialogue Design.

Dialogue Identification begins early in the project life-cycle and is completed by the end of Stage 3 with the creation of the User Role/Function Matrix.

Dialogue design has already been discussed briefly with regard to Specification Prototyping, but it is in Step 510 that all dialogues are fully defined.

6.3.1 Dialogue Identification

To help place Dialogue Design in context it is worth recapping briefly on the activities of Dialogue Identification as illustrated in Figure 6.3. The gentle reader will recognise that most of what is contained in this section is a reiteration of what was said during the Definition of Job Specifications (Step 335). The difference here is that we specify dialogues from the system's perspective while in Step 335 we were more interested in the human aspect of each dialogue.

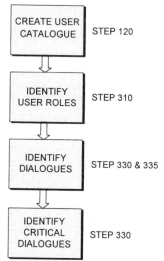

Figure 6.3 - Dialogue Identification Tasks

User Catalogue

In Step 120 (Investigate and Define Requirements) we create a User Catalogue, containing details of all job holders who require access to the system. Thus each job holder is a potential user who will engage in dialogues with the automated system.

User Roles

In Step 310 User Roles are identified. Each User Role represents a collection of users who will carry out similar (or the same) automated tasks, and thus require access to the same functions. Thus each user belonging to a particular User Role will use a common set of dialogues.

User Role/Function Matrix

Following the definition of functions in Step 330 we create a User Role/Function Matrix. This documents which functions each user role will require access to, thereby identifying all required dialogues. The responsibilities of each user role are defined in Step 335.

Critical Dialogues

We then identify which of these required dialogues are regarded as critical to the success of the system. This helps us to select dialogues for prototyping in Step 350, and possibly to evaluate the impact of different TSOs in Stage 4.

6.3.2   Dialogue Design

The design of dialogues at this stage is concerned with logical issues, not physical ones such as screen layout, colour usage, etc. The technique is built on the concept of logical screen components which may eventually be implemented over more than one physical screen, or form just one part of a single physical screen.

Our main aim in designing dialogues is to support the way in which users wish to interface with the system. Clearly the best way to achieve this is to involve users in the process as much as possible.

Although we should not be driven by physical considerations at this point, we should take into account some style issues, such as the maximum number of data items on a screen. Information on this sort of thing will usually be available from an organisation's standards manual or 'Style Guide'.

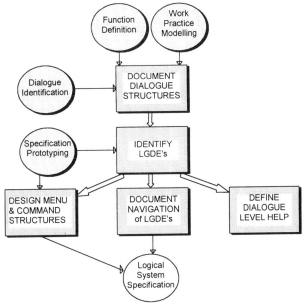

Figure 6.4 - Dialogue Design Tasks

Some dialogues may have already been prototyped in Step 350. However, our primary concern in Specification Prototyping is to validate user requirements, not to design final dialogues. We can use the dialogues or menu structures produced in Step 350 as input to Step 510, but we should always review them before doing so (and in any case they will usually need further expansion and integration with other dialogues or menus).

Figure 6.4 illustrates the activities involved in dialogue design in Step 510.

Document Dialogue Structure

We have already looked briefly at drawing Dialogue Structures in Chapter 5 when discussing Specification Prototyping. We will now discuss Dialogue Structure documentation in a little more detail using the dialogue for the function Book Delivery as our example (Figure 6.5).

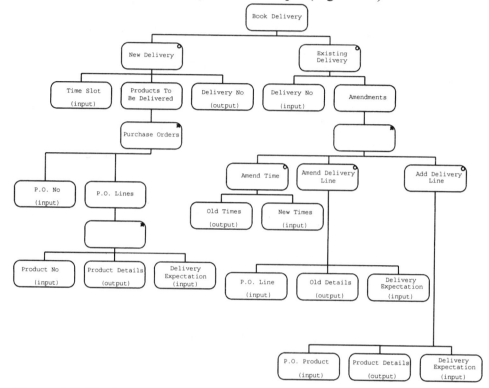

Figure 6.5 - Dialogue Structure

The I/O Structure for Book Delivery is carried forward to form the basis for the Dialogue Structure (Figure 6.5). We then begin to fill out a Dialogue Element Description form (Figure 6.6) by copying all of the data items from the I/O Structure Description; each Dialogue Element being equivalent to an I/O Structure Element.

Note that the Dialogue Structure does not replace the I/O Structure, it is merely based on it.

Dialogue Element Descriptions			
Dialogue Element	**Data Item**	**Logical Grouping of Dialogue Elements**	**Mandatory/ Optional LGDE**
Time Slot	Supplier Number Delivery Date Delivery Start Time Delivery End Time		

P.O. No	P.O. Number		
Product No	Product Number		
Product Details	Product Name P/S Reference Quantity Ordered		
Delivery Expectation	Quantity Due		
Delivery No	Delivery Number		
Old Times	Delivery Date Delivery Start Time Delivery End Time		
New Times	Delivery Date Delivery Start Time Delivery End Time		
P.O. Line	P.O. Number Product Number		
Old Details	Product Name P/S Reference Quantity Ordered Quantity Due		

Figure 6.6 - Dialogue Element Description Form

Identify Logical Groupings of Dialogue Elements (LGDE)

We now examine the Dialogue Structure in order to identify groups of dialogue elements that logically belong together, as components of the dialogue. The views of users are paramount at this point, but individuals may well differ on the question of what constitutes a logical grouping for their purposes. Representatives of different User Roles, all requiring access to the same function, could require different paths or navigation through the dialogue, reflecting the ways in which they operate. It is quite acceptable to produce more than one set of LGDEs for a given Dialogue Structure, leading to more than one Logical Dialogue for the function.

In the case of Book Delivery we will assume that only one dialogue is required for all User Roles with the LGDEs shown in Figure 6.7.

Identifying which elements should be logically grouped together is really a matter of discussing with users which elements 'feel right' together. Elements that are always input as a set, which form a group of inputs and resultant outputs or reflect tasks which are always carried out in sequence are candidates for grouping. Clearly there should be a close relationship between LGDEs and the components of the relevant Function Navigation and Window Navigation Models.

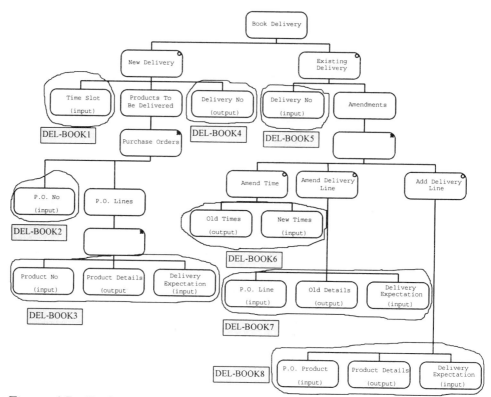

Figure 6.7 - Dialogue Structure with LGDEs

A few other points to bear in mind when looking for LGDEs are:

- Never group together elements that have elements outside the group between them.
- Each element must belong to one and only one LGDE.
- Avoid grouping elements together which represent mutually exclusive selections.

Once the LGDEs have been added to the Dialogue Structure we should update the Dialogue Element Description form as shown in Figure 6.8.

Dialogue Element Descriptions			
Dialogue Element	**Data Item**	**Logical Grouping of Dialogue Elements**	**Mandatory/ Optional LGDE**
Time Slot	Supplier Number Delivery Date Delivery Start Time Delivery End Time	DEL-BOOK1	
P.O. No	P.O. Number	DEL-BOOK2	
Product No	Product Number		
Product Details	Product Name P/S Reference	DEL-BOOK3	

	Quantity Ordered		
Delivery Expectation	Quantity Due		
Delivery No (o)	Delivery Number	DEL-BOOK4	
Delivery No (i)	Delivery Number	DEL-BOOK5	
Old Times	Delivery Date Delivery Start Time Delivery End Time	DEL-BOOK6	
New Times	Delivery Date Delivery Start Time Delivery End Time		
P.O. Line	P.O. Number Product Number	DEL-BOOK7	
Old Details	Product Name P/S Reference Quantity Ordered Quantity Due	DEL-BOOK8	

Figure 6.8 - Adding LGDEs to the Dialogue Element Descriptions

Complete Dialogue Control Table

The LGDEs provide us with logical screen components. Whenever a user interacts with the function they will navigate through a number of these components.

For example the most frequently used or default path through the Book Delivery dialogue will be to enter an agreed delivery time, followed by a group of delivery lines arranged by purchase order and finally by confirmation of the delivery, i.e. DEL-BOOK1, DEL-BOOK2, DEL-BOOK3, DEL-BOOK4.

However this is not the only path. For example we may begin by entering an existing delivery number just to change the delivery time, i.e. DEL-BOOK5, DEL-BOOK6. This happens about 15% of the time.

The default path and any alternatives can be documented using a Dialogue Control Table, as in Figure 6.9.

As well as indicating possible pathways we can use the table to document the frequency (or 'percentage path usage') of each path, and to show the minimum, maximum and average number of occurrences of each LGDE in a typical execution of the dialogue. Clearly any LGDE with a minimum number of occurrences of greater than zero will be present in all alternative pathways, and is known as *mandatory*. Where the minimum number of occurrences is zero the LGDE is *optional*.

The Dialogue Element Description form should be updated to reflect whether LGDEs are optional or mandatory (Figure 6.10).

Note that any LGDEs consisting of sequence boxes only must be mandatory. If an LGDE covers just part of a selection or a whole selection

Dialogue Control Table								
Function: Book Delivery								
LGDE	**Occurrences**			**Default**	**Alternative pathways**			
	min	**max**	**ave**	**Pathway**	**alt1**	**alt2**	**alt3**	**alt4**
DEL-BOOK1	0	1	0.8	X				
DEL-BOOK2	0	6	2	X				
DEL-BOOK3	0	20	6	X				
DEL-BOOK4	0	1	0.8	X				
DEL-BOOK5	0	1	0.2		X	X	X	X
DEL-BOOK6	0	1	0.1		X	X	X	
DEL-BOOK7	0	6	4			X		X
DEL-BOOK8	0	6	2				X	X
% path usage				80	15	2	2	1

Figure 6.9 - Dialogue Control Table

Dialogue Element Descriptions			
Dialogue Element	**Data Item**	**Logical Grouping of Dialogue Elements**	**Mandatory/ Optional LGDE**
Time Slot	Supplier Number Delivery Date Delivery Start Time Delivery End Time	DEL-BOOK1	O
P.O. No	P.O. Number	DEL-BOOK2	O
Product No	Product Number		O
Product Details	Product Name P/S Reference Quantity Ordered	DEL-BOOK3	O
Delivery Expectation	Quantity Due		O
Delivery No (o)	Delivery Number	DEL-BOOK4	O
Delivery No (i)	Delivery Number	DEL-BOOK5	O
Old Times	Delivery Date Delivery Start Time Delivery End Time		O
New Times	Delivery Date Delivery Start Time Delivery End Time	DEL-BOOK6	O
P.O. Line	P.O. Number Product Number	DEL-BOOK7	O
Old Details	Product Name P/S Reference Quantity Ordered Quantity Due	DEL-BOOK8	O

Figure 6.10 - Complete Dialogue Element Descriptions

containing a null box it must be optional. Iteration LGDEs can be mandatory or optional depending on whether the possibility of zero iterations is allowed in the particular dialogue under scrutiny.

Design Menu and Command Structures

Once we have completed the documentation of possible pathways within each dialogue, we turn our attention to pathways through the system as a whole (i.e. between different dialogues and menus).

We encountered Menu Structures when developing Specification Prototypes, and indeed we may carry forward the structures used then as input to this step. Menu Structures provide a good idea of how the system fits together from a user's point of view, but do not strictly specify all the alternative ways of accessing any given dialogue. This function is fulfilled by Command Structures, which provide details of where a user may go to in the Menu Structure once a dialogue is finished.

Menu Structures

Menu Structures are fairly straightforward, and do not require much explanation beyond that given already in section 4.8.

SSADM suggests that a Menu Structure should be constructed for each User Role. The bottom level in a Menu Structure hierarchy will then consist of the dialogues required to interface with all of the functions identified for the appropriate User Role in the User Role/Function Matrix. For example, taking the user role 'Delivery Scheduler' the required dialogues are:

- Book Delivery
- Update Delivery
- Maintain Schedule
- Overdue Delivery Query
- Check Available Slots
- Delivery Query
- Book Transfer

Dialogue names will normally be taken from the name of the function they represent. If a function is accessed by more than one User Role then it may be represented by more than one dialogue. In this case the dialogue name for each User Role will consist of the function name plus a qualifier indicating the User Role to which it belongs.

Once the bottom level of the Menu Structure is known we can construct intermediate levels in the hierarchy by grouping dialogues that belong together logically under sub-menus.

There are no strict rules for doing this, and in the extreme case we could hang all of the dialogues from the top of the User Role main menu as in Figure 6.11.

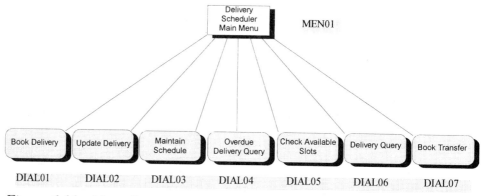

Figure 6.11 - Menu Structure

Alternatively we could group dialogues together under intermediate levels of menus. As a general guide any groupings of dialogues should aim to support the way in which activities are carried out by users. In the absence of firm requirements from users we might consider groupings based on the following:

- Functions of a similar type (e.g. group all updates under one menu, and all enquiries under another).
- Functions that access the same data.
- The grouping of processes on the Required System DFM.

In the case of the Delivery Scheduler we will produce three main groups based on delivery data, Schedule Maintenance and Enquiries (Figure 6.12).

Command Structures

The Menu Structure gives us a fair idea of how we can navigate to the dialogue we require by following the menu hierarchy. However this does not give us the whole picture. We may frequently wish to jump from one dialogue to another dialogue, or back to the beginning of the same dialogue without returning to a menu.

For example on completion of the dialogue DIAL001 (Book Delivery) in Figure 6.12 we may wish to do any of the following:

- Book another delivery
- Check slot availability
- Return to the main menu
- Enquire on overdue deliveries
- Return to the Delivery Bookings menu

We document this information using a Command Structure. Each dialogue in the Menu Structure will have its own Command Structure detailing all of the places that control can pass to upon completion of the dialogue.

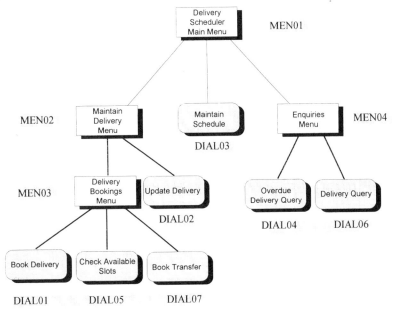

Figure 6.12 - Menu Structure

Figure 6.13 shows the Command Structure for DIAL01 (Book Delivery).

Command Structure		
Dialogue Name *Book Delivery*	Dialogue Id. *DIAL 01*	
Option	Dialogue or Menu	Name/Id.
Book another delivery	Dialogue	*Book Delivery DIAL 01*
Check Slot Availability for new delivery	Dialogue	*Check Available Slots DIAL 05*
Quit to Main Menu	Menu	*Delivery Scheduler Main Menu MEN 01*
Quit to Maintain Delivery	Menu	*Maintain Delivery MEN 02*

Figure 6.13 - Command Structure for DIAL01

Command Structures include no details of how each completion option is to be implemented (e.g. using a function key or mouse button), this is an issue for Physical Design. If the technical environment is known at this point we might need to take certain constraints into account regarding possible navigation, e.g. it may not allow us to jump directly to dialogues below other sub-menus.

Define Dialogue Level Help

While designing logical dialogues we will also consider the question of where dialogue level help might be required.

By dialogue level help we mean help with navigation problems, i.e. how to exit, where to go next, etc. The level of help needed will depend largely on the complexity of the system and will be driven by the needs of users.

Once again we are operating at a logical level so will not consider the format of help screens or the procedure for obtaining them. The main thing at this point is to identify where help is required.

6.3.3   Summary (Step 510)

The SSADM tasks carried out in Step 510 are:

Task

10   Translate I/O Structures into Dialogue Structures and identify LGDEs.

20   Describe possible navigations through each dialogue in a Dialogue Control table.

30   Create a Menu Structure for each user role, and document possible paths through the structure in Command Structures (one for each dialogue).

40   Identify where dialogue level help is required.

6.4   Step 520 - Define Update Processes

Having defined the required logical system interfaces in Step 510, we now turn our attention to the detailed specification of internal system processing. Through the use of Entity Life Histories and Effect Correspondence Diagrams during Requirements Definition we have painted a picture of the impact of events on the system's logical data model. For many projects the Effect Correspondence Diagram will suffice as the model of update processing to be input to Physical Design. However, the Effect Correspondence Diagram is not a proper Jackson Structure, and for more complex processes it can be slightly ambiguous as to the precise order of processing. If it is deemed necessary the Effect Correspondence Diagram can be converted into an Update Process Model which will represent exactly the same set of effects using Jackson notation.

Update Process Models are developed using a sub-technique of Conceptual Process Modelling with the unsurprising name of Update Process Modelling.

As with all Conceptual Process Models, the Update Process Model assumes that the Required System Logical Data Model exists as an implemented database - a logical database. In environments where the final system is to be built using non-procedural code the process models can act as actual program specifications, since the translation from logical processing and databases to physical processing and databases is handled by the development software itself. Where procedural coding is to be used the process models will be translated into environment-specific program specifications during Physical Design.

As well as serving as the basis for Physical Design and implementation of the new system, conceptual process models act as effective maintenance documentation once the system is running live. Any future changes to the system can be evaluated against, and applied to, the underlying logical (or business oriented) model before any physical amendments are made.

6.4.1   Update Process Modelling

The notation for process structures is another variation on the now familiar Jackson-like structures of Entity Life Histories and I/O Structures. Each update process structure will describe the processing of a single event, and each end-leaf will represent a discrete module within that overall processing. To create an Update Process Model we go through the following steps:

Carry Forward the ECD

In Stage 3 we developed Effect Correspondence Diagrams to model the effects of a single event on the entities in our Required System Logical Data Model.

Effect Correspondence Diagrams provide a picture of how changes triggered in response to event (i.e. input) data are applied to and permeate through the Logical Data Model.

The purpose of each Update Process Model is to describe the processing which is to take place in response to an event: exactly the same as the Effect Correspondence Diagram for that event. Thus each Update Process Model is based on an Effect Correspondence Diagram. We will use the Effect Correspondence Diagram for the *Purchase Order Proposal* event, reproduced in Figure 6.14, to illustrate the creation of an Update Process Model.

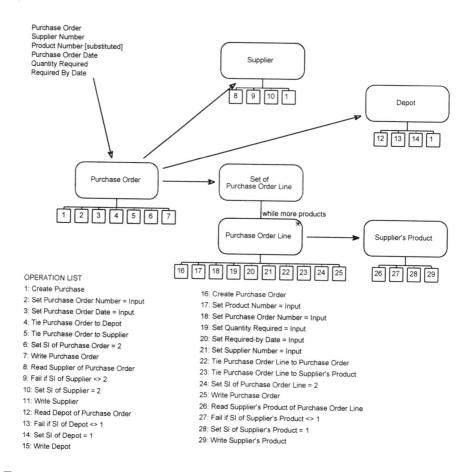

Figure 6.14 - ECD for Purchase Order Proposal

Group Effects in One-to-One Correspondence

All effects linked on an Effect Correspondence Diagrams by arrows are in one-to-one correspondence. This means that the affected entities can be accessed and processed unconditionally as a group.

In specifying the processing associated with each event we are interested in creating units of processing that can be designed and implemented in reasonably self-contained modules or blocks. By grouping together effects on each Effect Correspondence Diagram that are in one-to-one correspondence we have the basis for such modules.

Groups are added to an Effect Correspondence Diagram by drawing a boundary around all effects linked by correspondence arrows, and giving them a name that reflects the processing carried out for them. Any effects that stand alone, i.e. are not linked by arrows, automatically become single element groups.

Figure 6.15 illustrates the Effect Correspondence Diagram for Purchase Order Proposal with processing access boundaries added.

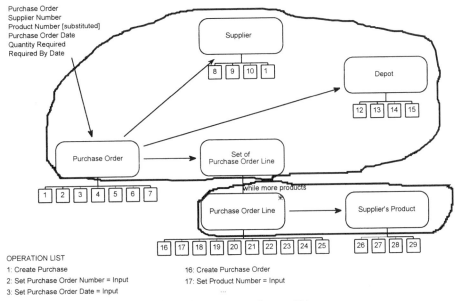

OPERATION LIST

1: Create Purchase   16: Create Purchase Order
2: Set Purchase Order Number = Input   17: Set Product Number = Input
3: Set Purchase Order Date = Input   ...

Figure 6.15 - Grouped Effect Correspondence Diagram

Convert to Jackson-like Structure

This is a fairly simple and somewhat mechanical procedure. Firstly we draw a root node containing the name of the event whose processing is being described. The wording is of the form 'Process <event name>'.

The entry point processing group becomes a child of this root node. Then we add any subsequent processing groups. The resulting structure must adhere to the usual rules regarding combinations of box types, so a few new structure boxes may need to be added: in this case the processing of Purchase Order Lines is iterated, so this group will need a structure box above it.

The structure now represents all of the processing required to apply the updates generated by the event, and to provide the required output.

Allocate Operations and Conditions to Processing Structure

In Figure 6.16 the Effect Correspondence Diagram's operations have been carried across just as they were, as have the conditions. Where several effects have been merged into one processing group, all the operations of those effects have been placed together, in the order in which they are to be processed. Thus the processing of Supplier will take place before the processing of Depot, although in this instance the order in which these two entities are processed is not important.

Once again, a good CASE tool should be able to perform an automatic transformation from Effect Correspondence Diagram to Update Process Model.

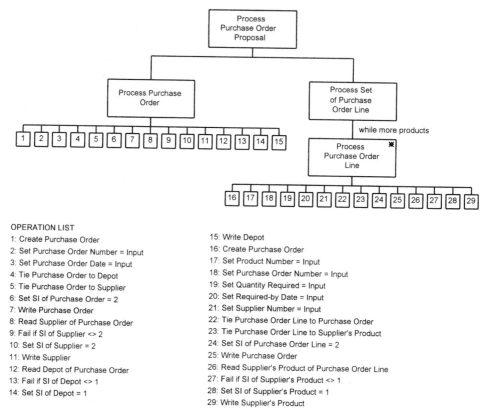

OPERATION LIST

1: Create Purchase Order
2: Set Purchase Order Number = Input
3: Set Purchase Order Date = Input
4: Tie Purchase Order to Depot
5: Tie Purchase Order to Supplier
6: Set SI of Purchase Order = 2
7: Write Purchase Order
8: Read Supplier of Purchase Order
9: Fail if SI of Supplier <> 2
10: Set SI of Supplier = 2
11: Write Supplier
12: Read Depot of Purchase Order
13: Fail if SI of Depot <> 1
14: Set SI of Depot = 1

15: Write Depot
16: Create Purchase Order
17: Set Product Number = Input
18: Set Purchase Order Number = Input
19: Set Quantity Required = Input
20: Set Required-by Date = Input
21: Set Supplier Number = Input
22: Tie Purchase Order Line to Purchase Order
23: Tie Purchase Order Line to Supplier's Product
24: Set SI of Purchase Order Line = 2
25: Write Purchase Order
26: Read Supplier's Product of Purchase Order Line
27: Fail if SI of Supplier's Product <> 1
28: Set SI of Supplier's Product = 1
29: Write Supplier's Product

Figure 6.16 - Update Process Model

Walk-through Structure

Once conditions and operations have been added the resulting Update Process Model should be 'walked through' with users to verify that they actually make sense. Each organisation will probably have its own set of guidelines on walk-throughs, and these should of course be followed.

6.4.2   Summary (Step 520)

The SSADM tasks carried out in Step 520 are:

Task

10   Convert each Effect Correspondence Diagram into a processing structure.

20   Allocate operations to the processing structure for each event. Allocate conditions to selections and iterations in the processing structure. The conditions and operations are based on those of the Effect Correspondence Diagrams.

30   Specify error outputs.

6.5   Step 530 - Define Enquiry Processes

An enquiry process is a Jackson-like structure that describes in a procedural manner one of the new system's enquiries.

7.5.1   Enquiry Process Modelling

Enquiry Process Modelling is carried out in exactly the same way as Update Process Modelling, except that the starting point is an Enquiry Access Path rather than an Effect Correspondence Diagram.

Carry forward the EAP

The Enquiry Access Paths developed in Step 360 are designed specifically to illustrate Logical Data Model access and navigation. It is these which now form the basis for our processing structures.

The Enquiry Access Path for the Purchase Order Query is reproduced in Figure 6.17.

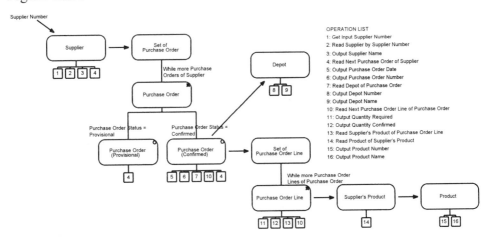

Figure 6.17- Enquiry Access Path for Purchase Order Query

Group Accesses on the EAP

As with update processes, we are interested in grouping together processing that can be carried out unconditionally as a single module. We do this by grouping those accesses on the Enquiry Access Path that are in one-to-one correspondence, i.e. those that are linked by a single-headed access arrow.

All such groups should be given a meaningful name, and any accesses that stand alone will form a group of their own.

Figure 6.18 illustrates the addition of access groups to the Enquiry Access Path for Purchase Order Query.

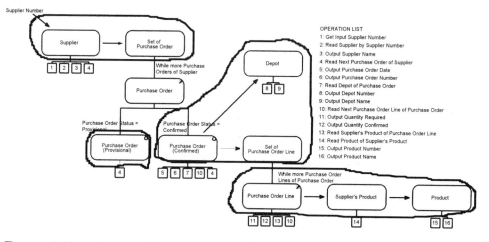

Figure 6.18 - Grouped Enquiry Access Path

Convert to Jackson-like Structure

We now convert each grouping to a box on a Jackson-like structure. We follow the same method as for Effect Correspondence Diagram conversion. In this example we have added some extra structure boxes. These ensure that the structure conforms to the normal rules of Jackson structures, with which the reader will be very familiar by now.

Allocate Operations and Conditions to Processing Structure

Operations are carried across from the Enquiry Access Path to the Enquiry Process Model just as they were from the Effect Correspondence Diagram to the Update Process Model.

Care should be taken with the placement of *read* operations for an iteration. We need an initial read operation to access the first record. If no record exists then the condition governing the iteration evaluates to false, otherwise processing of the first record can take place, at the end of which the next record has to be read. Thus each iteration is preceded by a *read next* operation, and the same *read next* operation is repeated as the last thing in the sequence under the iteration. Careful readers should note that this rule explains why operations 4 and 10 each appear twice on the Enquiry Process Model of Figure 6.19.

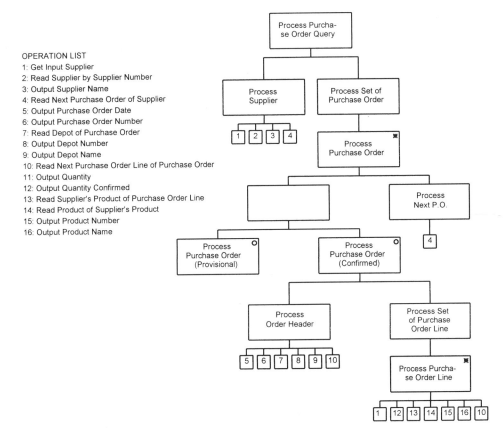

OPERATION LIST
1: Get Input Supplier
2: Read Supplier by Supplier Number
3: Output Supplier Name
4: Read Next Purchase Order of Supplier
5: Output Purchase Order Date
6: Output Purchase Order Number
7: Read Depot of Purchase Order
8: Output Depot Number
9: Output Depot Name
10: Read Next Purchase Order Line of Purchase Order
11: Output Quantity
12: Output Quantity Confirmed
13: Read Supplier's Product of Purchase Order Line
14: Read Product of Supplier's Product
15: Output Product Number
16: Output Product Name

Figure 6.19 - Enquiry Process Model for Purchase Order Query

Walk-through Structure

Once the Enquiry Process Models are complete we should hold a walk-through meeting with users, to check that they make sense. In practice this will probably be done at the same time as for Update Process Models.

6.5.2 Summary (Step 530)

The SSADM tasks carried out in Step 530 are:

Task

10	Transform each Enquiry Access Path into a processing structure.
20	Allocate operations and conditions to the processing structure based on those from the Enquiry Access Path.
30	Specify error outputs.

6.6 Assemble Logical Design

The assembly and publication of the Logical Design will cover all of the products of Stage 5, plus many of those of Stage 3, which will also be carried forward to Physical Design.

The Stage 5 products to be checked for consistency and completeness are:

- Command Structures
- Dialogue Control Tables
- Dialogue Structure
- Enquiry Process Models
- Menu Structures
- Update Process Models

The Stage 3 products to be checked are:

- Effect Correspondence Diagrams
- Enquiry Access Paths
- Entity Life Histories
- Function Definitions
- I/O Structures
- Required System Logical Data Model
- Requirements Catalogue
- User Role/Function Matrix

Together with the Technical Systems Architecture and Action Plan from Stage 4 (Technical System Options), the Logical Design provides all of the information needed to begin Physical Design (Stage 6).

6.7 Logical Specification Exercises

6.1 *(Update Process Models)* Produce an Update Process Model for the event 'Respond to Estimate' using the solutions to exercises 4.3 and 4.12.

Add relevant operations from the Entity Life History for Estimate, and try to make reasonable guesses as to other operations and to appropriate conditions (the Logical Data Structure from exercise 2.27 may be helpful).

6.2 *(Enquiry Process Models)* Produce an Enquiry Process Model for the Treebanks enquiry used in exercises 4.1 and 4.14. Again make reasonable guesses about operations and conditions.

6.3 *(Process Models)* Produce Process Models for the ECDs of question 4.18 and for the EAPs of question 4.20.

7   Physical Design

7.1   Stage 6 - Physical Design

The products of Logical Design provide a system specification that could be implemented in a wide variety of technical environments. The Technical System Architecture resulting from Stage 4 will identify the chosen implementation environment. Our aim in Stage 6 - Physical Design - is to map our logical system specification onto our target environment.

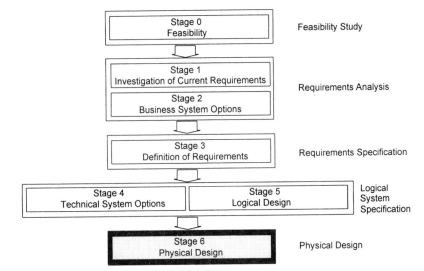

Figure 7.1 - The Stages of SSADM

By the end of Stage 6 the non-procedural aspects or components of the system will have been implemented, and no further specification will be necessary for the procedural components. In transforming the logical design into a physical design we will need to balance various competing factors such as performance, space usage and development time in order to achieve the optimum implementation. Throughout this process we will aim to preserve as direct a mapping as possible between the logical and physical designs.

To help co-ordinate and document the mapping of logical functions onto physical function components we will develop a Function Component Implementation Map (FCIM); while on the data side any mismatches between the logical database and its final implementation will be handled by specifying a piece of software called the Process Data Interface (PDI).

We will then be able to design physical processing which acts as if the logical and physical databases are one and the same, with any mappings between the two being handled by the PDI. In many relational database environments (using query languages such as SQL) the role of the PDI is largely taken by the Database Management System itself.

SSADM provides mainly generic guidelines on Physical Design, which should be applicable or tailorable to most environments. These are separated into data and process design steps, although in many cases the two are interdependent. In some 4GL or application generator environments the developers may have little or no control over how the system is built or the tuned; in these cases the guidelines will be largely redundant.

There are a few physical design tasks that are applicable to a wide range of technical environments. Where this is the case SSADM offers a set of more rigorous techniques (notably those of first-cut data design), and these will be discussed in greater detail during this chapter.

Physical Design can be highly technical and the involvement of database and programming specialists is likely to be essential (particularly in 3GL environments). However the presence of analysts and users from earlier in the project is also crucial to ensure that the final design satisfies user requirements.

7.2 Structure

Step 610 - Prepare for Physical Design

The implementation environment is studied and its facilities are classified and documented (with emphasis on its strengths, weaknesses and optimisation mechanisms), Application Development Standards are drawn up, and a Physical Design Strategy agreed with management.

Step 620 - Create Physical Data Design

The Required System Logical Data Model is converted to a first-cut data design using techniques based on assumptions common to many Database Management Systems. Product-specific rules are then used to produce an environment-specific data design.

Step 630 - Create Function Component Implementation Map

The specification of functions is completed with the addition of physical components such as system error handling routines.

A Function Component Implementation Map is drawn up listing the components of each function and how they map onto physical function components.

Non-procedural function components are implemented.

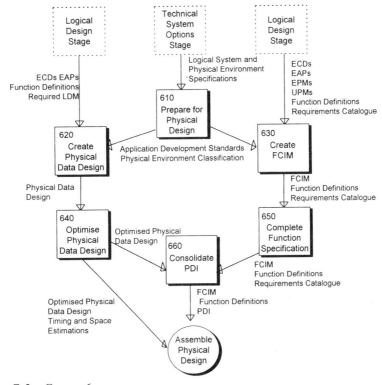

Figure 7.2 - Stage 6

Step 640 - Optimise Physical Data Design

The Physical Data Design from Step 620 is tested against the performance objectives set out in the Requirements Catalogue and Function Definitions. If necessary the design is optimised, using the facilities of the implementation environment rather than by compromising the data structure wherever possible.

Step 650 - Complete Function Specification

Program specifications are produced for any function components that are to be implemented in procedural code.

Step 660 - Consolidate Process Data Interface

The optimised Physical Data Design is examined to identify where mappings are required from logical database operations to physical database operations. A Process Data Interface is developed to handle these mappings if necessary.

7.3   Step 610 - Prepare for Physical Design

Before Physical Design begins in earnest there are some basic preparations to be carried out. These are intended to equip the project team with as great an understanding of the physical environment as possible, and to set a strategy for the entire Physical Design process. Where a lot of specialist help is available there may be a great deal of knowledge already within the team on how to exploit the strengths and overcome the weaknesses of the physical environment. However, it is still the job of the analysts present to gain an overall understanding of its facilities in order for them to be able to participate in Physical Design.

7.3.1   Classify the Physical Environment

The facilities offered by the physical environment will clearly affect the extent to which the logical design can be directly preserved in the physical design, and therefore determine the need for software to map between the two.

SSADM recommends that a relatively formal classification of facilities is undertaken to ensure that they are fully understood, and hence can be fully exploited. This classification is divided into three areas: DBMS Data Storage, DBMS Performance, and Processing System. In practice most of the information covered by these areas will be provided by database and programming specialists or suppliers of hardware and software.

In order to help classify facilities SSADM provides a checklist of mechanisms that are common to many Database Management Systems. The idea then is to examine the physical environment to identify the way in which it supports these mechanisms. In some environments (notably non-procedural or 4GL) these mechanisms will be present but may be entirely hidden from the developer. Nevertheless it is worth checking if any of them are visible and so capable of manipulation.

DBMS Data Storage Classification

This concentrates on establishing how data is stored, accessed and updated. It is also crucially concerned with how relationships are implemented. The basic questions to be answered are:

- How are relationships represented?
- Where is relationship data held?

- Are relationship keys symbolic or physical, i.e. based on attribute values or physical pointers?
- What mechanisms are used to locate records?
- Can the Database Management System place related records near each other physically?
- What restrictions are placed by the Database Management System? e.g. on the maximum number of tables or level of the detail-master hierarchy.

DBMS Performance Classification

This concerns questions relating to the timing of Database Management System operations. In order to satisfy non-functional performance requirements we will often need to adjust our physical data design to balance the time overheads of these operations.

Time overheads may be associated with the following:

- Transaction logging.
- Recovery logging i.e. the automatic backing up of the database at regular intervals, so that it can be restored to an uncorrupted state if a disaster occurs.
- Standard operations: read, write.
- Commit mechanisms.
- Space management.
- Data sorting (on input or for output).

Once the DBMS classifications have taken place it is a good idea to design forms for recording the timings and space requirements of the physical design. These will then be used later in testing that design against performance objectives.

Processing System Classification

The final area of classification is concerned with identifying the features and facilities of the processing environment. These may differ for development and production, e.g. if different hardware is used, or if special development 'front-ends' are provided, and so we may need to carry out two classifications.

Our major aim is to understand how each function component i.e. dialogues, logical processes, etc. can be implemented, with emphasis on whether the mechanism is procedural or non-procedural.

Points to be considered include:

- What tools are available and what can they generate? (For example, screen or report generators).
- Can procedural and non-procedural code be mixed?
- Can on-line and off-line function components be mixed?
- What error handling facilities are available?
- How are success units defined?
- What database access facilities exist?
- How can data be grouped on screens and reports?
- What types of interface can be generated?
- How can command structures be implemented?
- How can a PDI be constructed, or can its creation be automated?
- To what extent is the designer aware of physical data distribution?

7.3.2 Specify Naming Standards

In most organisations, naming standards will already exist for objects such as programs, data tables, records, etc. If the physical environment is new to an organisation, naming standards may need specifying from scratch. In this case *all* function components should be subject to review with management to decide on acceptable naming conventions.

7.3.3 Develop Physical Design Strategy

Once the physical environment is understood a strategy for creating the Physical Design can be developed. This will include customising Physical Design activities to fit with the requirements of the project, and assigning personnel to relevant activities. Particular attention should be paid to:

- The implementation method of each function component i.e. procedural or non-procedural.
- The mapping between logical processes and actual programs or program modules i.e. will one logical process equal one program, or a suite of programs?
- What tools within the processing system will be used, and for what?
- The extent to which physical data design can be automated, or optimised.
- Relative priority of timing, space and maintainability objectives, etc.

- Timing and space estimation methods.
- The mechanism for storing business rules i.e. with the data, or using validation processes.

The level of detail required in the Physical Design Strategy will depend largely on the experience of the design team, and the level of control over the above issues allowed by the physical environment.

7.3.4   Summary (Step 610)

The SSADM tasks carried out in Step 610 are:

Task

10	Classify the chosen physical environment (processing system, data storage facilities and DBMS performance characteristics).
20	Design DBMS space and timing estimation forms.
30	Specify standards for the use of the physical environments processing and data facilities.
40	Establish the product-specific data design rules.
50	Specify naming standards for the project.
60	Produce a Physical Design Strategy for the physical design and specification of the system. Tailor the SSADM steps to fit with the physical environment.
70	Start preparing the user, training and operations manuals.
80	Agree the Physical Design Strategy with the project board.

7.4   Step 620 - Create Physical Data Design

The Required System Logical Data Model provides a picture of how users view system data and of its underlying business meaning. It does not tell us how this system data should be physically organised or stored.

In SSADM the transformation of the Required System Logical Data Model into physical data design takes place in two steps: first-cut data design, where general and product-specific rules are applied to create a data design which matches the Required System Logical Data Model as closely as possible; optimised data design, where the first-cut design is tested against performance objectives and tuned as necessary.

In Step 620 we are concerned with first-cut data design. It should be noted that the Required System Logical Data Model is *not* replaced by the physical data design. Indeed it is by far the most permanent of the two data models and could be used to generate a number of physical data designs over the lifetime of the system as the physical environment alters.

The technique of first-cut data design involves applying a number of transformations based on general assumptions about the target Database Management System, followed by product-specific rules as embodied in the DBMS Data Storage Classification.

It is in the first stage, applying the general rules, that the analyst will be able to participate fully in Physical Design. The activities involved are fairly straightforward and quick to apply, and a knowledge of the system as a whole will be helpful. The application of product-specific rules may be a specialist activity.

7.4.1 DBMS Assumptions

To be a suitable candidate for the application of first-cut data design SSADM assumes a Database Management System will have the following properties:

- Entities are stored as record types.
- Records are accessed in blocks.
- Records that are likely to be accessed together are stored as groups. In practice this means physically grouping together hierarchies of masters and details, with the record type at the top of a hierarchy being known as its root.
- Relationships between masters and details within a physical group are supported.
- Relationships between records in different groups are supported.

This is not to say that all Database Management Systems will make these properties visible to the developer. In many non-procedural environments they will be hidden, and a first-cut data design generated automatically from the Required System Logical Data Model (using application generators, data definition screens or languages).

7.4.2 Develop Physical Data Design

The Required System Logical Data Model is transformed into the Physical Data Design by carrying out the following eight activities. The first seven produce an intermediate design known informally as a physical data model. The eighth activity (applying product-specific rules) then uses this to create the Physical Data Design.

1. Adapt Required System Logical Data Model

We begin the transformation of the Required System Logical Data Model by identifying those aspects of the Logical Data Structure that are not required in a physical data model (i.e. those that deal with business rules that are not relevant to Physical Data Design).

We can then produce a physical data model to be used as a working document throughout the step.

The features of a Required System Logical Data Model that are not needed in a physical data model are:

- Relationship names.
- Master to detail optionality (not maintainable in Relational Database Management Systems).
- Exclusion arcs.

There are some notational differences between logical and physical data models:

- Round cornered, or soft boxes are converted to square cornered, or hard boxes in order to differentiate between the two types of structure.
- Detail to master optionality is denoted by an "o" on a solid relationship line, rather than a dashed line (see Figure 7.3).

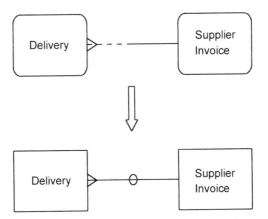

Figure 7.3 - Detail to Master Optionality in Physical Design

- Detail to master exclusion arcs are replaced by an "o" on the relationship line (see Figure 7.4).

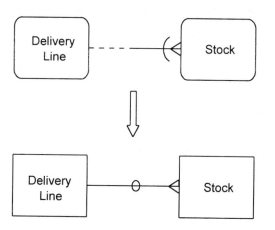

Figure 7.4 - Detail to Master Exclusion Arcs in Physical Design

If entity and relationship volumes have not yet been added to the Logical Data Structure they should be established and added to the physical data model. The entity volumes show the average number of occurrences of each entity. This information should have been collected as part of Logical Data Modelling, and documented in the Entity Descriptions.

The relationship volumes indicate how many detail entity occurrences each master entity will have. Often the ratio of detail entity volume to master entity volume will give a reasonably accurate figure but where optional relationships exist this guideline has to be used with care: there are not 250 Stock occurrences per Transfer Line, because most Stocks result from Deliveries, not Transfers.

2. Identify Required Entry Points

Access entry points can be identified by looking at Effect Correspondence Diagrams and Enquiry Access Paths. Each entry point is indicated on the physical data model by an arrow pointing to the relevant entry, with the input data items listed alongside. The access data items are then compared with the key of the entity, and if they do not match we have a non-key entry point. Each non-key entry point is indicated by adding a lozenge-shaped box to the entity as shown next to the Delivery entity in Figure 7.5.

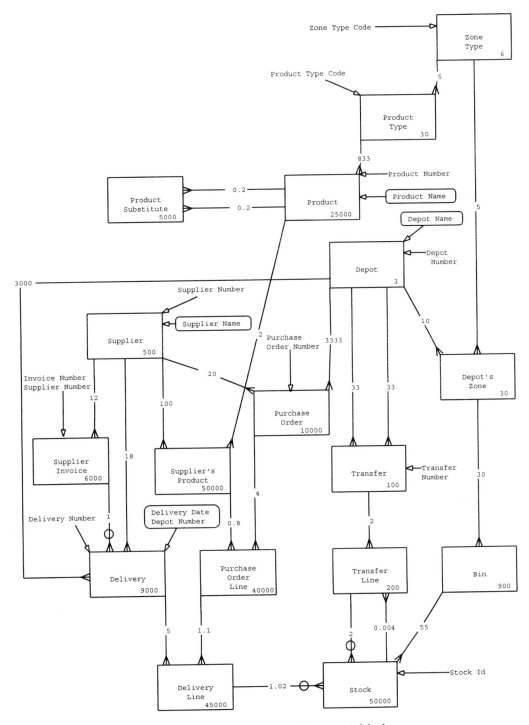

Figure 7.5 - Physical Data Model With Entry Points Added

3. Identify Roots of Physical Hierarchies

Root entities lie at the top of the physical groupings based on master-detail hierarchies. There are two stages to identifying roots.

Firstly:

- An entity is a root if it has no master.

Secondly:

- An entity is a root if it is a direct entry point; *unless* it has a compound key which contains the key of a root entity.

Each root entity is identified by adding a stripe to the top of its box (Figure 7.6).

Applying the first rule, Supplier, Zone Type and Depot become roots.

Applying the second rule, notice that Supplier Invoice is a direct entry point, but its key contains the key of Supplier which is already a root. Therefore Supplier Invoice is not a root. The other direct entry points become roots.

Secondary or non-key access is ignored when determining groups.

4. Identify Allowable Groups For Non-Root Entities

We now look at the physical data model to identify which root entities each non-root entity could allowably be grouped with.

- A non-root entity can only belong to a group if the group contains one of its mandatory masters.
- If a non-root entity has two mandatory masters and it is a direct entry point, it should be grouped with the one whose key is part of its own key.

Each allowable grouping should be drawn on the model. 'Stand-alone' root entities, i.e. those with no non-root details, will form single entity groupings on their own. Allowable groups are shown in Figure 7.6.

5. Apply Least Dependent Occurrence Rule

If a non-root entity can allowably be placed in more than one group, we choose the one in which it occurs the least. This is done by working up from the non-root entity to the root of the group, and multiplying together the volumes of the relationships connecting all of the entities in the hierarchy. The non-root entity is then placed in the group with the lowest total.

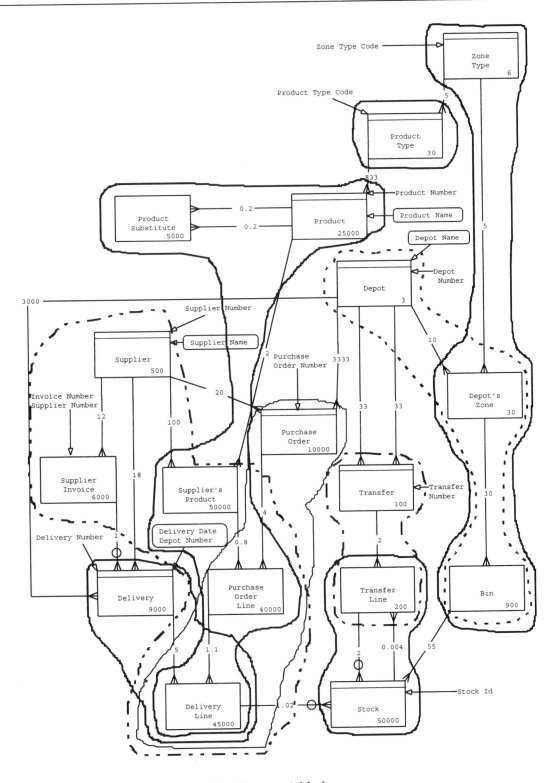

Figure 7.6 - Roots and Allowable Groups Added

For example, Delivery Line could be grouped with one of four groups: Product, Supplier, Purchase Order or Delivery. The relationship volume with Delivery is five (i.e. there are an average of five Delivery Line occurrences for each Delivery). For every Purchase Order there are 4.4 Delivery Lines (Each Purchase Order has four Purchase Order Lines, and each Purchase Order Line has 1.1 Delivery Lines). For every Supplier there are 88 Delivery Lines. For every Product there are less than two Delivery Lines, so Delivery Line is grouped with Product.

Continuing in this manner for the rest of the model results in the groupings shown in Figure 7.7.

6. Establish Block Size

We now need to establish the standard block size to be used in Physical Data Design. Choosing a suitable block size involves considering the sizes that can be handled by the Database Management System, the amount of memory available for reading blocks into (blocks must be smaller than the available memory) and the size of the most commonly used groups. In practice there may be little choice, due to installation standards or physical constraints. Ideally the block size will be large enough to accommodate even the largest groups. For SRW we will assume that a block size of 2000 bytes is the most suitable.

7. Split Physical Groups to Fit Block Size

We now need to examine each block in the physical data model to see if it will fit into the chosen block size.

The size of each record is calculated by adding up the lengths of the attributes in the entity description. The number of records accessed in each block is calculated by starting at the root of the block (which will occur once) and working down the hierarchy multiplying the number of occurrences of the previous entity by the connecting relationship's volume.

The total space required for the block is then arrived at by adding up the space required for each record type (the number of occurrences multiplied by the length of the record), and allowing for any space overheads involved in maintaining relationship and disk maintenance.

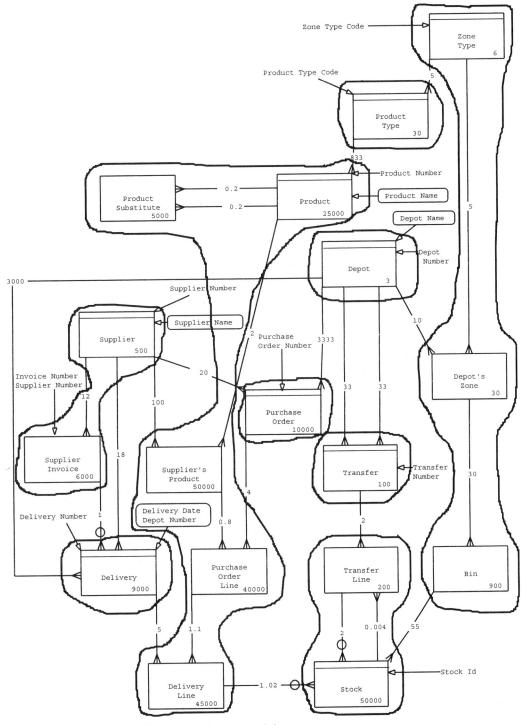

Figure 7.7 - Grouped Physical Data Model

For example let us look at the group containing Product, Supplier's Product, Purchase Order Line and Delivery Line:

Record Types in Group	Length (bytes)	Records per block	Size (bytes)
Product	100	1	100
Supplier's Product	45	2	90
Purchase Order Line	64	1.6	102
Delivery Line	48	1.8	86
		Total size of group	378
		Add 20% overhead	453

Figure 7.8 - Sizing of Product Group

Clearly a group which is 453 bytes in size will fit into the chosen block size of 2000 bytes.

Any group that will not fit into the block size must be split into smaller groups. We do this by working from the bottom of the grouping until the largest sub-group that will fit into the block size is reached, which we then split off to form a new group. This means that when we need to access the original grouping the necessary number of accesses is kept to a minimum.

For instance, the sizing for the Zone Type group is as follows:

Record Types in Group	Length (bytes)	Records per block	Size (bytes)
Zone Type	32	1	32
Depot's Zone	8	5	40
Bin	14	150	2100
		Total size of group	2172
		Add 20% overhead	2606

Figure 7.9 - Sizing of Zone Type Group

The size of the Zone Type group exceeds the given block size, so we must split off Bin into a group of its own.

8. Apply Product Specific Rules

The physical data model is now transformed into our first-cut Physical Data Design by applying product-specific rules. Most of these rules will have been identified as part of the DBMS classifications, and the extent of their application will be included in the Physical Design strategy.

7.4.3   Summary (Step 620)

The SSADM tasks carried out in Step 620 are:

Task

10	Convert the Logical Data Model into a physical data model by removing elements which are not needed for physical data design.
20	Identify required entry points.
30	Identify roots of physical hierarchies.
40	Identify allowable groupings for non-root entities.
50	Apply least dependent occurrence rule.
60	Establish block size.
70	Split physical groups to fit block size.
80	Apply product-specific data design rules.

7.5   Step 630 - Create Function Component Implementation Map (FCIM)

This is a rather curiously named step, as we actually do a great deal more than simply create the Function Component Implementation Map. It is here that we carry out most of the physical processing design activities. Indeed by the end of Step 630 the only processing design elements left to complete are the specification of procedural programs and the Process Data Interface.

The main parts to this step are:

- Complete the specification of each function.
- Create the Function Component Implementation Map.
- Implement non-procedural fragments of the system.

The word *fragment* refers to the physical implementation of a logical function *component*.

7.5.1   The Function Component Implementation Map

SSADM is very firm in its promotion of the Function Component Implementation Map as a design control and mapping concept, but rather vague on how it should look or be organised. Therefore the Function Component Implementation Map elements and diagrams presented in this section should be taken as suggestions only. The general idea is that each organisation will develop its own standards depending on the target physical environment.

The Function Component Implementation Map acts as the central reference point for tying together all of the physical fragments of the system and relating them to the logical components as identified in the Universal Function Model. As such it underpins the entire physical process design activity.

A Function Component Implementation Map should satisfy three principal objectives:

(i) Map Logical Components to Physical Fragments

Each logical component of a function will be implemented as at least one physical fragment. In practice it is likely that many components will be split into several fragments, e.g. a logical dialogue may be implemented as several screens, or a logical process as several programs or modules.

(ii) Identify Common Components or Fragments

Ideally we should be aiming to maximise re-use of fragments such as modules or screens. Common processing fragments will often (but not always) reflect common logical processing as identified in Elementary Process Descriptions and Function Definitions. It may also reflect the grouping of functions into 'super functions', e.g. the batching together of several off-line functions into a single execution of a super function. Duplicate I/O fragments may reflect the appearance of a single event in more than one function (resulting in the duplication of I/O Structure Elements), or the re-use of physical screen layouts in more than one function.

(iii) Identify Implementation Route

It is extremely important to fully consider which of the available implementation routes are applicable to each function component and/or fragment. The Function Component Implementation Map can assist in this by supplying a matrix that lists fragments down one side and all possible implementation methods along the other. The implementation route of each fragment can be further documented by allocating personnel to its development, and by linking it to relevant program specifications.

The concept of a Function Component Implementation Map is all well and good; it does enforce controls and rigour over the development of the physical design. However, the layout of a Function Component Implementation Map poses quite a problem and most organisations are probably best advised to develop their own, suited to their project procedures and physical environment.

Figures 7.10 and 7.11 offer suggestions for a two-part Function Component Implementation Map. Part A deals with the mapping of logical components to physical fragments, and the make-up of super functions. As super functions can legitimately be made up of other super functions, they, along with functions themselves, will appear on both axes.

Part B deals with mapping physical fragments back to logical components, and in doing so identifies where they will be re-used. It also documents the implementation route of each fragment. Any processing fragments marked as N (Non-procedural) will actually be implemented in this step; those marked as P (Procedural) will be formally specified in Step 640. The number of the program specification that details its implementation is shown in the fourth column.

	Logical Component	Physical Fragment	Super Function Id SF 1	SF 2	SF 3
	Function 1 (F1)		X		
1	Input	1.1 (I/P)			
2	Input Process	1.2 (Proc)			
3	Event 1 Process	1.3 (Proc)			
		1.4 (Proc)			
4	Event 2 Process	1.5 (Proc)			
5	Error Process	1.6 (Proc)			
6	Valid Output	1.7 (O/P)			
7	Output Process	1.8 (Proc)			
8	Error Output	1.9 (O/P)			
	Super Function 1 (SF !)			X	
9	Function 2 Input (F 2)	1.1 (I/P)	X		

Figure 7.10 - FCIM Part 1

Physical Fragment	Logical Component	P/N	Specification No.	Screen	Report	Screen Painter	3GL	4GL
1.1 (I/P)	1, 9, 20		1	X		X		
1.2 (Proc)	2	N				X		
1.3 (Proc)	3	N						
1.4 (Proc)	3, 12	P	2					X
1.5 (Proc)	4	N					X	
1.6 (Proc)	5	N						X
1.7 (O/P)	6		3		X			X
1.8 (Proc)	7	N						
1.9 (O/P)	8		4	X				

Figure 7.11 - FCIM Part 2

7.5.2   Completing Function Specifications

Each element of the Function Component Implementation Map (with the exception of procedural program specifications and *physical* database accesses) must now be fully specified, and linked back to the Function Component Implementation Map. Looking at the Universal Function Model (Figure 7.10) there are several elements that have not yet been specified: syntax errors i.e. input data errors; I/O processes, including sorts; error outputs.

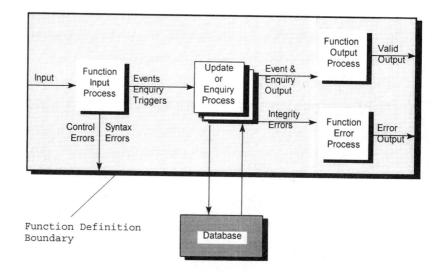

Figure 7.12 - Universal Function Model

In addition we must also decide on the physical formats of all inputs and outputs, e.g. printer, screen, file transfer system; and carry out actual physical dialogue design, i.e. the translation of Dialogue Structures, Menu Structures and Command Structures. This will involve many style issues and will usually be driven by a combination of installation standards and the capabilities of the physical environment.

In environments that contain an application generator and screen painter all of these fragments can usually be developed quickly and easily, once decisions on layout and style have been taken. However in entirely procedural environments each screen may need building by hand and be backed by complex input and output programs also developed with little or no automation. Every error message and all command structure translations are likely to require individual specification and construction. All of this can combine to form the largest part of the implementation phase.

Within each function we will need to decide on success units. A success unit is a set of inputs, outputs and processing that must succeed as a whole, i.e. that when complete will leave the system in a logically consistent state. Success units can be defined at event level i.e. all effects for a single event occurrence, or at the level of groups of related effects within a function. Success units will often relate directly to programs or program modules.

Any function fragments that are entirely non-procedural in nature can be implemented at this point. Further program specification of such fragments would be a waste of effort, as part of the justification of non-procedural development tools is that we do not need to specify *how* the program should process data, but merely *what* the program should deliver. Procedural processing fragments do need further detailed specification in Step 650.

7.5.3 Summary (Step 630)

The SSADM tasks carried out in Step 630 are:

Task

10   Review all functions to identify and remove as much duplicate processing as possible.

20   Review all functions to identify and maximise the sharing of common processing.

Repeat tasks 30 - 80 for each function:

30	Specify success units.
40	Specify syntax error processing.
50	Specify control mechanisms and error handling.
60	Specify the physical format of all system interfaces (with other systems, reports, data storage, users etc.).
70	Design the physical components of each dialogue, including report layouts, screens, menus etc.
80	Implement non-procedural function components using the physical environment's application generation facilities.

7.6   Step 640 - Optimise Physical Data Design

The first-cut data design produced in Step 620 is a more-or-less direct translation of the Required System Logical Data Model. If this could be implemented without amendment the resulting database should be easily understood and queried, maintainable and above all robust (as it would be based closely on the underlying data needs of the organisation). However, included in the non-functional requirements for the new system are pre-set performance objectives (relating to target data storage volumes and processing speed), and we may find that our first-cut data design would be unable to meet these objectives. In this case the design will need optimising.

Optimisation is a highly specialised activity and is well beyond the scope of both SSADM and this book; it is an activity that is really best left to database experts. The overall objective of optimisation is to meet performance objectives while preserving the one-to-one mapping between the Required System Logical Data Model and the final Physical Design as much as possible. Indeed, if we are forced to consider compromising the data structure we should try to negotiate reduced performance objectives with users first.

Clearly the extent to which data designs can be optimised will depend heavily on the physical environment concerned. As part of the DBMS classification we will already be aware of available mechanisms, and will have developed an approach to their use in the Physical Design Strategy. It should always be borne in mind that optimisation can be an expensive activity (especially if data structure changes lead to a complex PDI), and that the law of diminishing returns will apply. If optimisation leads to too much development effort and cost, it might be cheaper to purchase more efficient or powerful data management facilities.

The brief guidelines presented below are generic in nature, and relate more to a recommended approach to optimisation, than to optimisation techniques themselves. As well as trade-offs between development costs and performance improvements, there are often trade-offs to be made between meeting time and storage objectives, which may conflict. This all leads to an iterative process of optimisation as shown in Figure 7.13.

Identify Storage and Timing Objectives

Performance objectives are recorded in the Requirements Catalogue in Stage 3. We now carry these forward to test against our physical data design.

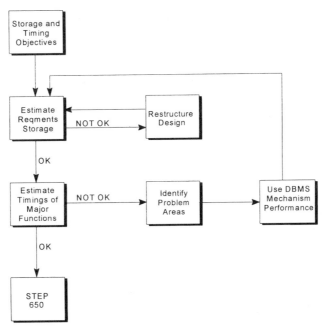

Figure 7.13 - Optimisation Cycle

Estimate Storage Requirements

The amount of storage required by our physical data model is estimated by calculating the size of all entities and multiplying by their estimated number of occurrences. We then add to this the storage required by data management mechanisms such as indexes, pointers and security measures. Finally we must allow some contingency for future expansion. The resulting storage requirement can then be checked against our objectives and if everything is OK we will proceed to look at timings. If our storage objectives are not met by Physical Data Design as it stands we will need to restructure it and carry out a re-estimation.

Restructure Design

Data Storage objectives are usually much less strictly defined than timing objectives (due to the relatively low cost of purchasing extra storage), so rather than restructuring the Physical Data Design we may be able to persuade users to relax them. If not then there are two possibilities:

Firstly, utilise data storage facilities:

- Improve data distribution.
- Change record types (e.g. from fixed to variable length).
- Pack data (by removing blank spaces).

Secondly, compromise one-to-one mapping:

- Reduce historical entity occurrences.
- Introduce summary records.
- Reduce attribute lengths.
- Delete derivable data.
- Eliminate 'classification' or 'type' entities.

Some of these measures (for example data packing) will have an adverse impact on timings, so may lead to problems and trade-offs with other performance objectives later on.

Estimate Timings of Major Functions

Estimating the timings of all functions in the system may be impractical, so we must pick only the *major* functions. To do this we will look for functions that are time critical or that are likely to involve large numbers of database accesses. The latter category is often associated with functions that create or read the most populous entities (usually those near the bottom of the Logical Data Structure hierarchy).

If the physical environment has automated database definition facilities we may be able to simulate the required accesses for each major function, and so compare actual timings with our objectives. If not, these timings will have to be estimated using specialist knowledge of the Database Management System's data access mechanisms (as identified in the DBMS Classification). This is not an easy task and is almost certainly a task for the experts.

If timings are assessed as acceptable then we can proceed to the next step in Physical Design; if not then we will need to identify which elements of the access mechanisms are giving us problems, so that they can be timed to achieve our pre-set objectives.

Improving Database Timings

Timings can be improved in two ways:

By using the Database Management System facilities:

- Changing access methods.
- Placing details near most commonly associated masters.
- Indexing.
- Sorts.
- Adjusting block sizes.
- Using faster access storage devices for critical data.
- Holding data in memory.
- Changing packing methods/application.

By compromising the data structure:

- De-normalising data (reduces read timings, increases update timings).
- Postponing updates.
- Adding redundant data (e.g. derivable data items).
- Alter processing to fit data hierarchy.

Most of these activities, and others like them, will be carried out (if the environment allows) by Database Managers or Data Administrators, so may be beyond the abilities of the SSADM analyst.

As mentioned earlier, compromising the data structure should always be a last resort and should certainly follow attempts to re-negotiate performance objectives. Whatever the outcome, once we have completed any timing optimisation activities we will need to make another pass through the storage estimation and checking tasks, to ensure that objectives in this area can still be met.

7.6.1   Summary (Step 640)

The SSADM tasks carried out in Step 640 are:

Task

10	Optimise the physical data design to fit with storage constraints, preserving the one-one mapping with the Logical Data Model wherever possible.
20	Optimise the physical data design to fit with timing objectives, preserving the one-one mapping with the Logical Data Model wherever possible.

7.7   Step 650 - Complete Function Specification

Any function components that have procedural fragments in them now need to be fully specified. Each organisation will have its own standards for procedural program design and specification, and these should be strictly adhered to. In largely 3GL environments this step is likely to form a substantial part of the Physical Design stage.

It is difficult to offer very much general guidance in this area without going into details of program design methodologies such as Jackson Structured Programming; see Jackson (1975).

One of the initial tasks, regardless of method, will be to identify how logical processes will equate with program or run-time units. Again this is likely to be an issue of organisational standards or physical environment characteristics, as set out in the Processing System Classification.

As well as the logical processes of the Universal Function Model, we may need to specify: input or output sorts; processes to resolve any structure clashes from Stage 5; and data optimisation processes identified in Step 640.

7.8   Step 660 - Consolidate Process Data Interface

Step 660 marks the end of the core SSADM development process. It also marks the coming together of Physical Data Design and Physical Process Specification (see Figure 7.14).

All of the processing elements in the Function Component Implementation Map view data as if the Required System Logical Data Model exists physically. In other words all data accesses are designed to operate on the logical database. As a result of Physical Data Design, particularly optimisation, we may not have been able to implement the Logical Database directly. So we now specify a Process Data Interface (PDI) which sits between our processing fragments and the physical database and acts as a translator or mapper from one view to the other (Figure 7.15).

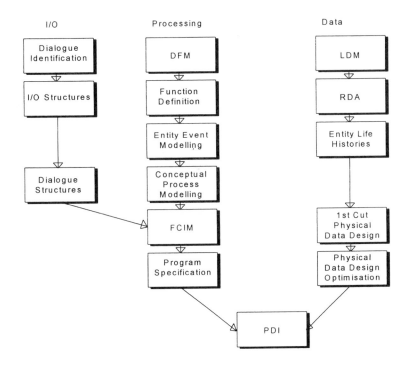

Figure 7.14 - Bringing Together the Physical Data Design and Physical Process Specification

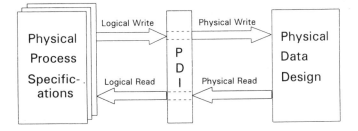

Figure 7.15 - Process Data Interface (PDI)

In effect we are adding a further optional component to the Universal Function Model (see Figure 7.16). It is optional in the sense that the Database Management System may well provide facilities for defining a logical view of the data and will then handle the physical mappings itself.

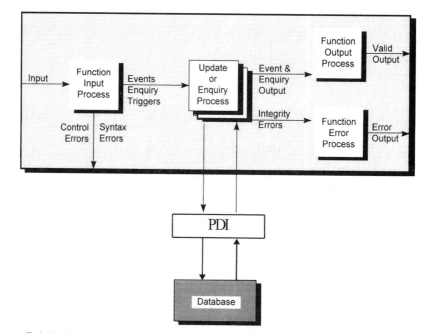

Figure 7.16 - Position of PDI Relative to the UFM

In cases where the Database Management System does not provide these facilities we will need to develop a Process Data Interface from scratch. This will involve examining the access requirements of each function component, identifying relevant physical data items (records, keys, etc.), and designing an access path to map between the two views. In some environments this may be a very complex and time-consuming task.

However, PDI development costs should be balanced against the likely benefits:

- **Logical/physical data independence.** By ensuring that processing is carried out on the logical data model we build in a degree of adaptability. Changes in the physical storage of data (e.g. reorganisation of disk packs, change of Database Management System) will be reflected in an updated Process Data Interface, but will leave functions unchanged. Similarly, new versions of a function or entirely new functions will lead to changes in the Process Data Interface, but should minimise necessary physical data reorganisation. In addition, by shielding users from physical data structures we enable them to take as full a part as possible in the design of processing and ad-hoc queries.

- **Documentation.** The Process Data Interface provides live documentation of physical design decisions.

- **Data design independence.** By building a buffer between data and processing, we can limit the impact of data optimisation activities. The Process Data Interface itself can then be optimised by efficient coding or choice of language.
- **Maintenance costs.** In most cases, despite the need to maintain the Process Data Interface itself, it will be less expensive and easier to maintain programs using a Process Data Interface than programs with hard coded data accesses.

Process Data Interface development is yet another area of Physical Design where specialist help is almost inevitably required. The extent to which a Process Data Interface is used is likely to be based on calculations of its net benefits, and its impact on system performance.

All Process Data Interface elements should be added to the Function Component Implementation Map (in the same way as any other fragment) in order to document which components they will interface with.

Finally, as Step 660 signals the end of Physical Design, we must update the Requirements Catalogue with details of any design decisions which have an impact on how well user requirements have been satisfied.

7.8.1   Summary (Step 660)

The SSADM tasks carried out in Step 660 are:

Task	
10	Identify mismatches between the logical view of data used in function specification and the physical database.
20	Identify the keys of all data subject to a mismatch.
30	Specify the mechanism to be used in mapping from one view to the other, thus resolving all mismatches.
40	Ensure that no elements of the Process Data Interface are duplicates.
50	Document the Process Data Interface processes in the Function Component Implementation Map.
60	Update the Requirements Catalogue to show where data requirements may have been compromised.

7.9   The Products of Physical Design

The final deliverables of SSADM are the Physical Design and Application Development Standards. The following products will need to be checked for completeness and consistency:

- Function Component Implementation Map
- Function Definitions
- Optimised Physical Data Design
- Required System Logical Data Model
- Requirements Catalogue
- Process Data Interface specification
- Space and timing estimations

Once these are complete, we can publish them, and move on to implementation.

But that is another story.

7.10   Physical Design Exercise

7.1 Carry out 1st Cut Data design on the Natlib Logical Data Structure from exercise 2.3, using the following volume information:

- Natlib keeps details of 500 titles.
- There are an average of 3.2 copies of each title.
- Natlib has 1000 registered readers.
- There are 2400 loan records.
- There are 250 recorded reservations.

The keys and lengths of each entity are as follows:

Title:	ISBN	400
Book Copy:	ISBN/Copy No.	100
Reservation:	Reservation No.	120
Loan:	Loan No.	60
Reader:	Reader No.	350

Direct entry is required to all entities, except Book Copy. Assume that the block size is 6000 bytes.

8 Feasibility Study

8.1 Stage 0 - Feasibility

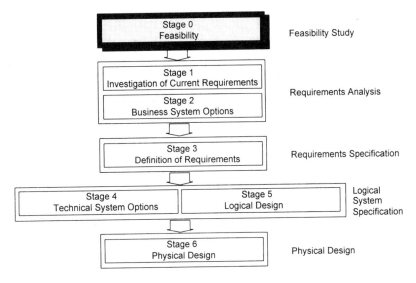

Figure 8.1 - The Stages of SSADM

Many of the proposals for new Information Systems that come out of strategy planning are vague and uncosted. Before we commit resources to their development we need to ensure that they are feasible. By feasible we mean justifiable in terms of net benefits compared to overall costs, and technically possible. Feasibility assessment is an activity that can take many forms, varying from informal studies carried out as part of strategy planning to high level systems analysis projects. The basic questions to be answered in any kind of feasibility study are:

- Is there a computer solution to the given business problem?
- Is the solution justifiable in business terms (organisationally and financially)? e.g. Will benefits outweigh costs? Will the proposed solution be politically acceptable? Can the solution be developed in time?

The approach adopted by SSADM is to carry out an overview systems analysis in order to answer the first question, and to gather quantitative information as we go along to help in answering the second.

SSADM regards the Feasibility Study as an optional stage as project feasibility may have already been established during strategy planning, or the study may be unnecessary where there is little risk or choice in commencing with a full study straightaway.

An SSADM Feasibility Study involves applying several core techniques at a very high level.

There are several points in the life cycle where a decision to drop the project might be made. The Feasibility Study stage provides easily the most cost effective point to do so and this provides the major justification for carrying it out. The Feasibility Study presents a low-risk strategy for commencing a full SSADM study, in that likely costs are low, while many of the outputs can form the basis for subsequent detailed analysis work.

8.2 Structure

The Feasibility Study module consists of a single stage, appropriately enough called 'Feasibility'

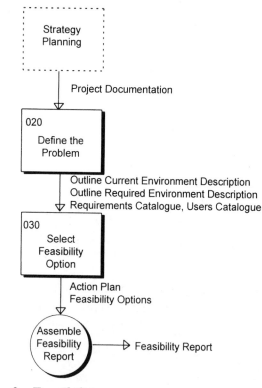

Figure 8.1 - Stage 0 - Feasibility

The Feasibility stage contains two steps which resemble the other two 'decision' stages of SSADM, namely Business System Options and

Technical System Options. The main difference between feasibility and the other two decision steps is one of emphasis and scope:

020 - Define the Problem

The business problem to be solved is defined by comparing required services with the current position and user representation is agreed.

The relevant project documentation, usually handed down through a strategy plan, is set into motion. An overview of the current system, with its associated problems and limitations, is fleshed out a little, and a catalogue of system users is set up.

The required system is also outlined using Logical Data Modelling and Data Flow Modelling, and more detail is collected on user requirements.

030 - Select Feasibility Option

Several options are developed to provide alternative solutions to the business problem as defined in Step 020.

A single option is selected and the direction of the rest of the SSADM study is agreed (or the project is terminated).

Assemble Feasibility Report

The products of the Feasibility Study are checked and put together for publication as the Feasibility Report.

8.3 Step 020 - Define the Problem

As soon as a fair idea of the scope and complexity of the proposed project is ascertained, plans for the rest of the Feasibility Study are drawn up. Any problems or inconsistencies with the terms of reference are also resolved.

Every project should have its own project management procedures or method (e.g. PRINCE), which we will now use to plan the main part of the Feasibility Study. A detailed discussion of the activities involved in this planning are beyond the scope of this book, but a few activities which must certainly be carried out are worth outlining.

- The key users and managers in the business area under investigation should be identified and their commitment sought for the rest of the Feasibility Study. User involvement in the study is essential to its success, so written confirmation of user participation is extremely desirable, if possible giving firm dates for meetings or secondments.
- The SSADM products and techniques to be used in the study must be identified and assigned to appropriate project team members.

- The scoping exercise will reveal areas of the system which will require particularly careful analysis, because of their complexity or importance to the success of the business. These areas will require special planning and may need more detailed investigation and additional fact finding.

The main aim is to investigate the requirements of the new system to a level which will enable the project team to define possible development solutions, and to evaluate the extent of new support compared with existing systems. To do this we will develop overviews of the current environment, adding a little more detail where necessary, and develop similar overview models for the required system.

To support the aim of the step we have several specific objectives:

- To gain a fuller understanding of the required functional support and information needs of the business area.
- To develop a more detailed picture of existing systems in order to identify problems and missing support.
- To identify the users of the new system, and their current responsibilities.

By the end of this step we should have a reasonable description of both the current and required systems. Using these descriptions we will then be able to draw up a Problem Definition Statement in agreement with management, which summarises and assigns priorities to the requirements of the new system and reveals the full extent of the work involved in moving from the current position to the required position.

During feasibility we must be careful to restrict analysis to the most important elements of function and information. Our purpose is to understand the fundamental requirements, not to specify the complete new system. The required system outline will consist of an overview LDS and a *logical* overview DFM.

Part of the purpose of Step 020 is to provide a statement of the 'ideal' required system, albeit in outline. In Step 030 we may find that it is not feasible to develop this ideal, but that it is feasible to develop an intermediate system, some way between the current and required systems. We must be careful to leave such decisions to Step 030 and concentrate now on building models encompassing all high level user requirements.

As outlined in Chapter 1, SSADM adopts an approach of specifying user requirements logically, and only later maps the resulting logical design onto a physical environment. The DFD created in Step 020 to reflect the required system will thus be a *logical* DFD.

When developing the Current Physical DFD we are able to verify its accuracy quite easily by checking that it mirrors what was actually happening on the ground. With required DFDs there is nothing 'real' with which to compare. Therefore we are likely to spend a great deal of effort in assessing users' often conflicting and sometimes rather vague wishes, in order to arrive at a sensible and accurate view of business requirements (and into agreeing this view with management).

This gives us the freedom to be creative as we are not restricted by any physical constraints, enabling us to describe an ideal picture of how the new system should function. On the other hand it means that the success of the model is highly dependent on our ability to ask the right questions of the right users.

A context diagram and/or a Business Activity Model might again be helpful in starting off DFD development, as it will identify the major logical data flows into and out of the system and its main external entities.

However rather than going about this in an ad-hoc fashion we can try to be a little more methodical by identifying the major functional areas that the system will be required to support, and using these as a checklist of high level processes to be covered by the overview DFD.

For example using the Project Initiation Document (PID), preliminary interview results and the Requirements Catalogue we draw up the following list of functional areas for the new SRW system:

- Placement of purchase orders
- Receipt of deliveries
- Recording of new stocks
- Despatch of customer orders
- Transfer of stock between depots
- Invoice matching
- Maintenance and monitoring of stock position
- Monitoring of supplier performance

Further interviews confirm the above list and add a new activity, distinct from Purchase Order placement, of maintaining a delivery schedule for each depot. At the moment deliveries are arranged for specific dates and suppliers are told whether to deliver in the morning or afternoon. This has led to frequent bottlenecks, so in the future deliveries will be scheduled in half hour slots.

While concentrating on the processing aspects of the system we should not neglect to maintain overview Logical Data Models at the same level of detail as the Data Flow Models we create.

During our investigations of the current and required environment in Step 020 we also expand the requirements catalogue considerably.

Any areas that require improved system support should be recorded in the Requirements Catalogue. Requirements for additional areas of support from the new system should be added to the Requirements Catalogue as well as the required system models.

By comparing the overview models of the required and current environments we should be able to identify most of the new required functionality, so providing a check that the Requirements Catalogue is complete.

While updating the Requirements Catalogue, a User Catalogue is also developed. In feasibility the main purpose of the User Catalogue is to support the identification of users in the current environment. If needed, the prevailing work practices are documented either in a separate Work Practice Model or in an extended Requirements Catalogue entry.

The current and required environment models, together with the Requirements Catalogue, provide a formal definition of the business problem. However, to present these products in isolation to users and project managers may make it difficult to obtain agreement as to their accuracy.

So a Problem Definition Statement is produced, providing a textual summary of requirements and their relative priority. It should include references to the formal SSADM products (which it does not replace but merely supplements), and should include a list of the minimum requirements.

Once the Problem Definition Statement is agreed by users and management the Feasibility Study can proceed to Step 030, where it is used to formulate options for the rest of the project.

8.3.1   Summary (Step 020)

The SSADM tasks carried out in Step 020 are:

Task

10   Review the PID. Establish scope and complexity of project by creating or extending overview models of current processing and data. Define high level requirements for the new system. Agree scope and user representation for Feasibility Study. Plan the Feasibility Study. Record problems with the current services in the Requirements Catalogue.

20   Create an Outline Required Environment Description using an overview LDS and, as necessary, a BAM and/or DFM.

30   Record prospective users of the required system in a User Catalogue.

40   Identify additional functional and non-functional requirements for the new system, and record them in the Requirements Catalogue.

50   Produce a Problem Definition Statement summarising the users' requirements.

60   Agree the Problem Definition Statement with the Project Board.

8.4   Step 030 - Select Feasibility Options

The main aims of Step 030 are to identify the best option in business terms for solving the problem defined in the PDS, and to provide an outline plan for development of the chosen option.

A Feasibility Option is really a high level combination of two standard SSADM products:

- **Business System Option (BSO).** A BSO defines the functional scope of a proposed solution. At its most basic level it consists of the set of Requirements Catalogue entries satisfied by the solution. All BSOs must satisfy the minimum requirement as identified by users (i.e. those with a priority of 'essential').
- **Technical Systems Option (TSO).** A TSO defines a possible technical environment for the implementation of the system. It will include descriptions of hardware and software, technical support arrangements, distribution of the system and development tools.

Step 030 consists of a series of distinct tasks designed to guide us through the process of selecting the most feasible option for the rest of the project. It is not a step that leads to the production of highly specified products, as with a lot of other SSADM steps. The creation of Feasibility Options involves the application of a range of general analysis and business techniques, which lie outside the scope of core SSADM.

The basic structure of the step is very similar to that used in the selection of fully fledged BSOs and TSOs later in the project, but the overall level of detail is much lower.

We begin by outlining several BSOs and TSOs for solving the business problem. We then produce composite options that combine the two, shortlist a number of them and flesh them out a little. Finally we present the options to management who will select one of them as the basis for the rest of the project.

In practice this whole process is unlikely to proceed in sequence like this. It is far more likely to be an iterative exercise, with new options being proposed throughout.

The organisation will often have a strategic policy on technical implementations, tied to particular hardware and software platforms, or to specific suppliers.

We should use any flexibility in these existing technical policies to provide as wide a range of suitable TSOs as possible.

The investigation and selection of technical environments is a specialised process and is outside the scope of SSADM and of this text.

However, a few pointers and guidelines as provided by SSADM are worth mentioning, largely to clarify the purpose and content of TSOs.

Outline TSOs should include consideration of:

- System distribution (often influenced by the organisation of system interfacing in the BSOs).
- Hardware platforms.
- Software, e.g. 4GL, 3GL.
- Development method.
- Technical support arrangements, e.g. in-house, software house, contract staff.

In the case of SRW there is no existing technical policy, but one of the physical constraints for any new system is that existing PC hardware in the depots should be used as much as possible. The hardware and software platform of the Supplier/Product and Accounts systems will need to be looked at where interfaces are needed. For the purposes of this study two TSOs are proposed:

TSO 1: The current stand-alone depot PCs will be networked. Additional PCs will be available for each office within the depot, and will all be attached to local printers. New software will be written in-house using the 3GL and database software used for the development of the Supplier/Product system. Each depot will be responsible for operating its own network, with technical support provided in-house.

TSO 2: This option consists of a single wider network of PCs managed centrally by the in-house computing division. It will cover all of the depots, and have live links to the Supplier/Product and Sales systems. Application software will be developed in-house using the same tools as option 1, but the network software will probably be supplied by a specialist outside organisation. Once the network is in place technical support will be provided by the in-house computing division.

At this stage TSOs might include details of specific suppliers or products if the proposed environment can only be supplied by one vendor (or if an organisation's policy dictates the choice of vendor).

We now combine the outline BSOs and TSOs to produce composite Feasibility Options.

Each TSO may be capable of supporting more than one BSO and each BSO may be supportable by more than one TSO. So we could produce a number of Feasibility Options that propose several different physical implementations of a single BSO.

A brief check on the viability of each composite option should prevent the number of options getting out of hand. Feasibility Options are compared with a view to eliminating those options which offer less obvious net benefits or which are impractical given the constraints of the project (maximum cost, time scale, etc.).

The remaining Feasibility Options are then expanded by high level descriptions of the following:

- Functional support. Textual descriptions can be supplemented with DFDs and LDSs showing the subset of functional requirements covered by the option.
- Technical overview. This should extend the outline TSO description and be tailored to the specific needs of the BSO. It may be necessary to produce outline configuration diagrams.
- Costs. These will be very approximate and must include hardware, software and development, maintenance and running costs.
- Organisational Impact Analysis. Again this will be at a high level.
- Approximate timings.
- Pros and cons of the option.

For each of the shortlisted options we should draw up proposals for a development project (or projects) for its detailed analysis, design and implementation.

When deciding on possible development approaches the following should be considered:

- Is SSADM the most suitable method for developing the option? If not, what method should be used?

- How many projects are necessary? If the proposed system is large or complex, a phased approach may be best.
- Who will develop the option? Possibilities include in-house project teams, contractors, software houses, package vendors, etc.

Once we have decided on the development strategy for each option, we will need to plan all of the necessary projects in outline using the organisation's standard methods (e.g. PRINCE).

Finally the shortlisted options are presented to the project board or management; hopefully in the form of a meeting rather than by circulating a proposal report (which is all too often the case).

Our task is to assist the board in assessing the relative merits of each option, so that they can make an informed selection of a single Feasibility Option. We must also ensure that the reasons for selection are fully documented.

It is quite possible that a combination or hybrid of the Feasibility Options will be selected by the board. In this case it may be necessary to take this option away to investigate its viability and to prepare it for presentation to management at a second selection meeting. It is also possible that none of the options will appear feasible to management and the project may be halted at this point.

When a choice is made we produce an outline development plan for the chosen Feasibility Option. In most cases the project plans prepared before selection will be carried forward and adjusted to allow for any decisions made by the selection meeting. If an entirely new option is adopted by management then we may need to produce development plans from scratch.

8.4.1   Summary (Step 030)

The SSADM tasks carried out in step 030 are:

Task

10	Establish minimum requirements for the new system.
20	Produce up to six outline BSOs.
30	Produce a number of outline TSOs to support the outline BSOs.
40	Combine the BSOs and TSOs to produce a range of composite Feasibility Options. Shortlist them to leave around three options.
50	Add more detail to the shortlisted options.
60	Produce outline project plans for each Feasibility Option.
70	Present the options to the project board for selection of a single, possibly hybrid, option.

80   Develop an action plan for the selected Feasibility Option. Halt the project if no options are found to be feasible.

8.5   Assemble Feasibility Report

The products of the stage are checked for completeness and consistency and updated as appropriate to ensure the integrity of the Feasibility Study before the results are published in the form of a formal report, consisting of a set of SSADM models and documents and accompanying textual report which links together the SSADM products and provides details of project decisions and approvals.

For the Feasibility Study the formal SSADM products that require checking (and cross-checking) are:

- Outline Current Environment Description.
- Outline Required Environment Description.
- Problem Definition Statement.
- Requirements Catalogue.
- Selected Feasibility Option.
- Action Plan.

The Feasibility Report will be used to initiate the full SSADM study and so will be signed off by users and IS management.

Appendix A   Case Study

Introduction

SRW is an organisation that buys fine foods in bulk from suppliers, for re-sale to small to medium sized food retailers, typically independent delicatessens and quality food shops. SRW only deals with relatively long-life foods, such as bottled or canned products.

Organisation

SRW is divided into four main divisions: Sales and Marketing, Purchasing, Warehousing and Administration. Each division is further subdivided into sections, as shown in Figure A.1.

Figure A.1 - SRW Organisation Chart

History

SRW began trading twenty two years ago, with a single storage depot, servicing local food stores with a range of continental foods.

Ten years later the business had expanded to three depots, each covering a local region. The number of products had increased substantially but was still restricted to mainly continental foods from a few major suppliers. Around this time computers were introduced to keep records of stock levels and to support the accounts section.

SRW now has four depots and plans to open several more over the next few years. The range of products has widened over the last twelve years to include many local products, and is being extended to cover wines and beers.

SRW is no longer tied to the same small number of suppliers. With the growth in its trade SRW has been able to negotiate deals with many specialist suppliers, many of whom compete to supply the same products.

Overview of Current Business Operations

SRW stock a range of quality foods and drinks, selected by purchasers from within the Purchasing Division.

Customers send orders for items from the SRW catalogue to the Sales and Marketing Division, who then direct them to the appropriate depot.

Each depot covers a geographic region, and stocks all of the items in the SRW catalogue.

If an item is out of stock, customer orders for that item are placed on hold until stock is received from a supplier.

Information on stock levels and estimated future customer order values is assessed by the Purchasing Division who place purchase orders with suppliers to cover anticipated demand for each depot separately.

Suppliers deliver a complete order at a time to the depot, who check and record the delivery of new stock.

Invoices from suppliers are matched with delivery records by each depot and sent to the Accounts Division where payment is made according to pre-arranged terms (e.g. within 30 days of delivery).

The Accounts Division also deals with the invoicing of customers following the dispatch of goods from a depot.

Within each depot, goods are stored in zones which may consist of areas of floor, shelving, or for very small items, large plastic bins.

Computer Support

The original computer systems of ten or more years ago still form the core of the current computer support. Many changes and additions have been made and the maintenance of the systems now forms a substantial part of SRW's business overheads.

With recent expansions, particularly into wines and beers, and plans to increase both the product range and number of depots, SRW have decided to review and re-develop the existing systems.

As part of the first phase the Accounts Division has purchased a package to manage its function, and the Purchasing Division has re-written part of its system, covering supplier and product information. The system that monitors customer sales is felt to be fairly effective and will be retained.

The second phase of the strategic review covers the depot system and purchase order placement.

Terms of Reference (taken from PID)

This second phase will consist of a single project to be undertaken by the computer services team from within SRW.

The areas to be investigated include the following:

- Recording of purchase orders placed with suppliers.
- Receipt of deliveries.
- Monitoring of stock at all depots.
- Despatch of customer orders.
- Monitoring of supplier performance.

The project will begin with a study to investigate and propose options for replacing or enhancing current systems (manual and computerised) in these areas.

Given the success of the accounts package implementation and the in-house development of supplier and product information systems, solutions similar to these should be considered. If the depot system is to be replaced it should make maximum use of the new Supplier/Product database.

Although the project will be carried out by the computer services section, users from the appropriate areas must be involved, and overall responsibility for the adoption of the final system will lie with the warehousing director.

Each depot contains a limited amount of computer equipment which should be re-used by any new systems.

Major Problems

As part of its high level strategic review, SRW management have identified some major problems with current system support which any new system must address:

(i) Currently suppliers must deliver an entire purchase order at a time. This means that delivery has to wait until all items in the order are available, causing unnecessary delay.

(ii) Stock is only recorded as being held in a particular zone. As each zone is fairly large this sometimes causes problems with the location of stock when assembling a customer order.

(iii) Current systems do not allow for the transfer of stock from one depot to another, to cover for shortages in one region while there is surplus in another.

(iv) Inadequate information is available on the performance of suppliers in:

- Promptness.
- Condition of delivered goods.

- Accuracy of order satisfaction.

(v) Expansion of trade over the next few years means that the current systems will not be able to cope with future volumes of data.

(vi) Many areas of the system are rather manual in nature, and interface badly with other computer systems, e.g. details of products have to be entered twice: once in the depot stock system, and once in the new Supplier/Product system.

(vii) Existing systems are inflexible, and difficult to adapt to new working practices.

Clearly many more problems and requirements will be uncovered during the project, but any proposed system *must* address the above points.

Initial Fact-Finding Results

Initial information gathering activities lead to the following textual summary of the *current* SRW depot system:

Purchase Order Placement: Purchasers examine estimates of future customer orders and compare these with the current levels of stock held in depots. Records of stock levels are available in the form of a daily computer generated report sent by the Stock Clerk which highlights products which have fallen below their 'standard' order points. The report also includes details of customer orders awaiting despatch. Purchasers decide if new supplies are required to supplement current stock and if so details of the required quantities are sent to each depot.

The Purchase Order Clerk at each depot groups these purchase requirements by supplier into purchase orders. The delivery date and time are agreed with the supplier of each order, either at order placement time or later if necessary.

Two copies of the purchase order are filed for later processing when goods are received.

Goods Receiving: Suppliers deliver a complete order at a time with a delivery note which is checked against the original copies of the purchase order.

If goods are in poor condition or fail to match the order the delivery may be rejected. In this case the purchase order copies are marked as 'Order Cancelled' and passed to the Purchase Order Clerk. The purchase order Clerk sends an official cancellation to the supplier, files one copy of the purchase order and sends the other to the Purchaser.

If the goods are accepted one copy of the purchase order is sent to the Purchasing department, and the other is placed in a tray for collection by the Stock Clerk.

Stock Keeping: The Stock Clerk enters details of the newly accepted items onto the depot PC system and assigns the goods to a zone depending on their type, e.g. wines and beers to the bonded store, spices to the small items zone, biscuit products to the biscuit and cereal zone, etc.

The Stock Clerk then passes the purchase order copy to the Purchase Order Clerk for future matching with invoices.

Stock Keepers are provided with a printout of where to store each product, and the products are put away.

Stock-takes occur regularly and totals of goods checked with the PC-held records. Any differences are entered as amendments to stock levels. Occasionally stock may pass its sell-by date resulting in further amendments.

Despatch: Customer orders are sent to the Despatch Clerk by the Sales and Marketing division. Each order may contain detail of several products and will refer to quantities required by a single customer. Although a customer may have several food outlets, each outlet is known to the system as a separate customer.

The Despatch Clerk matches customer orders with the delivery runs timed for the next week and assigns them to specific runs. Details are then entered on the depot PC and the customer order placed in a pending file.

Every morning a report of dispatches for the day is printed and given to the Despatch Supervisor by the Despatch Clerk. Delivery runs are put together using this report and a stock listing from the Stock Clerk. The despatch report is marked with quantities despatched and a copy sent to the Stock Clerk who updates the stock levels on the PC system.

The despatch report is then passed back to the Despatch Clerk who checks the quantities against the customer order and sends this back with details of despatched goods to Sales and Marketing. A second copy of the order is sent to accounts for invoicing.

Invoice Processing: Suppliers send invoices for completed purchase orders to the Purchase Order Clerk, who matches them against the annotated purchase order copy and sends them to accounts for payment.

This rextual information forms the basis for the Business Activity Model and the initial Requirements Catalogue.

Appendix B   Bibliography and Selected Reading

Further reading on SSADM

Robinson K. and Berrisford G.
Object-Oriented SSADM
Prentice Hall 1994

CCTA (Hall J. and Slater C.)
SSADM 4+ Reference Manuals
NCC Blackwell 1995

Hargrave D.
SSADM4+ For Rapid Systems Development
McGraw-Hill 1996

Interesting reads from three decades

Jackson M.
Software Requirements and Specifications
Addison Wesley 1995

Brooks F.
The Mythical Man Month
Addison Wesley 1975

Demarco T. and Lister T.
Peopleware: productive projects and teams
Dorset House 1987

Methods and methodologies

Avison D. E. and Fitzgerald G.
Information Systems Development Methodologies, Techniques and Tools 2/e
McGraw-Hill 1995

Stowell and West
Client Led Design
McGraw-Hill 1994

Checkland P. and Scholes J.
Soft Systems Methodology in Action
Wiley 1990

Tudor D.J. and Tudor I.J.
A Comparison of Structured Methods
NCC Blackwell 1995

Flynn D.J.
Information Systems Requirements: Determination and Analysis
McGraw-Hill 1992

Rumbaugh J. et al
Object-Oriented Modelling and Design
Prentice Hall 1991

Yates D., Shields M. and Helmy D.
Systems Analysis and Design
Pitman 1994

Jackson M.
Principles of Program Design
Academic Press 1975

Lejk M. and Deeks D.
An Introduction to Systems Analysis Techniques
Prentice Hall 1998

Patching D.
Practical Soft Systems Analysis
Pitman 1990

Checkland P.
Systems Thinking Systems Practice
Wiley 1981

IS Development Management

Gilb T.
Principles of Software Engineering Management
Addison Wesley 1988

Bradley K.
Prince: A Practical Handbook
Butterworth 1993

Useful publications from CCTA

Drummond I.
Estimating With Mk II Function Point Analysis
CCTA 1992

O'Neil P.B.
Prototyping Whithin a SSADM Environment
CCTA 1993

Databases

Elmasri R. and Navathe S.
Fundamentals of Database Systems
Benjamin-Cummings 1994

Date C.J.
An Introduction to Database Systems
Addison Wesley 1995

Stanczyk S.
Programming in SQL
Pitman 1991

Appendix C   Glossary

Access Path A route through a data structure that is navigated to give access to all entities required by an enquiry or update process.

Analysis of Requirements The module consisting of Stage 1 (Investigation of Current Services) and Stage 2 (Business System Options). Its products go to make up a comprehensive statement of user requirements.

Application Development Standards Standards to be adopted during the physical design and implementation phases of the current project.

Application Generator A set of software tools, usually with a user friendly graphical interface, that automate and speed up many aspects of software construction.

Application Style Guide Standards to be adopted in the design of the human-computer interface. Although they apply to the current project they will be heavily based on the organisation-wide Installation Style Guide.

Attribute A property or piece of information which describes an entity.

BAM Business Activity Model.

BSO Business System Option.

Business Activity Model (BAM) A model describing business activities, business events and business rules.

Business Activity Modelling The technique within SSADM to describe business activities.

Business Event A happening that triggers one or more business activities.

Business System Option (BSO) A BSO defines the functional scope of a proposed solution. At its most basic level it consists of the set of Requirements Catalogue entries satisfied by the solution. All BSOs must satisfy the minimum requirement as identified by users. Developed in outline in Step 030 (Select Feasibility Option) and in detail in Stage 2 (BSOs).

Business System Options (BSOs) BSOs (note the plural) is the technique or set of guidelines provided by SSADM for creating a set of BSOs. It is also the name of Stage 2, where an option is selected for the rest of the development.

Candidate Key An attribute or group of attributes which together could be used to uniquely identify the occurrences of an entity.

Central Computer and Telecommunications Agency (CCTA) The UK government agency responsible for the co-ordination of government computer systems development and the promotion of effective standards in computing.

Command Structure A document that specifies where control may pass to on completion of a dialogue.

Common Process A piece or unit of processing that is shared or carried out by more than one function.

Composite Key A key made up of foreign keys and a qualifier.

Component A self-contained part of a logical function, usually equivalent to one or more SSADM products.

Compound Key A key made up of foreign keys.

Context Diagram A diagram which represents a system as a single DFD process. It is used to define the system boundary and external entities for the system.

Cost/Benefit Analysis A financial analysis of the anticipated costs and benefits of a proposed system.

Current Environment Description A description of all aspects of a current system (manual and computerised), together with a definition of its shortfalls and problems.

Current Services Description A logicalised view of the current environment. The complete output from Stage 1 (Investigation of Current Services).

Database Management System (DBMS) A software product for managing and controlling data within a computer system. It should govern the integrity, security and access to an organisation's data.

Data Catalogue A catalogue of information about the attributes and data items used or created by the system.

Data Flow A component of a Data Flow Diagram (DFD) illustrating where information is passed to and from in a system.

Data Flow Diagram (DFD) A diagram illustrating the flow, storage and processing of data in a system. It is essentially snapshot in nature, showing all possible movements of data. A very powerful analysis technique (being easily understood and flexible), it is less useful for design purposes.

Data Flow Model (DFM) A model consisting of a hierarchy of DFDs plus textual descriptions of their constituent processes, external entities and data flows across the system boundary.

Data Item The equivalent of an attribute in physical models. Data items are the smallest pieces of information held in data stores and passed around in data flows.

Data Store A place where data is held in DFDs. Data Stores may be permanent or transitory (i.e. temporary), physical or logical, and manual or computerised.

DBMS Database Management System.

DBMS Data Storage Classification Documentation describing the storage and retrieval mechanisms of a DBMS.

DBMS Performance Classification Documentation describing mechanisms and factors affecting the efficiency and performance of a DBMS.

Definition of Requirements Stage 3 of an SSADM project.

Dependent An attribute X is dependent on another attribute Y if, given the value of Y, we can always determine the value of X.

Detail Entity The entity at the 'm' end of a 1:m relationship.

Determinant An attribute Y is the determinant of X if, given the value of Y, we can always determine the value of X.

DFD Data Flow Diagram.

DFM Data Flow Model.

Dialogue The on-line interaction between a user and the computer system when executing a function.

Dialogue Control Table A table detailing the allowable navigations within and through a dialogue.

Dialogue Element A logical component of a dialogue consisting of one or more attributes.

Dialogue Element Description A form detailing the attributes that make up a dialogue element.

Dialogue Structure A diagrammatic representation of the structure of a dialogue, detailing the sequence, selection and iteration of its dialogue elements.

Document Flow Diagram A working document detailing the sources, recipients and flows of actual documents around the current system, and which can be used in the development of DFDs.

Domain The range of values that an attribute or data item may take.

EAP Enquiry Access Path.

ECD Effect Correspondence Diagram.

Effects The set of changes to an entity caused by an event. Represented in ELHs by the bottom leaves of the structure.

Effect Correspondence Diagram (ECD) A diagram illustrating all of the effects of a given event. An ECD will show all of the entities affected by an event, and the ways in which they interact. ECDs are used to define 'update access paths'. Developed in Step 360.

Elementary Process The lowest (most detailed) level of process in a DFM. Elementary Processes are those which will reveal no further understanding of the system if decomposed.

Elementary Process Description (EPD) A textual description of an Elementary Process.

ELH Entity Life History.

Enquiry A retrieval of data that has no updating effects on the system.

Enquiry Access Path (EAP) A model of the formal navigation through the Logical Data Model to access all data required by an enquiry. Developed in Step 360.

Enquiry Process Model (EPM) A model of all logical database processing required to retrieve the data for an enquiry. EPMs are derived from EAPs and are drawn using Jackson-like notation. Developed in Step 530.

Enquiry Trigger The data that initiates or triggers an enquiry.

Entity Any object or concept about which a system needs to hold information. Entities provide the core concept for Logical Data Models. Each entity must have a number of real world occurrences.

Entity Description A textual description of an entity, including its attributes, purpose and relationships with other entities.

Entity-Event Modelling The analysis of events and their effects on entities. It consists of two techniques: ELH analysis and Effect Correspondence Diagramming.

Event/Entity Matrix A matrix illustrating which entities are affected by which events. Each correspondence between an entity and an event is described as Create, Delete or Modify. Developed in Step 360 as input to ELH analysis.

Entity Life History (ELH) A Jackson-like structure diagram showing all of the events that can affect an entity, from creation to deletion. ELHs detail the allowable sequence, selection and iteration of these events, as well as detailing the operations carried out on the entity as a result. Developed in Step 360.

Entity Role If more than one occurrence of an entity can be affected by a single event, and in different ways, then the entity is said to be adopting different Entity Roles (denoted on an ELH by square brackets).

EPD Elementary Process Description.

EPM Enquiry Processing Model.

Event A real world event that causes the data within a system to be updated. Thus an event will act as a trigger for update processing.

External Entity A source or recipient of data for or from the system under consideration.

FCIM Function Component Implementation Map.

Feasibility Option An option for taking a project forward into full analysis and design. A Feasibility Option consists of a combination of a high level BSO and a high level TSO.

Feasibility Study Stage 0 of an SSADM project. An optional, but highly recommended stage.

First-Cut Data Design A technique for transforming the Logical Data Model into a first-cut physical data design, based on a standard set of assumptions about the facilities provided by the target DBMS. Used in Step 620.

Foreign Key An attribute of one entity which is also the primary key of another is called a foreign key. It is by maintaining foreign keys that detail to master relationships are established.

Fragment A piece of physical processing, usually corresponding to a logical function component or operation.

Function A user defined unit of system processing. Functions represent the system's functionality from the perspective of activities carried out by users in the same time frame. Functions become the basic unit for specification of processing. First developed in Step 330, but constantly updated and supplemented throughout the rest of the project.

Function Component Interaction Map (FCIM) A mapping of the logical design (represented by function components) onto the physical design (represented by fragments).

Function Definition The identification of all components of a function. The product of Function Definition (also called a Function Definition) is a package of specification products that together define a function.

Function Navigation Model A representation of the navigation through the components of a function.

Functional Requirement A requirement to provide a service or facility for users.

Hierarchical Task Model A breakdown of the tasks involved to perform an activity.

Impact Analysis An analysis of the effects of a BSO or TSO on an organisation's working practices and social structure.

Installation Style Guide Standards to be adopted in the design of the human-computer interface, throughout an organisation.

Investigation of Current Environment Stage 1 of an SSADM project.

I/O Description A description of all of the data items carried by a data flow (which crosses the system boundary).

I/O Structure A model of the structure and logical content of a user interface with a function. There are two components: a Jackson-like structure diagram (the I/O Structure Diagram), and descriptions of the data content of the interface (the I/O Structure Description).

IS Information System.

LDM Logical Data Model.

LDPD Logical Database Process Design.

LDS Logical Data Structure.

LGDE Logical Grouping of Dialogue Elements.

Logical Data Flow Model A logical DFM representing the current system. Derived from the Current Physical DFM in Step 150.

Logical Data Model (LDM) A rigorous model of the data requirements of an organisation, free from physical constraints and implementation considerations. It consists of a Logical Data Structure and accompanying textual descriptions. A Logical Data Model details the content, true interrelationships and business rules applicable to an organisation's data.

Logical Data Store/Entity Cross Reference A document detailing the correspondence between the entities in the Logical Data Model and the data stores used in the Logical DFM. Logical data stores must be based on a whole number of entities from the Logical Data Model.

Logical Data Structure (LDS) A diagrammatic representation of the true structure of an organisation's data.

Logical Design The output from Stage 5 (Logical Design), consisting of the requirements catalogue, logical process models and the Required System Logical Data Model. It defines a logical view of the final system, and will provide the input for physical design in Stage 6.

Logical Database Process Design (LDPD) The technique of modelling the logical processing of data input to and output from the system. It is based on operations carried out on a logical database as defined in the Logical Data Model, and makes use of Jackson-like notation. Its products are Enquiry Process Models (EPMs) and Update Process Models (UPMs).

Logical Grouping of Dialogue Elements (LGDE) Groupings of dialogue elements within a Dialogue Structure for use in Dialogue Design.

Logicalisation The technique of transforming the Current Physical DFM into a Logical DFM.

Master Entity The entity at the '1' end of a 1:m relationship.

Menu Structure A hierarchical diagram illustrating how menus and dialogues will be put together in the required system.

Non-Functional Requirement Requirements for the new system covering non-functional aspects, such as timings, performance, security and volumes. They may be used to qualify functional requirements or be applied to the system as a whole.

Non-Procedural Program code in which the developer states a desired result (e.g. a screen layout), without having to specify how it will be achieved.

Normalisation The technique of refining unstructured tables of data into smaller tables based on the principles of Relational Data Analysis. Each refinement is known as a Normal Form.

Off-Line Function A function that is carried out mainly 'off-line', i.e. without user interaction.

On-Line Function A function that is carried out mainly 'on-line', i.e. with constant user interaction.

Operation Discrete units of processing carried out on the Logical Data Model, which together constitute the effects of an event.

Optimisation The technique of tuning a Physical Data Design to meet with performance or space requirements.

Outline Current Environment Description The product of the Feasibility Study that describes an overview of current processing and data within the business area under investigation.

Outline Required Environment Description The product of the Feasibility Study that describes an overview of required processing and data for the business area under investigation.

Parallel Structure A structure used in ELHs to show where events can occur in parallel with the main life of an entity, without altering the course of that main life.

PDI Process Data Interface.

Physical Data Design The design of the physical database to be implemented as part of the final system. The product of Physical Data Design techniques applied in Steps 610, 620 and 640.

Physical Data Model The product of first-cut data design in Step 620.

Physical Design The output from Stage 6 (Physical Design).

Physical Design Strategy The strategy arrived at in Step 610 for transforming the logical design into implementable physical fragments.

Physical Environment The implementation environment for the required system.

PID Project Initiation Document.

Problem Definition Statement A statement of user requirements for the new system produced in the Feasibility Study. It ties together the Outline Current and Required Environment Descriptions, the Requirements Catalogue and the User Catalogue.

Procedural A term applied to program code that explicitly states how every result is to be achieved.

Process Activities that transform or manipulate data in the system.

Process Data Interface (PDI) A definition of how the Logical Data Model maps onto the Physical Data Design. It is then used to translate between processing which acts on the Logical Data Model and the DBMS which controls the physical database.

Process/Entity Matrix A matrix that illustrates which processes access which entities. It can be used to group processes during logicalisation.

Processing System Classification A description of the implementation and, if possible, the development processing environment.

Program Specification A document that details how a fragment of the system should be coded and implemented.

Project Initiation Document (PID) A document used to launch an IS project. It will usually include Terms of Reference, personnel details, high level requirements and objectives for the project.

Prototype A simulation of what the system might look like. Used to provide a demonstrable statement of requirements for verification by users.

Prototype Pathway A simple flowchart showing how the components of a prototype will be demonstrated.

Quality Assurance (QA) The process of checking products against pre-determined quality criteria.

Quit and Resume Notation used in ELHs to cater for departures from predictable patterns of events which cause changes to the normal life of an entity.

Random Event An event that can occur at any time in the life of an entity.

RDA Relational Data Analysis.

Relation A collection or table of attributes, identified by a unique key.

Relational Data Analysis (RDA) The technique of transforming groups of data items or attributes into relations that obey rules of relational data design, giving rise to increased flexibility and reductions in duplication and data redundancy. In SSADM RDA involves applying the process of normalisation to produce tables in Third Normal Form (3NF), which can then be translated into mini Logical Data Structures for comparison with the Logical Data Model.

Relationship A logical association between two entities (or between an entity and itself) on the Logical Data Structure.

Relationship Degree (cardinality) An indication of the number of occurrences of the entities involved in a relationship that can take part in a single occurrence of that relationship. Possible degrees are 1:m, m:n and 1:1.

Required System Data Flow Model A DFM illustrating the required processing for the new system.

Required System Logical Data Model A Logical Data Model illustrating the required data for the new system.

Requirements Catalogue A catalogue of all user requirements (functional and non-functional), including details of measures of success, final solutions and priority.

Requirements Definition The technique of identifying and documenting all user requirements (in the Requirements Catalogue).

Requirements Specification The product of Stage 3 (Definition of Requirements). It is made up of all the models developed during requirements definition and provides a detailed non-procedural specification of the new system.

Resource Flow Diagram A variant on the DFD, illustrating the flow of physical goods or items rather than data.

SI State Indicator.

Specification Prototyping The technique of presenting prototypes of the new system as a method of confirming or identifying requirements.

SSADM Structured Systems Analysis and Design Method. The UK government's standard IS development method.

State Indicator (SI) An additional attribute added to entities in Step 510, which make the position of an entity occurrence within its life explicit. They are used to re-express the allowable sequence of events as defined in an ELH.

Success Unit A unit of processing which must succeed or fail as a whole.

Super Function A function which consists of two or more whole functions.

System Boundary The boundary of a system. In the current physical environment it will equate with the boundary of the area under investigation, i.e. will define the extent of all manual and computer systems in that area. In a logical environment it will equate with the extent of the computerised (or 'computerisable') system.

Task An activity can be broken down into tasks.

Technical System Architecture (TSA) A description of the technical (or physical) environment specified and chosen in Stage 4 (Technical System Options).

Technical System Option (TSO) A TSO defines a possible implementation route for the Requirements Specification.

Technical System Options (TSOs) TSOs (note the plural) is the technique or set of guidelines provided by SSADM for creating a set of TSOs. It is also the name of Stage 4, where an option is selected for input to Stage 6 (Physical Design).

Third Normal Form (3NF or TNF) The product of RDA is a set of tables in 3NF, in which all attributes depend on 'the key, the whole key and nothing but the key'.

Transient Data Store Data stores on a DFD that exist to hold data temporarily, until read once. The classic example of a manual transient data store is an in-tray.

TSA Technical System Architecture.

TSO Technical System Option.

Universal Function Model An SSADM model of the standard logical components of a function.

Update Process Model (UPM) A model of all logical database processing required to access and update data in response to an event. UPMs are derived from ECDs and are drawn using Jackson-like notation. Developed in Step 520.

User Catalogue A catalogue of all the prospective users of the new system, detailing their job titles and responsibilities.

User Role A collective term for a set of users who share common tasks and system access requirements.

User Role/Function Matrix A description of which functions each user role will need to access. Each such access gives rise to a required dialogue. Developed in Step 330.

User Object Model A model following the user's perception of the system's functionality.

Windows Navigation Model A model showing a function's navigation through a Windows interface.

Work Practice Model (WPM) A mapping of business activities onto the organisation structure.

Work Practice Modelling The technique through which a user-centred view of the system is achieved.

WPM Work Practice Model

Appendix D   Suggested Solutions to Selected Exercises

2.1

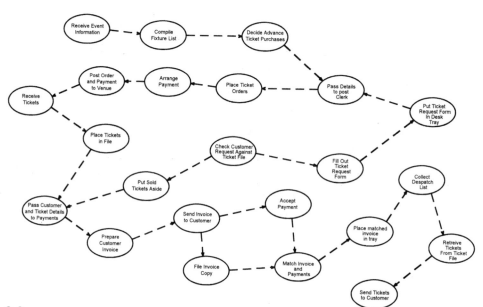

2.2

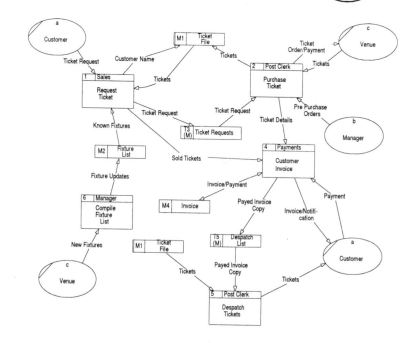

2.3

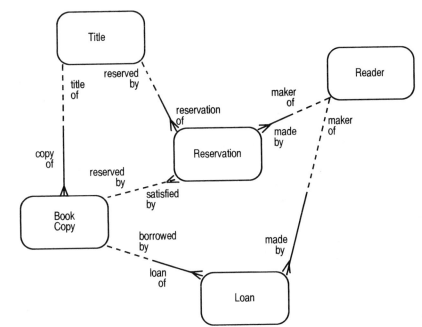

2.4

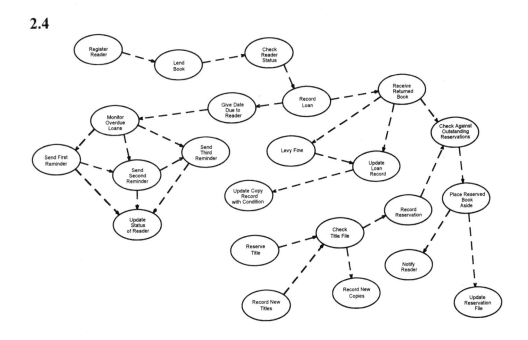

2.5

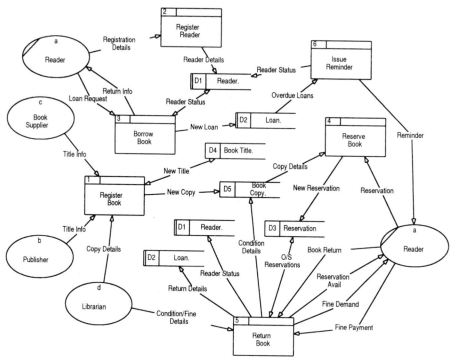

2.6

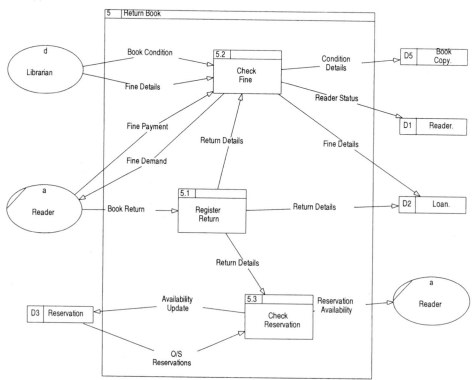

2.8

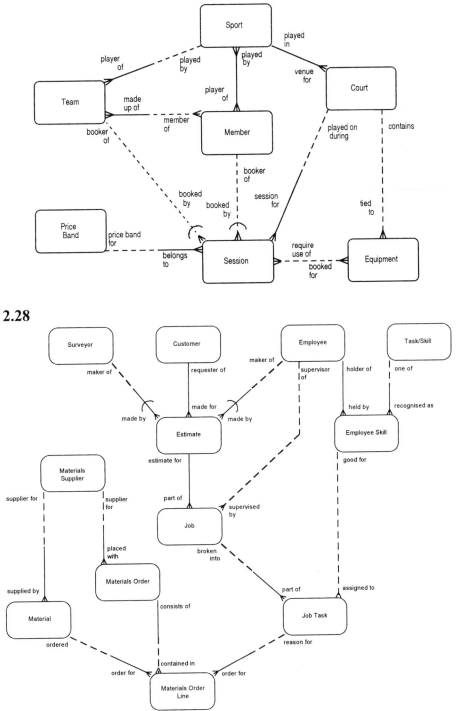

2.28

2.29

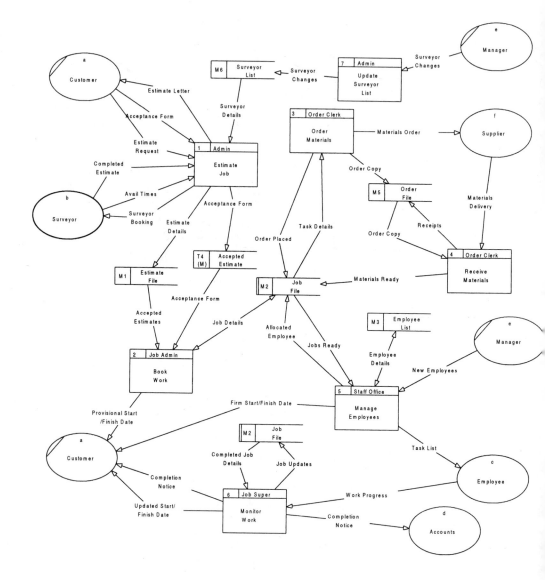

2.30

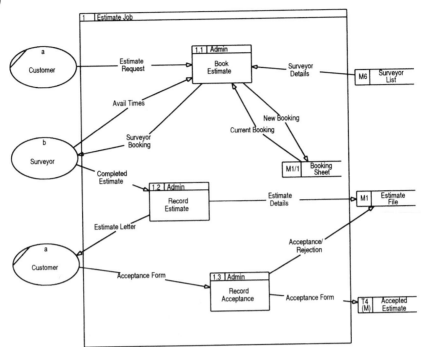

2.31

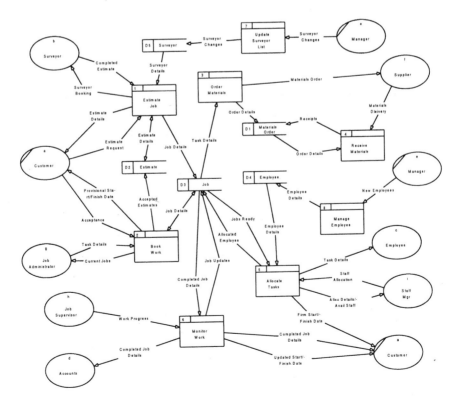

3.2

$$UFP = 0.58 \times 120 + 0.26 \times 120 + 1.66 \times 60 = 200.4$$
$$S = 130.26$$
$$Weeks = 25.3$$
$$Effort = 1195$$
$$H = 2.07$$

4.1

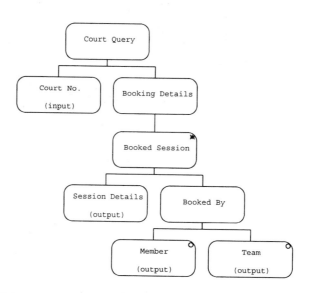

I/O Structure Description		
I/O Structure Element	Data Item	Comment
Court No.	Court No.	
Session Details	Session No. Session Start Time Session End Time	
Member	Member No. Member Name	
Team	Team No. Team Name	

4.2

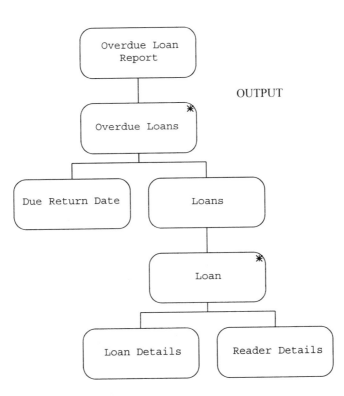

OUTPUT

I/O Structure Description		
I/O Structure Element	Data Item	Comment
Due Return Date	Due Return Date	Latest First
Loan Details	Loan No. Book ISBN Book Title Book Copy No.	
Reader Details	Reader No. Reader Name Reader Address Reader Tel. No.	

4.3

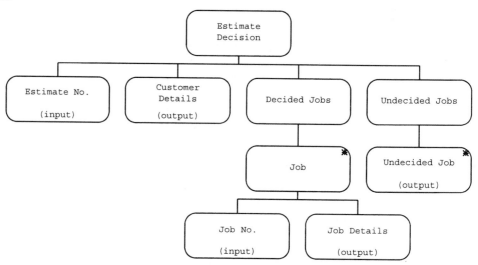

I/O Structure Description		
I/O Structure Element	Data Item	Comment
Estimate No.	Estimate No.	
Customer Details	Customer No. Customer Name Customer Address	
Job No.	Job No.	
Job Details	Job Description Job Decision	
Undecided Job	Job No. Job Description	

4.4

UNF	Lev	1NF	2NF	3NF
Court No.	1	Court No.	Court No.	Court No.
Session No.	2			
Session Start Time	2	Court No.	Court No.	Court No.
Session End Time	2	Session No.	Session No.	Session No.
Member No.	2	Session Start Time	Member No.	*Member No.
Member Name	2	Session End Time	Member Name	*Team No.
Team No.	2	Member No.	Team No.	
Team Name	2	Member Name	Team Name	Member No.
	2	Team No.		Member Name
	2	Team Name		
	2			Team No.
				Team Name
			Session No.	Session No.
			Session Start Time	Session Start Time
			Session End Time	Session End Time

4.5

UNF	Lev	1NF	2NF	3NF
Due Return Date	1	Due Return Date	Due Return Date	Due Return Date
Loan No.	2			
Book ISBN	2	Due Return Date	Due Return Date	Due Return Date
Book Title	2	Loan No.	Loan No.	Loan No.
Reader No.	2	Book ISBN	Book ISBN	* Book ISBN
Reader Name	2	Book Title	Book Title	*Reader No.
Reader Address	2	Reader No.	Reader No.	*Book Copy No.
Reader Tel. No.	2	Reader Name	Reader Name	
Book Copy No.	2	Reader Address	Reader Address	Book ISBN
		Reader Tel. No.	Reader Tel. No.	Book Title
		Book Copy No.	Book Copy No.	
				Book ISBN
				Book Copy No
				Reader No.
				Reader Name
				Reader Address
				Reader Tel. No.

Note: Book ISBN and Book Copy No. constitute a composite key.

4.6

UNF	Lev	1NF	2NF	3NF
Estimate No.	1	Estimate No.	Estimate No.	Estimate No.
Customer No.	1	Customer No.	Customer No.	*Customer No.
Customer Name	1	Customer Name	Customer Name	
Customer Addr.	1	Customer Addr.	Customer Addr.	
Job Decision	2			Customer No.
Job No.	2			Customer Name
Job Description	2			Customer Addr.
		*Estimate No.	*Estimate No.	*Estimate No.
		Job No.	Job No.	Job No.
		Job Description	Job Description	Job Description
		Job Decision	Job Decision	Job Decision

4.7

Customer Request Form:

UNF	Lev	1NF	2NF	3NF
Cust. Name	1	Cust. Name	Cust. Name	Cust. Name
Cust. Addr.	1	Cust. Addr.	Cust. Addr.	Cust. Addr.
Cust. Tel.	1	Cust. Tel.	Cust. Tel.	Cust. Tel.
Perf. Desc.	2			
Venue Name	2	Cust. Name	Cust. Name	Cust. Name
Preferred Date	3	Perf. Desc.	Perf. Desc.	Perf. Desc.
Preference Ind.	3	Venue Name	Venue Name	Venue Name
Upper Price	2	Ticket Qty	Ticket Qty	Ticket Qty
Lower Price	2	Upper Price	Upper Price	Upper Price
Ticket Qty	2	Lower Price	Lower Price	Lower Price
		Cust. Name	Cust. Name	Cust. Name
		Perf. Desc.	Perf. Desc.	Perf. Desc.
		Venue Name	Venue Name	Venue Name
		Pref. Date	Pref. Date	Pref. Date
		Pref. Ind.	Pref. Ind.	Pref. Ind.

Customer Invoice:

UNF	Lev	1NF	2NF	3NF
Invoice No.	1	Invoice No.	Invoice No.	Invoice No.
Invoice Date	1	Invoice Date	Invoice Date	Invoice Date
Cust. Number	1	Cust. Number	Cust. Number	*Cust. Number
Cust. Name	1	Cust. Name	Cust. Name	Total Price
Cust. Addr.	1	Cust. Addr	Cust. Addr.	Pay. Method
Cust. Tel. No.	1	Cust. Tel. No.	Cust. Tel. No.	Card Number
Perf. Number	2	Total Price	Total Price	
Perf. Name	2	Pay. Method	Pay. Method	Cust. Number
Venue Name	2	Card Number	Card Number	Cust. Name
Venue Addr.	2			Cust. Addr.
Perf. Date	2			Cust. Tel. No.
Perf. Time	2			
Ticket Price	3	Invoice No.	Invoice No.	Invoice No.
Ticket Qty	3	Perf. Number	Perf. Number	Perf. Number
Total Price	1	Perf. Name		
Pay. Method	1	Perf. Date	Perf. Number	Perf. Number
Card Number	1	Perf. Time	Perf. Name	Perf. Name
		Venue Name	Perf. Date	Perf. Date
		Venue Addr.	Perf. Time	Perf. Time
			Venue Name	*Venue Name
			Venue Addr.	
				Venue Name
				Venue Addr.
		Invoice No.		
		Perf. Number	Perf. Number	Invoice No.
		Ticket Price	Ticket Price	Perf. Number
		Ticket Qty	Ticket Qty	Ticket Price
				Ticket Qty

4.10 and 4.11

Request Estimate (from Surveyor)	(C)
Request Estimate (from Employee)	(C)
Book Estimate	(M)
Complete Estimate	(M)
Receive Response	(M)
Send Reminder	(M)
Estimate Expires	(M)
Complete Last Job	(M)
Archive Estimate	(D)

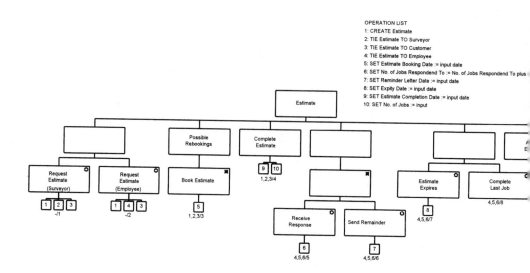

OPERATION LIST
1: CREATE Estimate
2: TIE Estimate TO Surveyor
3: TIE Estimate TO Customer
4: TIE Estimate TO Employee
5: SET Estimate Booking Date := input date
6: SET No. of Jobs Respondend To := No. of Jobs Respondend To plus
7: SET Reminder Letter Date := input date
8: SET Expiry Date := input date
9: SET Estimate Completion Date := input date
10: SET No. of Jobs := input

4.12

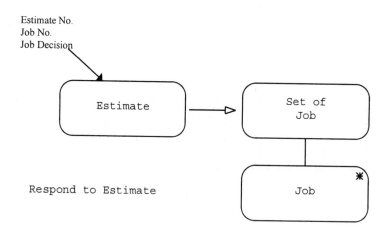

Estimate No.
Job No.
Job Decision

Respond to Estimate

4.14

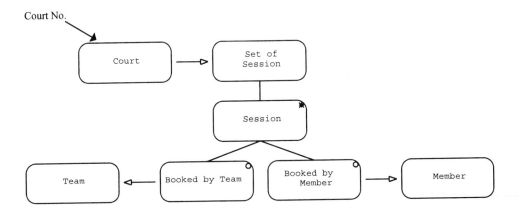

4.17

The completed matrix looks like this:

ENTITY EVENT/ENQUIRY	Video Title	Video Store	Member	Video Copy	Video Rental Period
Copy Purchase	M	M		I	
Copy Sale or Destruction	M	M		B	B
Membership Approval			I		
Membership Removal			B		B
Store Closure		B/M	M	M	
Store Opening		I			
Title Release	I				
Title Withdrawal	B				
Video Rental			M	M	I
Video Return			M	M	M

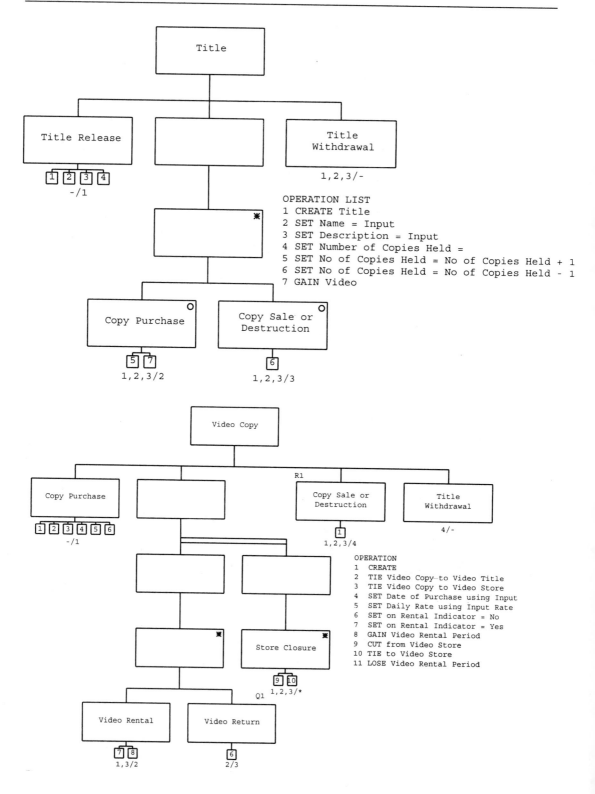

Title

Title Release

Title
Withdrawal

1,2,3/-

| 1 | 2 | 3 | 4 |

-/1

✳

OPERATION LIST
1 CREATE Title
2 SET Name = Input
3 SET Description = Input
4 SET Number of Copies Held =
5 SET No of Copies Held = No of Copies Held + 1
6 SET No of Copies Held = No of Copies Held - 1
7 GAIN Video

Copy Purchase ◯

Copy Sale or
Destruction ◯

| 5 | 7 |

1,2,3/2

| 6 |

1,2,3/3

Video Copy

Copy Purchase

R1

Copy Sale or
Destruction

Title
Withdrawal

| 1 | 2 | 3 | 4 | 5 | 6 |

-/1

| 1 |

1,2,3/4

4/-

OPERATION
1 CREATE
2 TIE Video Copy to Video Title
3 TIE Video Copy to Video Store
4 SET Date of Purchase using Input
5 SET Daily Rate using Input Rate
6 SET on Rental Indicator = No
7 SET on Rental Indicator = Yes
8 GAIN Video Rental Period
9 CUT from Video Store
10 TIE to Video Store
11 LOSE Video Rental Period

✳

Store Closure ✳

| 9 | 10 |

Q1   1,2,3/*

Video Rental

Video Return

| 7 | 8 |

1,3/2

| 6 |

2/3

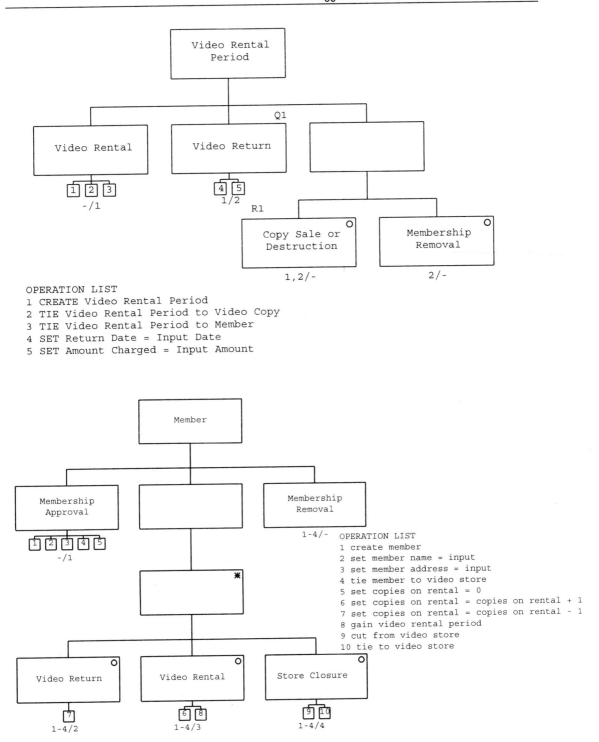

OPERATION LIST
1 CREATE Video Rental Period
2 TIE Video Rental Period to Video Copy
3 TIE Video Rental Period to Member
4 SET Return Date = Input Date
5 SET Amount Charged = Input Amount

OPERATION LIST
1 create member
2 set member name = input
3 set member address = input
4 tie member to video store
5 set copies on rental = 0
6 set copies on rental = copies on rental + 1
7 set copies on rental = copies on rental - 1
8 gain video rental period
9 cut from video store
10 tie to video store

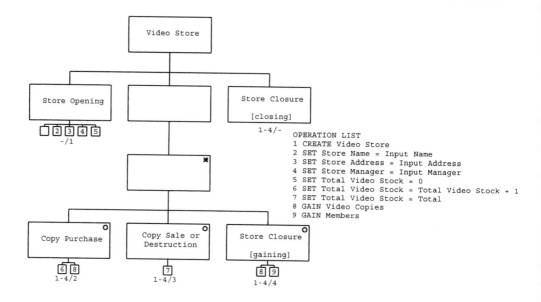

OPERATION LIST
1 CREATE Video Store
2 SET Store Name = Input Name
3 SET Store Address = Input Address
4 SET Store Manager = Input Manager
5 SET Total Video Stock = 0
6 SET Total Video Stock = Total Video Stock + 1
7 SET Total Video Stock = Total
8 GAIN Video Copies
9 GAIN Members

4.18

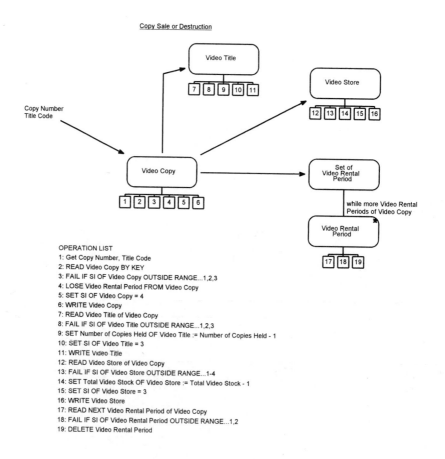

Copy Sale or Destruction

OPERATION LIST
1: Get Copy Number, Title Code
2: READ Video Copy BY KEY
3: FAIL IF SI OF Video Copy OUTSIDE RANGE...1,2,3
4: LOSE Video Rental Period FROM Video Copy
5: SET SI OF Video Copy = 4
6: WRITE Video Copy
7: READ Video Title of Video Copy
8: FAIL IF SI OF Video Title OUTSIDE RANGE...1,2,3
9: SET Number of Copies Held OF Video Title := Number of Copies Held - 1
10: SET SI OF Video Title = 3
11: WRITE Video Title
12: READ Video Store of Video Copy
13: FAIL IF SI OF Video Store OUTSIDE RANGE...1-4
14: SET Total Video Stock OF Video Store := Total Video Stock - 1
15: SET SI OF Video Store = 3
16: WRITE Video Store
17: READ NEXT Video Rental Period of Video Copy
18: FAIL IF SI OF Video Rental Period OUTSIDE RANGE...1,2
19: DELETE Video Rental Period

4.20

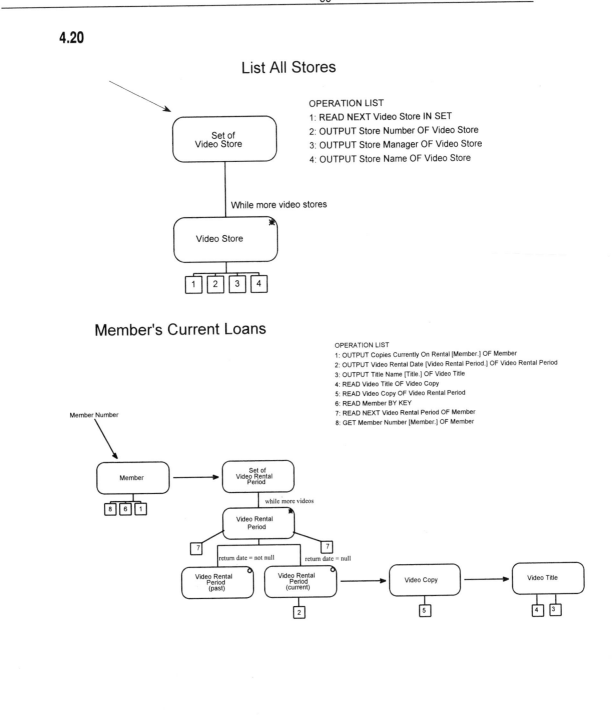

List All Stores

OPERATION LIST
1: READ NEXT Video Store IN SET
2: OUTPUT Store Number OF Video Store
3: OUTPUT Store Manager OF Video Store
4: OUTPUT Store Name OF Video Store

Set of
Video Store

While more video stores

Video Store

1 2 3 4

Member's Current Loans

OPERATION LIST
1: OUTPUT Copies Currently On Rental [Member.] OF Member
2: OUTPUT Video Rental Date [Video Rental Period.] OF Video Rental Period
3: OUTPUT Title Name [Title.] OF Video Title
4: READ Video Title OF Video Copy
5: READ Video Copy OF Video Rental Period
6: READ Member BY KEY
7: READ NEXT Video Rental Period OF Member
8: GET Member Number [Member.] OF Member

Member Number

Member

8 6 1

Set of
Video Rental
Period

while more videos

Video Rental
Period

7   7

return date = not null   return date = null

Video Rental
Period
(past)

Video Rental
Period
(current)

2

Video Copy

5

Video Title

4 3

6.1

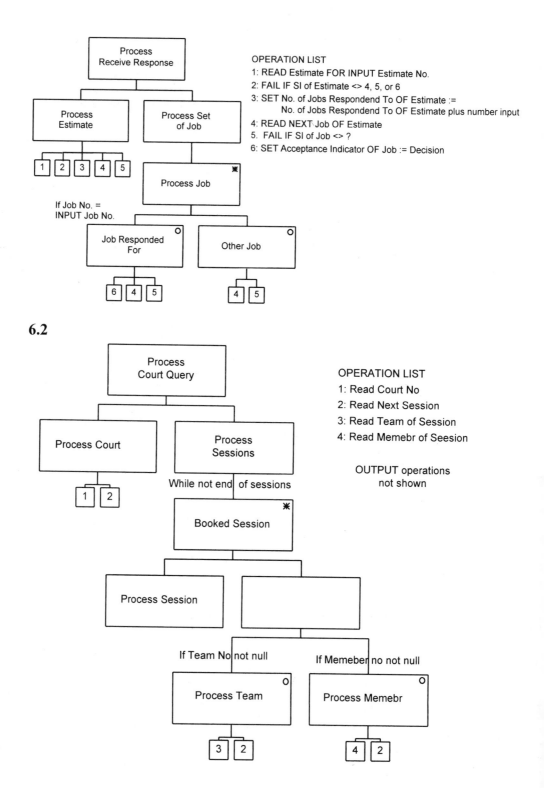

OPERATION LIST
1: READ Estimate FOR INPUT Estimate No.
2: FAIL IF SI of Estimate <> 4, 5, or 6
3: SET No. of Jobs Respondend To OF Estimate :=
   No. of Jobs Respondend To OF Estimate plus number input
4: READ NEXT Job OF Estimate
5. FAIL IF SI of Job <> ?
6: SET Acceptance Indicator OF Job := Decision

6.2

OPERATION LIST
1: Read Court No
2: Read Next Session
3: Read Team of Session
4: Read Memebr of Seesion

OUTPUT operations
not shown

6.3

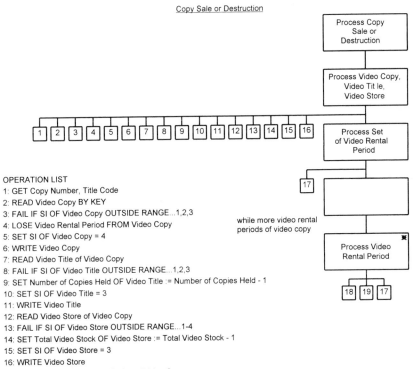

Copy Sale or Destruction

OPERATION LIST
1: GET Copy Number, Title Code
2: READ Video Copy BY KEY
3: FAIL IF SI OF Video Copy OUTSIDE RANGE...1,2,3
4: LOSE Video Rental Period FROM Video Copy
5: SET SI OF Video Copy = 4
6: WRITE Video Copy
7: READ Video Title of Video Copy
8: FAIL IF SI OF Video Title OUTSIDE RANGE...1,2,3
9: SET Number of Copies Held OF Video Title := Number of Copies Held - 1
10: SET SI OF Video Title = 3
11: WRITE Video Title
12: READ Video Store of Video Copy
13: FAIL IF SI OF Video Store OUTSIDE RANGE...1-4
14: SET Total Video Stock OF Video Store := Total Video Stock - 1
15: SET SI OF Video Store = 3
16: WRITE Video Store
17: READ NEXT Video Rental Period of Video Copy
18: FAIL IF SI OF Video Rental Period OUTSIDE RANGE...1,2
19: DELETE Video Rental Period

Member's Current Loans

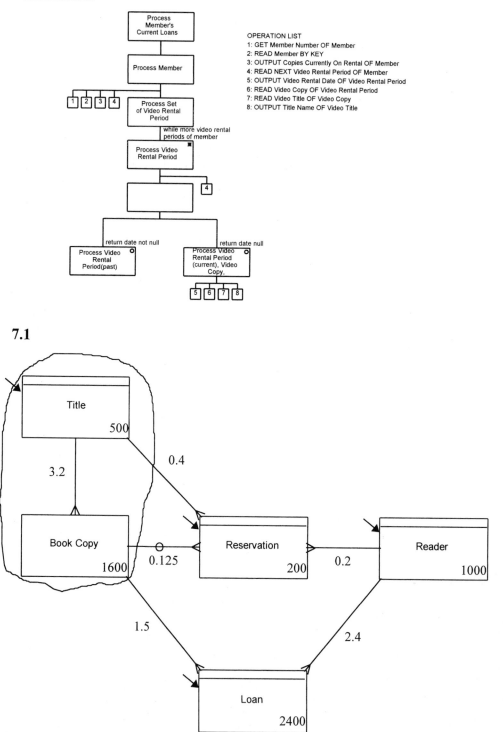

OPERATION LIST
1: GET Member Number OF Member
2: READ Member BY KEY
3: OUTPUT Copies Currently On Rental OF Member
4: READ NEXT Video Rental Period OF Member
5: OUTPUT Video Rental Date OF Video Rental Period
6: READ Video Copy OF Video Rental Period
7: READ Video Title OF Video Copy
8: OUTPUT Title Name OF Video Title

7.1

Appendix E   Useful Addresses

International SSADM Users Group

The International SSADM Users Group is the largest representative group of SSADM users and providers and is involved in all aspects of the industry surrounding SSADM and its use in application development.

Sue McGowan
Administration Officer
11 Burlings Lane
Knockholt
Kent
TN14 7PB
01959 534337

University of Westminster

Cavendish School of Computer Science
115 New Cavendish Street
London W1M 8JS
0171-911-5000 x3600

CCTA

SSADM has been developed under the management and sponsorship of the CCTA.

CCTA, the Government Centre for Information Systems, is responsible for promoting business efficiency and effectiveness through the development and use of information systems by Government departments and agencies.

Customer Services Manager
CCTA Information Systems Engineering Group
Rosebery Court
St Andrew's Business Park
Norwich
NR7 OHS
01603 704704

UK Academy for Information Systems

The aims of The UK Academy for Information Systems are to promote a better knowledge and understanding of information systems within the United Kingdom, and to improve the practice of information systems teaching and research.

UKAIS
Tom Gough (Membership Secretary)
Head of Teaching
School of Computer Studies
University of Leeds
Leeds
LS2 9JT
0113 233 5468

Rules and Patterns Group

The Rules and Patterns Group aims to promote the detection and reuse of common patterns in systems analysis and design. The goals are to raise the quality of both teaching and practical work: to help teachers turn students into experts; to produce better systems and constrain databases so they do not fill up with garbage.

Graham Berrisford (Chairman)
Validata
6 Lower Downs Road
Wimbledon
London
SW20 8QB
0181 947 0930
email: gberrisford@macline.co.uk

Information Systems Examinations Board

The ISEB is an independent and nationally recognised body which oversees and administers accreditation and certification in SSDAM qualifications (amongst others).

The latest qualifications structure is a modular one enabling practitioners to obtain a Foundation Certificate in SSADM 4+ upon which practitioners can build with further specialist qualifications in the area of information systems development.

ISEB Course Accreditation and Training
Pat Harris (Secretary)
Information Systems Examinations Board
1 Sanford Street
Swindon
SN1 1HJ
01793 417 417

For Professional Help

For those seeking professional advice on the application of SSADM, we can recommend:

SCOLL Methods Limited
The White House
70 High Road
Bushey Heath
Hertfordshire
WD2 3JG
0181 421 8960
email:
100413.3414@compuserve.com

Braille Support

RNIB
224 Great Portland Street
London
W1N 6AA

Appendix F Step/Technique/Product Cross Reference

Stage 0 - Feasibility Study		
Step	**Technique**	**Product**
020 - Define the Problem	Data Flow Modelling	Overview Data Flow Model - Required Environment
		Overview Data Flow Model - Current Environment
	Logical Data Modelling	Overview Logical Data Model - Required Environment
		Overview Logical Data Model - Current Environment
	Requirements Definition	Requirements Catalogue
	Dialogue Design	User Catalogue
030 - Select Feasibility Option	Business System Options Technical System Options Logical Data Modelling Data Flow Modelling	Feasibility Option

Stage 1 - Investigation of Current Environment		
Step	**Technique**	**Product**
115 -Develop Business Activity Model	Business Activity Modelling	Business Activity Model
	Work Practice Modelling	User Catalogue Work Practice Model
120 - Investigate and Define Requirements	Requirements Definition	Requirements Catalogue
	Dialogue Design	User Catalogue
130 - Investigate Current Processing	Data Flow Modelling	Current Physical Data Flow Model
	Requirements Definition	Requirements Catalogue
140 - Investigate Current Data	Logical Data Modelling (Relational Data Analysis)	Current Environment Logical Data Model
	Requirements Definition	Requirements Catalogue

150 - Derive Logical View of Current Services	Data Flow Modelling	Logical Data Flow Model Logical Data Store/Entity Cross Reference Requirements Catalogue
	(Logical Data Modelling)	Current Environment Logical Data Model
Assemble Investigation Results		Current Services Description

Stage 2 - Business System Options		
Step	**Technique**	**Product**
210 - Define BSOs	Business System Option (Logical Data Modelling) (Data Flow Modelling) (Work Practice Modelling)	Business System Options
220 - Select BSO	Business System Option	Selected Business System Option

Stage 3 - Requirements Specification		
Step	**Technique**	**Product**
310 - Define Required System Processing	Data Flow Modelling	Required System Data Flow Model Logical Data Store/Entity Cross Reference
	Dialogue Design	User Roles
	Requirements Definition	Requirements Catalogue
320 - Develop Required Data Model	Logical Data Model (Relational Data Analysis)	Required System Logical Data Model Data Catalogue
	Requirements Definition	Requirements Catalogue
330 - Derive System Functions	Function Definition	Function Definitions I/O Structures Task Scenarios Hierarchical Task Models Function Navigation Models Window Navigation Models
	Dialogue Design	User Role/Function Matrix
	Requirements Definition	Requirements Catalogue
335 - Develop User Job Specifications	Work Practice Modelling	Work Practice Model

340 - Enhance Required Data Model	Relational Data Analysis (Logical Data Modelling)	Required System Logical Data Model
		Data Catalogue
350 - Develop Specification Prototypes	Specification Prototyping	Prototyping Report
	Dialogue Design	Menu Structures
		Command Structures
	Requirements Definition	Requirements Catalogue
360 - Develop Processing Specification	Entity Behaviour Modelling	Entity Life Histories
	Conceptual Process Modelling	Effect Correspondence Diagrams
		Enquiry Access Paths
370 - Confirm System Objectives	Function Definition	Function Definitions
	Logical Data Model	Required System Logical Data Model
	Requirements Definition	Requirements Catalogue
Assemble Requirements Specification		Requirements Specification

Stage 4 - Technical System Options		
Step	**Technique**	**Product**
410 - Define TSOs	Technical System Option	Technical System Options
420 - Select TSO	Technical System Option	Technical System Options
		Technical System Architecture
		Application Style Guide

Stage 5 - Logical Design

Step	Technique	Product
510 - Define User Dialogues	Dialogue Design	Dialogue Structures Menu Structures Command Structures Dialogue Control Tables Dialogue Level Help Requirements Catalogue
520 - Define Update Processes	Conceptual Process Modelling	Update Process Models
530 - Define Enquiry Processes	Conceptual Process Modelling	Enquiry Process Models
Assemble Logical Design		Logical Design

Stage 6 - Physical Design

Step	Technique	Product
610 - Prepare for Physical Design	Physical Data Design Physical Process Specification	Application Development Standards Physical Design Strategy
620 - Create Physical Data Design	Physical Data Design	Physical Data Design (1st-cut) Space Estimation
630 - Create FCIM	Physical Process Specification	FCIM Function Definitions Requirements Catalogue
640 - Optimise Physical Data Design	Physical Data Design	Physical Data Design Function Definitions Requirements Definition Space Estimations Timing Estimations
650 - Complete Function Specification	Physical Process Specification	FCIM Function Definitions Requirements Catalogue
660 - Consolidate PDI	Physical Process Specification	Process Data Interface FCIM Function Definitions Requirements Catalogue
Assemble Physical Design		Physical Design

Module/Technique Matrix

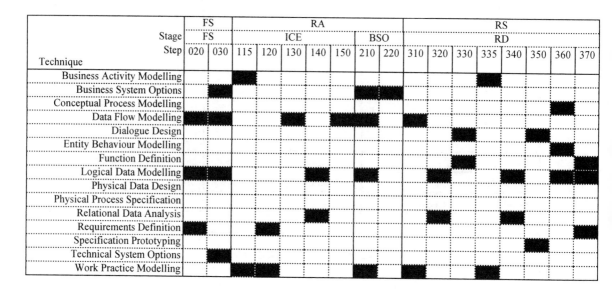

Technique	FS		RA (ICE)					RA (BSO)		RS (RD)							
Step	020	030	115	120	130	140	150	210	220	310	320	330	335	340	350	360	370
Business Activity Modelling			■										■				
Business System Options		■						■	■								
Conceptual Process Modelling																■	
Data Flow Modelling	■				■	■	■			■							
Dialogue Design												■			■		
Entity Behaviour Modelling														■			
Function Definition													■				
Logical Data Modelling	■					■			■			■			■		■
Physical Data Design																	
Physical Process Specification																	
Relational Data Analysis						■						■			■		
Requirements Definition	■			■													■
Specification Prototyping															■		
Technical System Options		■															
Work Practice Modelling			■					■		■			■				

Technique	LSS (TSO)		LSS (LD)			PD					
Steps	410	420	510	530	540	610	620	630	640	650	660
Business Activity Modelling											
Business System Options											
Conceptual Process Modelling				■	■						
Data Flow Modelling											
Dialogue Design			■								
Entity Behaviour Modelling											
Function Definition											
Logical Data Modelling											
Physical Data Design	■					■	■		■		
Physical Process Specification	■					■		■		■	■
Relational Data Analysis											
Requirements Definition											
Specification Prototyping											
Technical System Options	■										
Work Practice Modelling			■								

Index